D1058092

EVERYTHING
Reminds Me of Something

Also by Adam Carolla

I'm Your Emotional Support Animal:
Navigating Our All Woke, No Joke Culture

Daddy, Stop Talking!
And Other Things My Kids Want
but Won't Be Getting

President Me:
The America That's in My Head

Not Taco Bell Material

Rich Man Poor Man

In Fifty Years We'll All Be Chicks…
And Other Complaints from an Angry
Middle-Aged White Guy

EVERYTHING

Reminds Me of Something

Advice, Answers...
But No Apologies

ADAM CAROLLA

Post Hill
PRESS

Post Hill Press
New York • Nashville
posthillpress.com

Published in the United States of America
1 2 3 4 5 6 7 8 9 10

Contents

Contents

Introduction

Welcome, dear reader, to my sixth book. If you had told me in 2010 when I wrote *In Fifty Years We'll All Be Chicks...And Other Complaints from an Angry Middle-Aged White Guy* that I'd crank out five more volumes of said complaints, I wouldn't have believed you. So thanks.

This one's going to be a bit different. I'm going back to basics. The great Jimmy Kimmel created an idea for my stage show: having audience members write one word on a ping-pong ball for me to riff on. They would then shoot those ping-pong balls out of their vaginas at me onstage. When Jimmy sobered up, we decided it would be cleaner, literally and figuratively, if we just put those ping-pong balls in a bingo hopper and pulled them out at random for me to pontificate on. The name of the show is *Unprepared*, and I perform it along with some more prepared stand-up comedy throughout the country.

At my core I'm an improvisor. I flamed out of the Groundlings, the famous improv troupe in Los Angeles that gave us greats like Paul Reubens, Kristen Wiig, Lisa Kudrow, and Phil Hartman, but later went on to cofound the ACME comedy theater. More important, I did the lion's share of the work on the radio show *Loveline* for over a decade with Dr. Drew, who can name every bone in the body but doesn't have a funny bone in his. So I thought I'd kick it old school in this book and do things a bit more free-form, answering questions and doling out advice.

The audience questions throughout this book are all real; nothing is cooked. We solicited them on my podcast and on Twitter, weeded out the dead wood, and in various hours stuck in miserable L.A. traffic I riffed, ranted, and raged and turned them into the following tome. There are going to be many improvised tangents along the way, thus the title. It was originally going to be called *Ask an Asshole: Advice and Answers from the Least Apologetic Man in Comedy*. But smarter people than me realized that would be a marketing problem. Even though it's true that I am an unrepentant asshole, it would have been hard for Tucker Carlson to say the book title on air when I went to plug it on his show. So we decided to clean up the language a bit for sales. That was actually the biggest complaint from my last book, the language. If you read the Amazon reviews for *I'm Your Emotional Support Animal*, you'll see that people generally agreed with the sentiments, but many wished I had expressed them with a few less cuss words. My favorite was this email sent directly to my publisher. Let it be the first I address in this book.

> *I am writing you today to let you know how disappointed I am with your new Carolla book "I'm Your Emotional Support Animal." I bought it hoping for some humor in this now humorless society and to support Post Hill Press.*
>
> *I am truly disgusted by the filthy language in this book. Just a few pages into the book the profanity started. There should be a disclaimer for those of us who are offended by this offensive language. I returned the book at Amazon and will get my money back. I will never buy another of your books, as I find I can't trust them. I just don't know why, when we are such an educated society, we are now resorting to the most vile of language.*

Linda, Ohio

Introduction

As a proud asshole, let me say, fuck your delicate sensibilities. You do the thing I hate the most: say "I like humor as much as the next person" before you call for censorship and cancelation. You clearly have no sense of humor. I'm not going to apologize; shitty times call for shitty language. I wrote that book in 2019 when things sucked and our society was going off a cliff, but even I, with my crystal ball of a brain, couldn't have seen just how bad things would get after the twin viruses of COVID-19 (and the accompanying government ineptitude and overreach) and the post–George Floyd infection of "antiracism," critical race theory, and police defunding. That book hit the virtual shelf (because no one could go out to an actual bookstore at the time) and sold 11,292 hardcovers in our first week. Yet we did not make the *New York Times* bestseller list. Hmmm…

For June 14–20 of 2020, *I'm Your Emotional Support Animal* was the forty-eighth-bestselling book in the country, according to Bookscan, and the twelfth-bestselling nonfiction book on Amazon. It made the bestseller lists of *USA Today*, the *Wall Street Journal*, and *Publishers Weekly*. But more important, it sold more copies than eight books on the *Times* list, including the following. (I've included the publishers' descriptions from the list to add to the nausea).

- *Me and White Supremacy* (10,994 copies sold): "This eye-opening book challenges you to do the essential work of unpacking your biases, and helps white people take action and dismantle the privilege within themselves…"

- *Between the World and Me* (10,020 copies sold): "[A] bold and personal literary exploration of America's racial history…"

- *Hood Feminism* (3,672 copies sold): "A potent and electrifying critique of today's feminist movement announcing a fresh new voice in Black feminism."

Seeing a trend there?

I bring this up not out of bitterness but out of a need to call bullshit. So, like the great Babe Ruth, I'm calling my shot now. There is no way I'll get on the *New York Times* list again. And I now take that as a badge of honor. I never in my wildest or darkest fantasies would ever think that anything I said onstage or wrote on the page would ever be considered "important," but in times such as these, simply speaking your mind—as I'll do in the following pages, prompted by your questions—is considered an act of defiance and, potentially, patriotism.

As you likely know—and if not, then you'll know by the end of this book—I'm into vintage racing. I was at an event at the track at Pebble Beach last year, and people kept coming up to shake my hand and stroke my ego. It used to be that when I was stopped at an airport or an event like Laguna Seca, they'd say, "Hey, *Man Show*! Where are the Juggies?" or "I grew up listening to *Loveline*." In 2021 the same number of people came up to me, but no one brought any of that up. What they said was, "Thank you for what you're doing." I tried to stay humble and just reply, "I'm just talking. I'm a comedian just doing my job," but they'd push back: "No, it's important what you're doing."

I still have a hard time accepting this, but I'm glad if you think it. I can't say every moment in the following chapters is going to be a profound speaking of truth to power. There are still plenty of fart joke arrows in the Ace Man's quiver. But hopefully you'll enjoy some pearls of wisdom and nuggets of joy, and have some moments when you think, *I'm afraid people would think I'm an asshole for saying that, but I'm glad* he *did.*

Chapter 1

Auto Correct

know everything, but I really know cars. Between collecting vintage Paul Newman Datsuns, being a two-time Toyota Pro/ Celebrity Race champion, or simply being an infuriated Los Angeles native who has spent the better part of his life stuck in traffic, I'm uniquely qualified to answer your automotive questions. So, questioners, start your engines.

• •

What's the craziest crap that you've seen being hauled in a car or truck going down the highway (or that you hauled in your POS pickup truck back in the day)?

Mike, 50, Maryland

I have seen some crazy crap being hauled around in my time driving the highways and byways of SoCal. (How long before the LGBTQIA+ community decides that "byway" is problematic, by the way?) That crazy crap was not so much building materials or equipment, but what people used to haul in the form of homemade camper shells. I'm talking the kind of DIY in which you could get a DUI. Before Amazon shipped us cheap Chinese

1

plastic and every pot had a lid, people needed to use ingenuity. You'd have a pickup truck, and no camper shell existed for your model. Or the ones that did were half the price of what you paid for the pickup. This is when guys would get out the plywood, one-by-six tongue-and-groove knotty cedar, a sixer of Hamm's, and some ingenuity. You don't see that anymore.

This is a larger symbolic problem with modern America. Dig. We used to be a gritty country in which people made their own stuff. I grew up in an America where we fixed shit and made shit. Stuff was bespoke. Individualism used to be part of our world. My kids see a bunch of a beige Priuses going down the street, each one no different than the other. I grew up in a time when people took out the acetylene torch and made stake-bed pickup trucks out of VW bugs.

We're losing our individuality. It's the Starbucks-ing of our culture. Think about it. There's a Starbucks on every corner. There used to be coffee shops with names. There were a hundred thousand different places with a hundred thousand different names. Sometimes they were clever movie or literary references, or just some dude's name, like "Al" or "Ed." Usually they were mediocre coffee puns centered around the word "grind." The friends on *Friends* went to Central Perk. Nowadays they'd just go to a Starbucks that's two blocks away from another Starbucks.

A quick tangent. How many people do you think know that Starbucks is named after a character from Moby Dick? It's just become synonymous with coffee. Like Kleenex, Dumpster, and Google are brand names that have become synonymous with what they are. But it could have been different. If instead of a minor character from Moby Dick, what if the brand that overtook the coffee world were Moby Dick himself? Would we text our friend, "While you're out, grab me a grande Dick with heavy cream"? Would we have to chug a Dick before we got to airport security?

Another thing I've seen hauled around that you don't anymore that proves our society is declining is kids in jump seats facing the wrong direction. If you were behind them in the car, you'd be looking them in the eye for seventy miles and they'd be making faces at you the whole time. We're *way* too safety conscious now to do that. But back then, we all rolled around in the back of a station wagon hanging on for dear life if the old man took a turn too fast in the family truckster.

You'd see loose dogs in the backs of pickups too. When was the last time you saw some mutt wandering around the back of a moving pickup truck? That'd never happen today. I guarantee that your average American dog has spent more time strapped into an air-conditioned car this year than I did during my entire childhood.

This automotive modernization and homogenization also mean we've lost our connection to each other. When I was a kid, everyone drove with their windows down during the summer. You could tell what brand of cigarette the guy was smoking in the next car over when you pulled up to the stoplight. There was more eye contact. Now everyone is just hiding behind sunglasses and a COVID mask and a 25 percent tint on their windows. You used to know who people were by what they drove. When I was a kid, we all knew when Dr. Fagenbaum drove by, because he had a Mercedes. That was a big deal. And if you read my memoir, *Not Taco Bell Material*, you might recall my mentioning the guy in my neighborhood who had a van with "Radical Rich" written on the side in rainbow tape. I would love to know what happened to that guy. If you want to see the last vestige of this, google the name Dennis Woodruff and enjoy.

Cars have always been symbolic of America. They used to be about progress, going forward. Hitting the open road and seeing the USA in your Chevrolet. Well, now they're about comfort and entertainment—massaging seats and built-in iPads for all. And they're built to be disposable, not fixable or customizable. Plus, they're all about safety. Just like us, they're focused on all the wrong things. We'd be a better society if we dealt with a little discomfort, took a little more risk, and were a little more individual or even unique.

But to answer your question, Mike from Maryland, the things I hauled the most in my piece-of-shit pickup were ass and grass. No one rode for free. ∎

....

Why have I never seen and never will see a woman driving a man on a motorcycle?

Eric, 50, San Diego

A lot of it is about optics. Men don't want to be seen being their girl's bitch. Most guys would buy tampons for the wife at the CVS if everyone at the store wore those black pillowcases al-Qaeda makes you put over your head before they cut it off, or one of those hoods they put on falcons and hawks.

It's ironic. The wooden-bracelet-wearing, NPR-listening dads would be more than willing to get on a motorcycle their wife was piloting, because they're pussy-whipped enough to do whatever they're told. But they're also too scared to get on one. And they are too prone to anxiety disorders to let their old lady ride one. (And they'd never call her their old lady because that would be ageist and assume gender identification.) It's too big a risk, because their wife makes more than them. She's out there earning while he's trying to get his artisanal vegan cheese business off the ground. Kamala Harris's husband would never untuck his junk long enough to saddle up behind her on a hog.

Though if one of these homos ever did get on the back of his woman's bike, she could still wear the classic biker T-shirt that says on the back "If you can read this the bitch fell off."

4

You don't really see dudes riding with other dudes on the back of motorcycles that much. I was thinking about this not too long ago. A dude riding with a dude on a motorcycle is all about where you put your hands. It's connected to how gay you are. If you've got your arms around the waist of the man in front of you, not only are you gay but you're a bottom. If you have your arms around his shoulders, you've upgraded to bi. If you've got your arms folded, you're hetero. And if you've got your arms folded and a cigarette dangling out of your mouth, you're the straightest dude alive. ■

· ·

I want your thoughts on the landau top. Is it for people who don't really want a convertible but want people to think they have a convertible? It gives vandals something to slash, it's prone to rotting and sun fading, and when it comes loose from the roof it acts as a windsock so your '84 Skylark can somehow become less aerodynamic. Has there been a worse automotive concept than the landau top?

Aaron, 52, Louisville

All you need to know about how bad the landau roof was is that it came to prominence in the worst decade for everything. The height of the landau top was the late '70s, and it was exclusively on American cars. At that point we couldn't build an American car that would pass smog inspection or have consistently working power windows. The paint on the hood would blister after three years, and the vinyl on the dash would split after two. What made us think we could upholster the roof?

It was the magician's and politician's trick of misdirection. American car companies upholstered the outside of the car as a grand gesture because they didn't want you to know what was going on in their shitty engine design. Landau tops shouted, "Don't pop the hood; look at the love seat we've grafted onto the roof."

The people who had to be over the moon about this were the Japs. This must have sent a clear message to them that we were ripe for the picking. Just come in with your Datsuns and your Casio watches and kick the shit out of us. We've got a gas crisis, and we're carpeting the outside of the car. There's no sleeping giant to awaken here. We're a sleeping sloth. Think I'm exaggerating? At the height of the landau roof, the Japanese were good for only 8 percent of the market share for cars. By 1986 they had over 20 percent. We were asking for it, like when a woman is raped and the defense is "Did you see what she was wearing?"

Speaking of stupid car shit from the '70s, if you had a car with a landau roof, there was a pretty good chance you'd also have an opera window. I can hear the designers now: "What does this Coupe de Ville need in addition to a fake convertible top with useless snaps? An unusable window! Genius!" I guess it was there so if you passed out you could see the train light coming at you. And since no celebrity has ever driven a Buick Celebrity and no one from Malibu has ever driven a Chevy Malibu, do you think anyone has ever driven home to their mansion after attending the opera in a car that had an opera window?

What was with our obsession with unnecessary upholstery in the '70s? We had carpet kits for the lids of toilet seats. What the fuck? There was carpet in the bathroom. Who has ever left a bathroom and thought, *Hmm. That room where I fart, shit, and piss doesn't have enough shag carpet.* We were so nuts about carpeting in the '70s, you would think it had just been invented. Even toupees were called rugs back then. We were carpet-bombing Vietnam, and it was the big-bush era as far as porn was concerned. We loved all things carpeted.

But like a landau roof, I think I've covered this one more than I needed to. Next question. ■

. . . .

I don't think you've touched on stop signs on mall or other private property. I assume you ignore them since the cops can't do shit if it's not a real street?

Michelle, 50, Las Cruces, New Mexico

Of course. But cops wouldn't be there anyway. There's no place to hide in a mall parking lot. Traffic cops are cowards. These are the police that need to be defunded. Everyone I know has gotten a ticket for rolling through a four-way stop. It's always from a cop lying in wait at the bottom of the hill. Cops don't come to you; you come to them. They hang there and hide where they can light you up. No one thinks in terms of where they aren't. You'll never get a ticket going up a hill, because no one speeds going up a hill.

Your question about useless signs I ignore reminds me of those "Slow Down. Kids Live Here" signs. You know those A-frame yellowish-green signs that looks like a retarded turtle that's been pulled from its shell holding a flag? I've never seen any kids playing in streets with those signs. Maybe they all got run over, but it's more likely they're inside playing Fortnite and watching YouPorn while someone is setting up the sign. I've never seen kids playing within two thousand feet of one of these signs. It's ironic too, because I only see them in the good neighborhoods where the parents give a shit, but in those neighborhoods, at least one of the kids has a half-court basketball setup in the backyard, and that's where the kids are. Those kids don't play stickball in the street. They're in someone's in-ground pool or playing cornhole in the backyard by the fire pit. The garbage neighborhoods are where the kids are in the street, because the yards are the size of a Post-it note and full of weeds and dog shit. But nary a sign. Shouldn't some Good Samaritan go to the nice neighborhood and rescue these turtle signs and bring them to the poor neighborhoods where the kids are getting clipped by cars? It's overkill. Having these signs up in the good neighborhoods is like the guy with a small dick buying Magnum condoms.

By the way, my mom would not have put up that sign; she would have been waving motorists to my bedroom. "He's in there napping. It's easy pickin's." ∎

. . . .

Hi Adam, I need your help to argue my points. I want to contact the people who make gas pumps. When I pay cash at the gas station, the gas pump slows to a quarter speed when I get to 50 cents prior to the amount I paid. Why can't this happen at 10 cents prior?

Jason, 48, Huntington Beach, California

Good point. I feel the same way. You know you've arrived when you just walk away from that last half a buck. Certain things are too slow, like that last gas pump ejaculation. You know what else is too slow? The people mover at the airport. I always get on that thinking I'm going to save some time, but then I turn to my right and see guys hauling Samsonites, moving at a pretty good clip on the carpet and beating me on the people mover. Even when I'm moving, I get slowed down by someone who doesn't know there's a standing lane and a walking lane. Why are you standing on the people mover? Are you lazy or motivated? It's like the guy who wears a T-shirt and a scarf. Are you hot or cold?

But other things are too fast. For example, the time for entering the conference call fourteen-digit number. What would be the harm in giving me a beat to look down at the next round of digits I need to enter before you cut me off? You've decided I've lost interest in making the conference call because I took a humming-bird's heartbeat to see whether I wrote down a seven or a nine? It gives me anxiety. It's not five seconds; it's less than three. Why not give me thirty seconds? What would be the harm?

And while I'm in this area, I need to have a sit-down with Siri. When you're using the talk-to-text feature, if you inhale she decides you are done speaking and attempts to send the text. I'm sorry I'm not as artificially intelligent as you, bitch, but I actually want to compose my thought. So you end up shotgunning out your text because you're sick of getting cut off. Spelling and grammar be damned; you're going to spit out a run-on sentence and message your wife that you're stopping at the store for a gallon of MILF. ■

I made the mistake of not having a motorcycle when I got married in 2000. My life seems monotonous, and I fucking need something to blow off steam and decompress. Unfortunately, my wife thinks I will kill myself and leave her and our three kids without a father/husband. What should I do?

Ron, 48, Indiana

This is a mixed blessing. When they don't care if you get a motorcycle, that means they don't care if you get in a motorcycle accident. Think about it. If in week one of most relationships you said, "Would you care if I got a motorcycle?" most women would care greatly. But seven years in they'll say, "I'll drive you to the Honda dealership." So my advice is to get your relationship deteriorating to the point where she *wants* you to kill yourself on the motorcycle. ■

I am looking at leasing or buying the Model Y Tesla. Owning versus leasing...which do you think is the best move?

Lewis, 46, Dallas

I used to be an owning-oriented person. I'm now leaning toward leasing. I think it's smart to keep it to three years and always get something new. Think about anyone you've ever known who leased. They've never driven around in a twenty-year-old piece of shit. My mom had a Dodge Dart that was twenty years old, a VW Squareback that was twenty years old, and a VW bug that was twenty years old. If you utter the following phrase more than four times in your life, it's a bad sign: "I got a new car...well, new to me."

And that's why I know it's a self-esteem thing. She didn't, and people who buy versus lease don't feel like they deserve something new. You basically have to ask yourself if you're worth the extra expense. It doesn't make the most sense financially, but staying in a cheap motel versus a decent Marriott doesn't make the most sense either. Or coughing up for business class versus coach. Lots of things that don't make sense financially send the message to yourself that you can have nice new things and don't need to settle. Audi versus Mitsubishi. Eating at Morton's or Ruth's Chris Steakhouse versus Sizzler. Who cares? At a certain point you're going to die. Why not live a little before you do?

And when it comes to the Tesla specifically, I say lease. That car didn't even exist ten years ago. Electric is progressing at, pun intended, ludicrous speed. If you buy the Y, by the time your lease is up Elon Musk will have a new model you're going to want with all the latest tech. Who knows what he's got in R&D right now? Why own a donkey when a Model A is right around the corner?

A quick tangent. I've always been confused about the Model A. Why did the Model A come after the Model T? My fans know by now I'm not a great speller, but even I know the order of the alphabet. Well, I did a little research. The Model T was introduced in 1908. Letters A through T were designed before that, but not all of them went into production. The Model T was such a success and the next in line was so different that instead of going with a Model U, Henry Ford wanted to start over again with the letter A. Thus the Model A we all picture. I hope you enjoyed that educational tidbit. At first I googled "Model T and A," and a half-hour and an empty ballsack later I found my way over to Wikipedia to discover the above. ■

· ·

What items do you consider essential to have in your vehicle at all times?

Don, 57, Tempe, Arizona

There was an item for cars I'd always see while I was drunk, looking at the SkyMall catalog. You've probably seen it. It was called the LifeHammer. Designed to help you escape your car in an accident, it had a razor on one side to cut the seatbelt if it was jammed up, and a special hammer to break the window if you went full Chappaquiddick. I'm from North Hollywood and have always lived in Los Angeles—there's no body of water anywhere nearby. But I still felt like I needed it. Despite that, I didn't get it because I knew exactly what would happen. At some point I'd be going over a bridge at night, I'd be drunk, the fog would be rolling in, and I'd end up in the drink upside down. The water would be seeping in and I'd be freaking out, feeling under my seat, trying to open the glove compartment, looking for it in a panic. And with my last breath before sinking to Davy Jones's locker, I'd call my wife and say, "Where's the LifeHammer?" and she'd say, "I put it in the trunk." ■

· ·

Given the choice, would you rather drive in an IndyCar, F1, or NASCAR race?

Don, 57, Tempe, Arizona

You again, Don?

Normally I'm into European innovation and technology, but I'm going to surprise everyone by saying NASCAR. Open wheel is scary. You definitely feel safer inside the cage of a NASCAR vehicle. In NASCAR you can go bumper to bumper and door to door, and not worry about being launched into the air and likely to your death by bumping someone's tire.

Also, if Biden is still alive and president at the time, it could be exhilarating if I won a NASCAR race and during the postrace interview we could get chants of "Let's go Adam!"

A quick side note on NASCAR and race car movies in general. We don't need the scene where they're going down the back straight at Talladega and someone is bumping our hero from behind, and we get a close shot of him punching down the gear shift and leaving the other guy in the dust. In reality that guy is already in top gear, flat out and wide open. It's such a ridiculous idea. So everyone is just in the wrong gear the whole race? The professional driver you've based your movie on is feathering the gas? He doesn't know to put it into top gear?

Or, if he's not in the lead, they do that ultrafake moment when he decides he's sick of being in second place, upshifts from third to fourth gear, and slingshots around to take the lead. "Holy shit, this car has another gear?!!" Please. Or the other never-happened-in-real-life moment when he's looking in the rearview to see who's bumping him and realizes it's his archenemy. In reality, that guy has been behind him for seven laps.

But back to my NASCAR plans, because I have a brilliant idea for how to make a name for myself. Literally. It occurred to me years ago that it was a damn shame that Muhammad Ali changed his name from Cassius Clay. That's a strong name. And that Lew Alcindor changed his name to Kareem Abdul-Jabbar. Even Cat Stevens became Yusuf Islam. These guys had some of the coolest names of all time and changed them to Muslim monikers. Yet NASCAR legend Dick Trickle stuck with that name. (One of these days, I'm going to write a book called *What's Wrong with Rich?* and send it to Dick Trickle, Dick Butkus, and 1970s Red Sox and Mariners pitcher Dick Pole.)

I'm going to do what Rich Trickle never did. I'm going to join the NASCAR circuit, kick ass, get all the fans behind me, and then find my true faith in Islam and change my name to Muhammad Al

Sheikh just to see what the rednecks would do. They'd be so conflicted. Guys would be throwing beers at the track. I wouldn't race during Ramadan, and I'd refuse liquor sponsorships on my car. It'd be awesome. Then, to cap it all off, I'd take my fame, partner up with Shaquille O'Neal, and open a fast-food franchise serving soul food with Middle Eastern flair, like chicken shawarma and waffles. We'd call it Sheikh Shaq. ∎

· ·

Is there a bigger douchemobile than the Polaris Slingshot?

Tony, 55, Baltimore

Maybe the Mercedes-Benz G-Wagon. If not, it's a close second. If a Mercedes-Benz G-class collided with a Polaris Slingshot, it would be douche-on-douche destruction. The highway patrol wouldn't even investigate that accident; they would just assume both are equally at fault, both drivers being douches. And if that happens, two clubs are going to have to find backup DJs that night.

Let's sort this out. First, we have to factor in the per-wheel douche reduction. The Slingshot only has three wheels, so it's packing more douchiness on 25 percent less traction. That's just science. But while the Polaris packs a punch in the douche debate because of the reduced number of rims, the G-Wagon makes up for it with a higher price tag. A base-model 2021 G-Wagon has an MSRP of $131,750, compared to the highest-level limited-edition Slingshot's $32,799 suggested sticker price. Imagine the douchiness that it takes to pay four times a schoolteacher's salary for a vehicle that is essentially a box with Kardashians in it.

Then again, the G-Wagon has a roof and windows, so we don't have to hear Drake blaring out of it, while the Polaris douche is subjecting everyone to his horrible taste in "music."

Ooof. These are the difficult questions I was afraid I'd get when I started writing this book.

In the end, I'm going to have to go with the Polaris. Because it's made in America. At least the Mercedes is German. You can't blame the German engineers from Mercedes. They made it for off-roading. It should be on safari. They couldn't have anticipated that Scott Disik would give it a purple satin finish and then outfit it with 25-series tires and 27-inch rims he dings every time they hit a pothole in Malibu. The G-Wagon was made in Germany but douchified in America. The Polaris was born here but should have been aborted. ∎

Have you noticed that oversized pickup trucks have seemingly replaced expensive sports cars as the vehicle of choice for midlife crises? Trucks that were designed to haul tons of material to and from construction sites are now saturating strip mall parking lots when middle-aged dads need to make a run to the supermarket. I would love to get your crystal brain's take on this perplexing topic.

John, 38, Norfolk, Virginia

I've definitely noticed this myself. Like the G-Wagon in the previous question, this is all about image and status, but unlike that aforementioned douchemobile, it doesn't carry the stigma. You can get a Ford F-250 and option it up to a hundred grand these days but still seem like a normal person. It's like Mark Zuckerberg wearing plain T-shirts, cargo shorts, and flip-flops. It's saying, "I'm a rich guy but I drive a truck." "I might be a country music superstar, but I'm just like you." It's a humble brag. "I'm like one of you people who actually use it for its intended purpose." When Princess Di would hunt for land mines, she'd put on the flak jacket and take the photo, but a couple hours later she was blowing Dodi Al Fayed on a yacht.

Sports cars have always been status-related. Way back when, they were the obvious choice for aging dudes to feel young again.

Think of Sam Malone from *Cheers* and his Corvette fetish. That was the stereotype. Once it became the obvious trope, it had to shift a bit.

It's also impractical. The most Lamborghinis in the world are in L.A. And the most traffic in the world is in L.A. as well. Who would need a Lambo in L.A.? The top speed on a new Lamborghini is 191 miles per hour, but in L.A. you're not getting over 31. To get even more granular, the city with the most sports cars per capita is Malibu. You'll see them crawling down the Pacific Coast Highway. But at least in L.A., as long as we're not going anywhere, we might as well save a hundred grand and still make a statement. Sure, I'm not going 191 or hauling logs. That guy is not using the pickup to its full—or any—capacity, just like the other guy isn't taking the Lambo to Nürburgring. It's simply implying that you could be hauling timber you just chopped, but you're not.

But I think this ties to a deeper issue that I talked about in my last book. I wrote about where we are heading as a culture and a species, and I posited that one-half of us are heading to octagons and the other half are heading to safe spaces. As we go further into the margins, it's going to show up in lots of different ways. As I drive around L.A., for every Prius or Tesla I see, I also notice a Jeep with knobby tires. We're too extreme in our political and social identities. Nobody wants to be in the middle anymore. It's not exciting. It's not interesting. A Camry is the middle. It used to be that the highway was jammed with Accords and Camrys. Gone are the days when you'd buy a Tercel and just go to work. Now you buy a Tesla to make a statement. And for each one of the Tesla owners is a guy buying a Jeep with knobby tires and a suspension lift who's also making a statement. That statement is: "I'm not a Tesla guy." I bet if you pulled over anyone driving a Tesla and asked them what they thought about AOC, Biden, Tucker Carlson, or global warming, you'd get exactly the answers you'd expect. And it would be the same if you pulled over the Jeep-with-a-lift-kit guy. Each vehicle tells me who you are. I think the boom in pickup trucks you're noticing is the same phenomenon. These aren't guys in the trades going to the construction site. They're saying, "I still want to be comfortable, I want you to know I'm rich, but I don't want you thinking I'm one of those Biden-voting, electric car fags." ■

When driving, why do people slow down when the road in front of them is obviously clear?
—Alonzo Bodden

This is a great indicator that society at large is out of it. I was noticing it as I was driving through the 405 pass recently. It's a pretty steep grade going up and the opposite going down. I see people going seventy-two to seventy-five miles per hour toward the hill, but as soon as they hit that incline they go down to fifty-three. It's not that they don't know it. Most modern cars have a heads-up digital display on the windshield. You have it right in front of you—it's not like you have to stick your hand out the window and figure it out from the wind resistance. There's an easy remedy. It's not like the old days, when it'd be "I had to double-clutch it and drop it down into third." Your foot is on a pedal. If you depress it another three-sixteenths of an inch, you'll keep that speed you had before you hit the hill. It's probably safer going up a hill a little fast than down it fast, but after going seventy-five when the road has no grade, they drop down to fifty-three halfway up the incline, and then when they crest that hill they keep their foot in the same position and hit eighty-eight. Really, your brain can't talk to your foot enough to make this mild adjustment? Even with the big digital readout? It's probably the same group of assholes making the same commute every day.

Cars have never had more power or been easier to control, and they do all the shifting for you. You literally only need to apply a little more pressure with your right big toe. It's not like, "Oh, what is this mystery pedal that has appeared under my foot?!" You've been using it the whole time.

I wish the reason they were slowing down was fiddling with coordinates on their dashboard or texting. That would at least be an explanation. This is just pure fucking tune-out. "We were going seventy-seven, now we're going fifty-four. That's our new reality. We must accept it." It's a scary indictment of humanity. These aren't guys nodding off on fentanyl or illegal immigrant gardeners driving beat-up pickups that can't handle the hill who are afraid of getting a ticket and thus deported. These are affluent professional L.A. commuters driving BMWs and Lexuses (is the plural of Lexuses Lexi?).

There's a worse spot in SoCal called the Grapevine. It has a steep grade, about 6 percent for over five miles on the 5 freeway in Kern County heading into the San Joaquin Valley. People will slow down to about thirty up that bitch; meanwhile I'm playing Plinko dodging around them trying to maintain sixty-five by slightly altering the grade of my right toe.

What the fuck, people?

I think there's something to your question beyond the tune-out factor, Alonzo. It's the follow factor. If it's open road, nobody to follow. Something I've learned from COVID is we need someone to follow. Take the off-ramp from the 5 onto Flower, which is my exit to get to the podcast studio. There are two lanes to turn left. One will have fourteen cars, and the other will have one or two. People just queue up. Why? If this was the Disneyland Drive exit off the 5, I could explain it. It's tourists and they don't know. But this is Glendale. These are the same commuters going the same way daily. Obviously, there's something in the human psyche that wants to follow. Signs that are prominently displayed show two left-turn lanes. It's not a mystery. There's something in our DNA that compels us to do this. The open road for a minority of Americans such as yourself means it's time to get on it. For the rest, it causes a mild panic about not being told what to do by the person in front of them.

We also have a strange relationship with effort. Think about how people treat their own effort versus someone else's. A cyclist will blow through a four-way stop just about every time. And they could certainly get a ticket. So why do these middle-aged law-abiding citizens in my neighborhood blow through four-way stop signs on their bicycles? They don't want to brake and scrub off their own effort. They've been pedaling their ass off to get to that speed, and they don't want to lose it. The exact same person in a Tesla will come to a full stop at the same four-way even though they're covered in crumple zones. Those guys on the bike use their own sweat to get to that speed, and they're going to have to use more energy to get back up to speed. They're not thumbing their nose at the law; in fact, they're obeying the law—the law of conservation of energy. ■

···

What do you think of the accelerated efforts, especially in California, of phasing out the combustion engine in favor of electric?

Scott, 38, Costa Mesa, California

I'm not against it in principle. Most people are going to opt for electric cars by 2035 anyway. We just need to work out solar roof shingles that can feed the whole home battery. But I'm just not sure we can execute that. California doesn't have a power grid that can handle more than a third of the population's putting their air conditioner on in July. We have rolling blackouts and brownouts. (Where are the woke police on those "problematic" terms?) Every summer we're lectured by politicians and PSAs about only using appliances at certain times. It's like we're all forced to be Hassidic Jews on Shabbos. At this point Gavin Newsom and the Democrats running California *literally* don't want us to have any power.

These idiots want to phase out gas cars by 2035, and in 2020 former L.A. mayor Eric Garcetti was proposing an "urban air mobility partnership"—a.k.a. flying taxis. These idiots want to live in *The Jetsons*, but they're running the city like the Flintstones. (Thank Christ that Garcetti is off to be Biden's ambassador to India. I'll give him a ride to the airport and complain about traffic the whole time.)

Just like I was talking about earlier with the landau roof, it's misdirection. Newsom and Garcetti are so concerned with California "leading the world" that they forget to do normal shit that functional states do, like addressing the homeless problem, reducing traffic, and lowering crime. We're so busy trying to make Europe jealous with how progressive and regulatory we can be, actual shit that affects people falls through the cracks.

Newsom picks weird inane shit because it's what you would focus on if you were out of problems. If the schools were good, this is what you would focus on, but L.A. public schools are essentially prisons with a lot less exercise and a lot more sex. It would be as if you talked to a guy and he was bragging about how he was redoing his garage—"I'm putting in all stainless steel cabinetry with full Euro hinge and Accuride slides." You'd think, *I bet the rest of this guy's house is spectacular*. You wouldn't imagine a broken lightbulb in the socket, a pot with no handle full of moldy Ragu on the stove, and raccoons fucking on his couch. But that's what California under Newsom is. A lot of focus on shiny new things that make it seem like we're out of problems. Imagine a parent saying, "My son speaks Mandarin, but he doesn't speak Cantonese. We've got to get going on that." And you reply, "Isn't your son a junkie?" "Oh yeah, he's tying off in the pool house right now, but back to this Mandarin issue." That's Newsom.

The state is on fire, the homeless are building encampments on the freeway, which is at a standstill, and this is your plan? We need to reduce our carbon footprint? The state is on fire. Our carbon footprint is the size of Sasquatch wearing a waffle stomper. Cars aren't the problem; dead trees are the problem. How about focusing on that? Every year we have a forest fire that puts more shit into the air that causes global warming than all the cars that have ever driven on the 5 freeway. Newsom signed a law in 2021 announcing the state is outlawing gas-powered leaf blowers and chainsaws by 2024. Someone should have told him we already have a law against leaf blowers. It just wasn't enforced because we don't like the optics.

California, and Los Angeles specifically, doesn't enforce these laws because it's poor brown people being paid by rich white people to use these devices. The only people making a living with a leaf blower are Hispanic, and that's the Democrats' constituency and, as I know I've said before, they're empty bags. There's no money to ring out of the poor Latino selling flowers on Forrest Lawn Drive, but plenty to get from the guy driving the Lexus a little too fast on that same street. Which is worse for society: soccer moms going seven miles over the speed limit, or a vast underground, untaxed, unregulated economy of illegal immigrants who can't afford to see doctors, spreading God knows what while they sell unlicensed knockoff "SpiderDude" and "IronGuy" popsicles to kids from a van spewing toxic exhaust?

A quick but related side story to this on the danger of groupthink. I sat at a brunch table with a bunch of left-leaning people—showbiz people, husbands and wives—during a vacation in Maui a few years back. We were all friends. At some point the topic of leaf blowers came up, and I said something factual that I had read in the Los Angeles Times, that there had been a law against using them since 1998 but that we don't enforce the law because of the color of the skin of the people using them. Someone piped up that they thought it was kind of racist for me to say that. The rest of the sheep at the table just nodded along and made me the bad guy for my statement of fact. There was such a yearning to avoid talking about race and to get along that after the leader of the pack decided to contradict me, they all went like lemmings, one by one, off the retard cliff. It was me versus one guy and then eight other people. Did those eight other people ever have thoughts about leaf blowers and Hispanics and L.A. County municipal code enforcement before that brunch? No. What they did have was a need to feel like they were on the right side of an issue, which in this case was the left side of an issue, ignoring the law or the facts in favor of identity. They knew which way the leaves were blowing.

But back to Newsom and chainsaws. How about you use some of the chainsaws to manage the forests? We're going to outlaw them, but ten thousand chainsaws running for a thousand years still wouldn't put out the same amount of carbon into the atmosphere as the forest fires we have twice annually. So does Gavin Newsom care about the environment? No, he cares about getting reelected.

If California politicians wanted more electric cars, maybe they shouldn't have chased Elon Musk out of the state. When the top producer of electric cars threatened to take his big brain, big wallet, and big electric car factory to Texas because of overregulation, especially around COVID protocols, state assemblywoman Lorena Gonzalez tweeted "F*ck Elon Musk." She describes herself on her Twitter bio as "Mama, Labor Leader turned CA Assemblywoman, Proud Democrat." Good job, labor leader Lorena. You just tweeted a guy who creates thousands of jobs out of the state. It's not just him and his personal wealth you told to hit the bricks; it's the employees he pays, it's the outside contractors and suppliers he uses, it's the fucking guys who fill the vending machines at the factories.

So do I think we should phase out the combustion engine? Yes. Do I think California is going to be the leader on this? Fuck no. The people who will be able to afford a new electric car will have long since fled the state by 2035. All the taxpayers will be gone by then because the Democrats will have run the state into the ground. There will, however, be a large number of homeless people in the streets on bicycles jousting with rebar stolen from a construction site that was meant to be low-income housing and was supposed to be completed in 2024. ■

· ·

As a guy who's made a few racing docs, which is your favorite that you didn't direct or produce?
Jeff, 36, Baltimore

There are a lot of good ones, but I'm going to have to go with *Senna*.

There are not, however, a lot of good racing shows. People think there are a lot of car shows out there, and yes, there are entire channels dedicated to cars, but the truth is that for *actual* car guys like myself, the pickins are slim. Just because there are tattooed guys in a shop yelling, "Dude, we're gonna be late for SEMA!" at each other does not make it a car show. The people who create car shows work for car channels, and like all networks, they're staffed by chicks and gays who used to work for *Real Housewives of Orange County* and are trying to constantly infuse the shows with "drama." You know what's fucking dramatic? The Targa Florio. The oldest sports car racing event, it was discontinued in 1977 because too many people had been killed. It took place in Sicily on mountain roads and through villages and towns, where spectators watched from the sidewalks and sometimes even in the road. Over the years, many spectators and racers were killed or injured. That's gone now, but Group Rally5 is still around and that's dramatic as shit. We don't need fake staged interpersonal drama with the guys who race, modify, repair, and own race cars. The race is dramatic enough.

On that note, another quick fuck-you to the idiotic powers that be in the television industry. In 2008, I filmed the pilot for the American version of *Top Gear*, which could have been a good show for car guys. The British version was fun and had all the gearhead details we like. The shoot went well, and the pilot was good. It looked like it was going to be greenlit (car pun intended). But the network executives decided that year that people weren't into car shows. Why? At the time, NBC had recently brought back *Knight Rider* and it died a thousand deaths. So the head of the network declared, "No more car shows." Yes, because the cars were the problem. Not *Knight Rider*'s cheesy premise, music, and acting. People had generally decided that they weren't into things with four wheels. But the same mind that said yay to the project in the first place surely couldn't wrap their head around why it failed and apply it to my *Top Gear* pilot. I have no idea why someone would think this was a good idea. *Knight Rider* sucked in the '80s. Did you think it was like a fine wine that just needed some time to age? It was terrible when Reagan was president; it was going to be terrible when George W. was president. HBO was on season 5 of *The Sopranos* at the time. Look at the field and assess your competition. Just because you've heard of something doesn't mean you should bring it back. I've heard of polio and the Ford Pinto, but I don't think they're ripe for a comeback.

I'll end this chapter with a super tangent that will make you laugh. I have no idea what the context was, but in confirming the dates of the *Knight Rider* remake, I stumbled across a note from my old radio show that read: "Kitt from *Knight Rider* died of vehicular AIDS from a bad oil transfusion." ∎

Chapter 2

We're Going to Health in a Bucket, but at Least I'm Enjoying the Ride

There's a ton of shitty health advice out there, especially on social media. My newsgirl Gina was talking in 2019 about friends who were on celery-juice-only cleanses because they had listened to a "medical medium." Unless those hot chicks can show you a picture of themselves looking like Rhea Perlman one year before they started drinking celery juice, they should shut the fuck up. You have to take the source into account. Anyone claiming to be an expert should be ignored. So, listen to me. I'm not an expert.

I work in healthcare, and every year we need to watch videos on how to bring up weight in a nonthreatening manner to unhealthy overweight people. Yet every year our patients seem to be getting heavier and heavier. How would you bring it up?

Keith, 40, New Jersey

We used to run into this on *Loveline*. A guy would call up to complain about how his wife's pussy stank and ask how to bring it up to her. We'd always suggest talking to her from a pure-health, "I'm worried" angle. It conveys concern, and that always helps mitigate the shame that naturally comes up.

In the age of COVID, not being obese should be a no-brainer, but the people in charge who have no brains decided to not even discuss obesity and preexisting conditions. They just wanted to focus on their agenda—shutting shit down. We've entered some sort of weird zone where talking to someone about their health is considered an attack. Public health authorities, even the family doctor, have no problem hurting your liver and kidneys due to their fear of hurting your feelings.

As far as how to address this, I would compare it to smoking. Being fat is much more dangerous than being a smoker. We'd never tiptoe around the topic of telling a patient to quit smoking. People would be outraged if a physician wasn't trying to convince his patients to stop smoking and said, "I don't want them to feel shamed for smoking." That would be malpractice. If being fat has more health consequences than smoking, then you do the math. The candy cigarettes that used to exist when we were kids were much more harmful than actual cigarettes. It was essentially a sugar-infused piece of blackboard chalk. It's going to get to the point where doctors are going to have to recommend smoking so their patients can shed some pounds.

Smoking is a good boogeyman to use to get your point across. I've long said that we shame smokers much more than deadbeat dads. It occurred to me recently that the classic story of the abandoning father who went out for a pack of smokes and never came home is now considered quaint. Like a pickpocket or a cat burglar, it doesn't seem to exist anymore. Nowadays, we'd shame the dad more for smoking than rambling: "I'm sorry your dad left your family when you were seven, but at least that monster stopped exposing you to secondhand smoke." ■

· ·

What is your opinion on the ever-worsening, sorry state of napkins at restaurants?

Rob, 49, Missouri

I've never thought about it before, but there's an irony. The nicer the restaurant, the more apt you are to get cloth napkins—and they're slippery and shiny and not all that great. They're kind of stiff and slick, and they slide off your slacks and onto the steakhouse carpet. Plus, you're essentially getting a napkin that hundreds of people have used before you. It has the veneer of being nice, but it's like a handkerchief versus a Kleenex. It's actually more luxurious to be disposable. You don't want to think that someone used it before you. We don't do that with toilet paper in nice restaurants. You don't go into the can at Spago and get handed a cloth that Michael Douglas wiped his ass with the day before.

And they roll those things too tight. I never know how to get silverware out. Do you slide it through the hole or unravel it and have the silverware fall out onto the floor? Or do you try to dump it out like you're playing Yahtzee?

The thinning of napkins in the name of saving trees and reducing waste makes no sense. You end up using five times as many because they're practically translucent.

This is the slippery slope. Whenever you hear about people's travels to Third World countries, they complain about the TP. This is our descent, and it's starting with napkins. We're teetering on that Third World status, becoming like Turkey or something. Napkins used to be white and sturdy; now they're getting weak and brown. Just like America. ■

••

When filling a water bottle at the airport water fountain, there is often a line, yet no line in the bathroom. Bathroom sink water and water fountain water come from the same plumbing source, correct? Do you believe in saving time and calories by filling up in the bathroom?

Charlie, 38, Tacoma, Washington

We don't like the notion of getting water out of the bathroom. My dog Phil eats his own shit, but when he drinks out of a toilet, that's when my family freaks out.

The real problem with the bathroom water faucet is that it has the hand-motion activator and gives you a two-second burst. It would take hours to fill a one-liter bottle. Then it has to reset. There's no such thing as one and done with those. You couldn't put out a match with the amount of water that comes out, much less fill a canteen.

It's like the low-flow toilet. It essentially just means you'll flush three times. Are there water savings in using the same faucet spray five times on the installment plan?

It's especially egregious when you're at the airport, because you can go to the bathroom for free, wait at the water fountain at the cost of your time, or walk nine feet to the Hudson newsstand for a bottle of water that's thirteen dollars.

This doesn't freak me out at all. I'm the guy who drank from old SunnyD bottles full of water lined up at the boxing gym, took a swig of water out of a reused Clamato bottle in my fridge with my roommate John's false tooth in it, has taken any number of hits off the hose on any number of constructions sites, sucked off a school drinking fountain with a piece of gum stuck on it (which caused the water to jettison like from a clogged wiper spray nozzle), uses ice from the beer can–filled cooler to put into my drink, and in the dog days of summer as a kid biked around the San Fernando Valley taking draws of water off random sprinklers on people's front lawn. All of this was no problemo.

We got nuts with hydrating and water sources. Everything is triple-filtered, alkaline-balanced, and from a glacier or mountain spring in the Alps. Anyone who dies in their nineties today never saw a bottle of filtered water until they were at least seventy-five. They made it through fourteen-hour shifts in sweatshops in Brooklyn and stormed Normandy without a Poland Springs in hand. No one can draw a straight line between health and longevity and the contents of your water bottle.

One last H_2O-related tangent. The water bottle cage on ten-speed bikes has been around since the 1960s, but it never made it onto any other pedaled conveyance. Somehow, it was just decided that you didn't need water if you were on your Schwinn Stingray or Huffy. There were no water containers, no squeeze bottles made for the regular bike you use to get around and try to get some air with on a homemade ramp in the driveway. Why do the douchebags who dress in skintight Cinzano gear and block traffic get a special water bottle? ∎

....

Tacos or burgers?

Stephen, 30, Las Vegas

I love tacos. I grew up and live in Southern California, and we have some of the best Mexican food in the country. It's one of the only good things about living in L.A. There's nothing better than Lucy's El Adobe stringy BBQ beef on a deep-fried shell with guac, but here are the definitive taco rankings.

1. El Pastor
2. Carnitas
3. Steak
4. Chicken
5. Vegetarian

This list has been hotly debated on my podcast and Twitter. But in the end Danny Trejo, star of *Machete* and owner of Trejo's Tacos, settled it once and for all.

I think we got a little too far away into the soft taco realm. When I was a kid, soft tacos didn't comprise even 6 percent of the taco population. Now it's in the mid-'80s. We need to rediscover the majesty of the hard shell taco. It was never broken (pardon the pun).

I realize now, this happened about the time we made our way from hard cookies to soft cookies. When I was a kid, cookies were rock hard. You had to dunk them in milk just to make them edible. It was like hardtack. I think big cookie and big taco conspired.

And since I'm talking Mexican food, I must admit I'm not up to the burrito challenge anymore. Burritos are huge. They went in the same direction as cupcakes. They got massive. If your lunch is a burrito and a cupcake, you ain't eating dinner. I've seen rolled-up carpet with less heft than your average burrito. You could bludgeon someone to death with a modern burrito and then eat the murder weapon to cover your tracks.

But I must answer your question, Stephen, so it's time for some real talk re: tacos. I may lose some fans here. I love tacos, but I don't think there's anything that beats a killer hamburger. I feel like tacos have a ceiling on them. There are great tacos, but burgers have more potential.

Plus, America is built on burgers. Mexico is built on tacos. I'm just a patriot at (clogged) heart. Tacos are one of the greatest culinary contributions to the world. Burgers are as well. But the real question is: What's up, Canada? Where's your contribution to North American cuisine? Could you imagine the utopia we'd be living in if Canada had made the same culinary contributions Mexico has? What the fuck, Canucks? Your country is smart, successful, and bountiful. Mexico is struggling, but it's a cornucopia of awesome food. I could name fifteen Mexican delights off the top of my head. No one has ever uttered the phrase "Canadian cuisine." Have you ever said, "I could really go for some Canadian food tonight?" I can't think of a worse neighboring country. I'd rather be next to Hungary or Poland, or even a country in the Middle East and at least get some kabob going. I'm sure some Canadian readers are outraged now, so let me do a preemptive strike. Mayo on French fries and poutine are not contributions. Doing weird shit to French fries doesn't count. And Tim Horton's is just a doughnut shop. If you blindfolded someone and took them into a Dunkin' Donuts and then a Tim Horton's, they wouldn't be able to tell the fucking difference. Step it up, eh. ■

You seem to have a good balance between eating healthy and indulging in good but not good for you stuff. Between your earthy-crunchy hippie mom and living in Los Angeles, you were a prime candidate for buying into the all-natural organic vegan propaganda. How did you resist it?

Pete, 40, Amesbury, Massachusetts

Yes, when I was a kid with my mom, it was all holistic this and nature that. She and her earthy-crunchy friends would pontificate about how nature is going to heal everything. She'd watch Euell Gibbons talk about how you can eat pinecones and dandelions. It was real hippie shit. I never bought into it. I'm an atheist, and I think you only get one go-round, so why waste it eating foraged shit that tastes like crap? You could eat this book and get more flavor than the shit I was forced to eat growing up.

But a bigger and more current thought: My mom and her ilk's take was essentially, "You don't want to ingest a bunch of shit that The Man and big pharma cooked up. Homeopathic is the way to go." But in the flip-the-script department, the people like my mom, who talk the most about nature and healing, are suspiciously quiet about COVID and natural immunity. It's the right side of the country, the red states, that talk more about natural immunity. Those on the side that was anti–big pharma are all of a sudden very down with injecting something that Pfizer and Moderna cranked out and making fun of people who want to let nature take its course.

Fortunately, I have natural immunity to bullshit and see right through this. ∎

••

Does it bother you that "voluptuous" has been co-opted as a nice way to describe fat chicks?

Kevin, 37, White Plains, New York

I live by the mantra I saw on a bumper sticker: No Fat Chicks. I miss voluptuous. Sophia Loren, Gina Lollobrigida, and Marilyn Monroe were voluptuous back in the day. Now chicks who would have qualified for a sideshow at the turn of the century are being touted as voluptuous.

Appropriately enough, we're sugarcoating fat by calling it "voluptuous" and "a lot to love."

I was thinking about the '70s sitcom *The Facts of Life*. Everyone went from skinny to fat over the course of that show's run. No matter how Dove or Vogue tries to promote "body positivity," watch seasons three and nine of *The Facts of Life*. If all agree we want the girls as they looked in the early years, then mission not accomplished. Which version of Kirstie Alley did we all want to fuck? The Weight Watchers failure or the one Sam Malone was bagging on *Cheers*? Which version of Adele or Rebel Wilson do you want to wake up next to? Have you ever met a guy who said, "I want the version of Adele from her first album"? No. If that guy hasn't been born, then let's stop the charade.

Everyone has to fall over themselves about how "voluptuous" Lizzo is. I'm sorry, but I grew up in the '70s and '80s. I much prefer Thin Lizzy to Fat Lizzo.

And there's a double standard. We never make the body-positivity pitch for guys, as in, "I like the curvy Val Kilmer. He's owning it now."

As I was saying earlier, we're normalizing obesity. Take a look at pictures from the original Woodstock. That's what people used to look like. Now, everyone looks like they're in a funhouse mirror.

There's a difference between curvy and round. Biscuits are round, but they're not curvy. The curve has to curve back in order for the chick to be curvy. I think the ultimate reality check is porn. Ask yourself, if you filmed yourself fucking, what would the guys who run Pornhub file it under? (My video would be filed under "prodigious sack with low self-esteem," by the way.) You have to feel bad for the chick who uploads her homemade porn and is hoping to get labeled "busty" or "curvy" but ends up tagged "plumper" or "chubby." ∎

. . . .

Is peeing in the pool OK?

Adam, 38, Connecticut

Not only is it OK, it's mandated. The average public pool is 13,500 gallons, and the average amount of urination is 300 milliliters. How could you not?

The more gratifying piss is when you've just stepped out of the pool and piss on yourself and no one is the wiser. That's the much more satisfying endeavor. Sometimes I'll go in the pool just to get out and piss on myself.

We assume this is 100 percent the realm of the male, but in a world where most pools don't have an outdoor bathroom and guys can go to a nearby shrub, I bet women do it at least as much. Women get a free pass when it comes to this. If you said to a guy, "No peeing in the pool," he'd say, "I'll try," but if you said it to a woman, she'd slap you. We all know you're doing it. I think this is an offense to men. This is not the equality we've fought for. I'm starting a campaign to bring awareness: #peetoo.

Your best move if you're a pool pee-er is like my fake orgasm move, where a woman has to claim every ninth time that she just wasn't feeling it that night so the guy doesn't get suspicious that she's having sham orgasms. At the beginning of pool season, jump in and flop around for ten seconds, then get out and announce that you need to find the bathroom. Then you're off the list of pool pissers. You can happily pee in the pool for the rest of the summer. Ironically, you'll have marked your territory.

So yes, pee in every pool you can. You can urinate in a thousand pools, and no one will be the wiser. But take it from me, as I learned the hard way. Add the word "table" after the pool you pee in, and you're no longer welcome at the Burbank Y. ∎

Chapter 3

Relationshit

Whether it's from a decade-plus of doing *Loveline* or a lifetime with my own dysfunctional family, I feel over-qualified to answer your relationship queries. Bad dates? Been there, done that. Marital issues? Check. STDs? Absolu... You know what, Mike? Don't type that. Wait, you're not typing what I'm saying right now, are you?

....

What is the best response when before you even arrive at a social event your wife says to "be nice to everyone"?

Fred, 63, San Miguel de Allende, Guanajuato, Mexico

Obviously, she's basing it on past performance. You have to internalize it to some degree. But I would take the "be nice" comment as a feather in your cap. It means you have more going for you than the rest of the partygoers. If you've never been to a party with a bunch of supersuccessful business owners, ex-athlete superstars, or A-list actors, no one would ever have to tell you to be nice.

I don't know why we've created a society where the wife gets to tell the husband to be nice and how to dress and what's an appropriate gift to bring to the party, and it gets chalked up as a concerned wife supporting her man. If it were the man telling his wife to "be nice" and making her change into a different outfit, he would be considered a controlling dick and a pariah.

But let's talk about the concept of nice, because I have thoughts.

Nice is a two-way street. Not everyone is worthy of being nice to all the time. How many of your old associates, work partners, and friends from high school that you weren't nice to turned out to be douches and now you hate them? You were just ahead of the curve. While you should be nice to nice people, you should also get credit for being a douche to people you find out are douchey later.

Nice is also overrated. Nice can be the paper ribbon around the toilet seat in the hotel room. The idea is pleasant, but it doesn't serve a lot of function. Most people I would consider nice also aren't that innovative, creative, opinionated, or provocative. Nice has never won any wars or broken any speed records.

I would much prefer you to be fair than to be nice. If you're always fair, you'll always be nice, but if you're always nice, you might not always be fair. I'm very action-oriented. Nice can be a state of mind, but fair is where the rubber hits the road. Anyone can be nice. It's easy to say, "Oh, your hair looks good" or, "Have you lost weight?" when you go out to lunch with someone, but if you then suggest splitting the check even though you got lobster, two cocktails, and dessert and all they got was an iced tea, then you are unfair. I'd rather have a fair neighbor than a nice neighbor. Being pleasant to me is not as important as paying for my fence when the tree in your yard loses a limb and demolishes it. You'll most likely land on nice if you shoot for fair, but being nice doesn't always mean being fair.

Then there is the nuanced difference between nice and considerate. The longer I spend on this planet, the more I like considerate people. You can be nice without being considerate. Take, for example, the person who shows up a half-hour late every time you schedule a get-together. Even though they are apologetic and nice about it, the fact that they keep doing it shows they are not considerate.

Then there is nice that is being used to cover something, like Ellen dancing at the beginning of her show or Rosie O'Donnell launching Koosh balls into the crowd during her tapings and then as soon as the cameras are off berating and firing their staff. That's *using* nice. Using it mitigates it. The people who cultivate nice are doing it to take the place of being considerate or fair. Beware of those who are too nice. It's probably a smokescreen. It's covering fire. False nice can be a compensation for burning calories, spending money, or putting in unwanted effort to do things for people. Most so-called nice people end up just paying you back in some resentful, high-interest fashion. Nice can take the form of general proclamations about indigenous people and kids in need. Large, performative social media niceness is like a delicious frosting on a cupcake made of shit.

Being polite is fine, but this version of nice for you, Fred, often would just mean agreeing with every one of your wife's kooky friends. It's swapping out nice for agreeable. Most people are dumb and have stupid thoughts about why they need to fly with their dog, why Palestinians are just and Israelis are war criminals, or why Brett Favre is better than Tom Brady. You become a stupidity enabler when you agree just to be nice.

I'll admit that I'm not socially considerate. I'm not good with birthdays or anniversaries or finding the right words when someone's family member falls ill. But if I'm walking and I see a drywall screw in the middle of the street, I'm going to go out there and get it so someone doesn't destroy their tire. I may never meet the person whose tire gets saved or get thanked, but it's still a considerate thing to do. Again, nice can be an action. Considerate and fair are actions.

Here's the ultimate test. Go out for sushi with four people and order toro, that delectable fatty tuna. When four people are staring at the last piece, about eleven dollars' worth, and everyone's lost count of how many pieces they had, see what happens. Because no one is ever full from sushi. Everyone can handle one more piece. Who reaches for it? That's a true test of character. That will tell you if someone is nice or considerate and fair.

But since you're from Mexico and while we're on the topic, it makes me think of the border. Lot of shit going down there. The politicians on the left, the AOCs and Ayanna Pressleys of the world want to abolish ICE. For those of you who don't know, ICE stands for Immigration and Customs Enforcement. It makes it easy to villainize. It sounds cold and jagged and hard. The biggest douche in cinematic history was Val Kilmer's character in *Top Gun*, "the Iceman." But these ICE agents are just trying to do their job. They're just protecting us. So I figured out a genius way to keep ICE from being abolished. You just take the Immigration and Customs Enforcement and add National in front of it. Boom. You've now gone from ICE to NICE. Not even AOC would have the guts to stand on the floor of the House and declare that we need to abolish NICE. It'd be great for recruiting. Put that windbreaker on and you could get away with anything. "What's that NICE agent doing over there?" "He's beating the shit out of a Guatemalan grandma." "Well, she must have done something wrong. He's a NICE agent." ∎

∙∙

I recently bought a house, got married, and now I'm finally moving all of my stuff from my parents' house to our new house; however, there's one particular box my wife doesn't want me to bring with me because it contains all sorts of little keepsakes (photos, letters, gifts, etc.) I've collected over the years from my various relationships with ex-girlfriends.

I understand why my wife doesn't want me to keep these things, but I also don't just want to throw away some of my most meaningful and significant memories from my high school and college years. Is there another option that my wife and I would both be happy with?

Keith, 33, Detroit

Congratulations on successfully relabeling the spank bank as a "box of keepsakes." That's some high-level rebranding of the mobile masturbation museum. You should have been in the room when they were kicking around New Coke. This PR move is a step in the right direction. But I would go further.

I would transfer the contents of the "keepsake" box into another box and then take a Sharpie and write "Kirk Gibson Detroit Tigers Memorabilia" on it. You could leave that box on her side of the bed and she still wouldn't open it.

And if all else fails, I would caution her that there's still plenty of room in the box for another failed relationship. ■

• •

Since you've had both, what's more fun? Two dudes, one chick or two chicks, one dude. No cross-dick play included.

Jeff, 60, Leawood, Kansas

Your question is not quite accurate. I did have two chicks, one dude, but not the other option. It was the '90s, and I was living in Santa Monica. The two women were friends of friends who came to an ACME theater show, hung out at the after-party, and then went back to the Ace Man's pad for the after-after-party. One was a heavyset woman of color and the other a spindly white girl. I honestly don't remember much of it other than the white girl was in a little bit of a rush to get to church the next morning. She may have needed to douse herself in holy water after the unholy trinity with me the night before. I do remember being uptight because I had a female roommate at the time and she was a bitch about everything, never mind me bringing back two girls for a little ebony-and-ivory action. And to all you fucksticks who try to label me a racist and a conservative, how about that? I was way ahead of the game on diversity and equity.

The two-dudes, one-chick version didn't quite work out. I was living in a one-bedroom apartment on Laurel Canyon Boulevard in North Hollywood with The Weez (those of you familiar with the early days of my podcast or who read *Not Taco Bell Material* know all about him). He had a gal over who was, shall we say, "community property." She kind of slept with everybody. They were getting things started on the pullout sofa, and I thought, *She'd probably be down for a three-way.* So I came out of the bedroom and started rubbing her down a little bit, and it seemed like it was about to happen. But then there was a knock on the door to the apartment. It was the other town whore, and the hotter one at that. Sounds like the beginning of a great porno, right? Well, she was looking for my other roommate, Chris, who was a handsome fella who obliged all the ladies. She was making a late-night booty call, and I was the wrong number. This was around two a.m. on a Saturday. Chris wasn't around but yours truly was. I offered up my services, and she agreed. We hopped in her Jeep and went back to her place and ended up just talking all night. Nothing. I tried for the bird in the hand and didn't even get a handy when I could have gone for two and gotten some bush.

But to answer your question, I don't understand the allure of two dudes, one chick. I don't know why that's even a thing. Would you rather have one waffle cone and two scoops of ice cream, maybe even a vanilla-and-chocolate situation, if you catch my drift, or one scoop and two waffle cones?

I guess it comes down to, who is the second dude? Would you want to go with Dolph Lundgren and risk being humiliated but having a hell of a story, or go with Ken Jeong and not worry about looking bad? We all saw his dick in *The Hangover* and, ironically, it's so small it doesn't even hang over his balls. He doesn't have a penis; he has a pen*ish*.

And it's not just about physicality. How well do you know the other dude? Presumably you should know him, but if you know him too well, you might start talking shop in the middle of it. You might each be going to town on the girl in your own way, and then suddenly you remember that staff meeting tomorrow and ask him if he finished his PowerPoint before he finishes on the girl's tits. Or what if he owes you money for the Super Bowl bet and hasn't paid? These are all distractions in the two-guys, one-gal scenario. You'd like to know the guy well enough to know you're not gonna get stabbed, but not so well that you guys are finishing an argument you had about how Pat Benatar belongs in the Rock & Roll Hall of Fame while doing the Eiffel Tower with a runaway.

This question has prompted an even more interesting question, one that took me some time to nail down. I won't bother you with all the early machinations and algorithms. Suffice it to say, after a writing session that looked like the math equation on the blackboard in *Good Will Hunting*, I created this hypothetical question that is sweeping the nation.

Would you rather have sex with one person who's an "eight" or two partners who are a combined "ten"?

This question divided my staff, and my listenership. A Twitter poll had the one "eight" option coming in at 65 percent, while 35 percent would take the combo platter.

There's something to be said for checking the box of having had a threesome, but if you have to see a naked "three" in order to satisfy your "seven" urge, is it more harm than good? Are a "four" and a "six" even worth it?

These are the types of brilliant philosexual conundrums I like to come up with. They rank up there with my other hypothetical questions that will bend your mind and challenge your friend-ships when you force your buddies to answer them.

Would you rather your daughter be the girl onstage at the strip club but nobody you know would ever find out, or the hot chick on the billboard advertising the strip club even though she doesn't work there?

Would you rather have sex with the least attractive person in the office but none of your coworkers know it, or not have sex with that person but everyone thinks you did?

Would you rather have sex with your mother or blow your father?

With all that threesome talk and my whack down memory lane, I got turned on. Time to take a writing break and go have a *ménage à un.* ■

. . . .

What is your opinion on "friends with benefits"? What is your advice to someone who's been asked to be a "friend with benefits"?

Diana, 52, Seattle

Apparently, I have a lot of opinions I didn't know I had until hear-ing your question.

First, it's really a compli-sult. You're being told you're attractive but boring, or you have a bad personality. You should be flattered someone wants to fuck you and can tolerate you for short peri-ods but wouldn't want to live with you. It's kind of a backhanded compliment.

But if you think about it, friends with benefits is sort of the ultimate relationship situation. Because you are friends and you are having copious amounts of sex. Ask anyone who has been married fifteen years. They're having no sex, and even worse, they're having no sex with someone they're not friends with. They stopped being friends when they moved in together and started fighting about leaving the lights on and leaving dishes in the sink. This is the ultimate argument for friends with benefits. You get to stay friends.

But really, can it ever work? Is it ever possible that each person has the exact same interest level in the other person? Is it possible that neither one has any romantic notion about the other even though each enjoys the other as a friend and finds them attractive? What percentage of women who enjoy a guy as a friend and want to have sex with him have no designs on him and wouldn't be upset if he started dating one of their friends? Friends with benefits is like solar panels or recycling programs. It seems great on paper but never quite works out.

And "benefits" is the greatest euphemism for sex ever. A job with good benefits means a dental plan or a vending machine with 1950s prices, but you don't get to have sex with the receptionist. If the benefits that HR departments provide were the benefits a friend with benefits provides, we wouldn't be in the middle of "The Great Resignation" and the country's unemployment number would be negative. The "friends with benefits" phrase was most definitely coined by a man. If friends with benefits were called what it really is—"plowing someone when I get blackout drunk that I don't like enough to take on vacation"—it probably wouldn't get as much traction. "I would like to bang you now, but I think I could do better later" doesn't have as good a ring to it.

Perhaps this was the rebuttal to all the "just friends" talk over the years. Enough guys got the "I like you as a friend" line that we eventually had to come up with a counteroffer.

Then again, as a euphemism, being labeled a friend with benefits benefits women. For guys, it's a better way of saying "chick I fuck when I'm drunk," but for women it's camouflage for "I'm kind of a whore."

It's also a young person's game. No one over thirty-five is doing the friends-with-benefits thing. At that point you're ready to settle for friends *or* benefits. Either you want to still be having sex with your wife, or you want to be hanging around with your friends to get away from your sexless marriage.

But on that note about youth, how good can your friendship be if there are benefits? When you're young, all you talk to your friends about is who you're fucking. It would be incredibly awkward if you say, "I was banging this chick the other night...oh wait, that was you..."

By the way, in the gay community they don't bother with this nonsense. They just kind of do away with the charade. If you are friends, the benefits part is implied.

As far as advice for you, Diana, I think it's about self-esteem. Do the friends-with-benefits thing if you don't mind being treated like a rental car. That's essentially what it is. A guy who wants you to be his friend with benefits is basically saying, "This is a rental, not a purchase. I need transportation, but I don't want to pay for an Uber." ∎

....

I'm a middle-aged guy from Kansas who was adopted at birth nearly fifty years ago. I didn't find out until I was seventeen. Recently, by sending my spit to Ancestry.com, I found out that my birth father is a very successful, recently retired orthopedic surgeon who lives on the edge of the golf course in Pebble Beach, California. I have reached out to him via social media, but he ignored me completely, going so far as to delete his Facebook account or block me. I have spoken to his daughter (my half-sister), and she seems very open to having at least some kind of relationship with me, but our father seems to be a nonstarter. I'm not after his money, which I'm sure is the reason he is ignoring me, but how should I go about getting his attention? I'd just like to

*meet the guy and have an acknowledgment of some kind
that we are father and son. Is that asking too much? It is
weird knowing you have a flesh-and-blood father out there
who wants nothing to do with you. My adopted father was
a WWII veteran who passed when I was just twenty-three.
What would Adam do?*

Dan, 50, Kansas

First off, living on the edge of a golf course is a great addition to
my ever-growing "Rich Man, Poor Man" list—things the very rich
and very poor have in common. Either you are in a triple-gated
community with a private members-only golf course, or you live
next to the public driving range in a double-wide and are constantly dodging shanked Titleist 4s.

But to answer your question, my general rule is not to get too
hung up on the blood part of it. I wouldn't even look at it as blood.
I would just look at it as semen. He just wanted to bang your mom.

And there are so many examples of "blood" turning into bad
blood. Just because you are related to someone doesn't mean they
are going to like or care about you. Just ask Noel and Liam Galla-
gher of Oasis or the Robinson brothers of the Black Crowes.

I would let sleeping orthopedic surgeons lie, if he can even
sleep knowing of your existence. The burden should be on him.
He's the one who should be tossing and turning.

Even if he were to come around, it would be an awkward,
uncomfortable rendezvous somewhere that would ultimately be
unsatisfying. They say the best revenge is a life well lived. Just live
your life well.

You had a WWII vet who loved you enough to adopt you and
raise you. That's a lot more than most people have. My dad had
the blood connection with me minus the desire to act on it. Your
adopted father didn't have the blood, but he put in the sweat and
the tears. ∎

• •

Do men have preferences on vag size? Some women prefer a large penis, others not so much. I would argue if a woman has a large, stretched-out vag she would prefer a large penis, but if a man has a smaller penis and gets with a woman with a stretched-out vag, is he just happy to get some...or is he disappointed?

MeChelle, 47, Seattle

Methinks MeChelle doth protest too much. ■

• •

My sister-in-law married a 350-pound forty-year-old trucker without a truck, and they live in my in-laws' basement. He smells, has floppy fat arm wings, three teeth—give or take—and likes to hug the ladies. They play video games with their only two online friends, get drunk, smoke, and cook meat all day. How do we get Trucker Bob back on the road and out of the basement?

Rebecca, 38, New York

You've got me thinking about truckers. How the mighty have fallen. But maybe they shouldn't have been on a pedestal in the first place. Firefighters have always been heroes, and janitors have always been losers in the eyes of society, especially women. But being a trucker was just a regular job until the 1970s, when for some reason we turned them into folk heroes. This might be a little hard for the current generation to understand. If you grew up in the 1970s, you were inundated with images of truckers being hard-lovin' renegade outlaw poets. Their legend was told in movies, like *Every Which Way but Loose* and *Smokey and the Bandit*; on television shows, like *B.J. and the Bear*; and in songs, like "Keep on Truckin'" and "Convoy." They punched out their bosses; brought contraband cigarettes, booze, and women across state lines; and hung out with orangutans, and we were all-in. Everyone wanted to get on a C.B. and give a big 10-4 to their good buddies. Being a trucker was as likely to get you laid as being a fighter pilot or a bull rider. I think it was the down vest. That somehow made truckers cool. I've never seen someone get out of a truck in a down jacket. That makes you look like a skier, not a trucker. Somehow taking the sleeves off it made it cool.

So why did the trucker achieve mythical status in the 1970s? I think it was because society was so fucked-up that guys who rambled were seen as elevated. They said no to being The Man and having all those things "squares" had, like a house, a steady paycheck, and 2.5 kids. (Though truckers today might have 2.5 kids—the two they know about, and the half is the kid the bitch claims is his but he ain't paying child support for.)

But dig this thought. Maybe they were elevated in our eyes because they were actually elevated. You're on the road as a kid in the back of your parents' station wagon facing the wrong direction, and you give the pull-the-chain-for-the-horn signal and he does! That's a great moment for a kid. And where is the guy giving the kid that everlasting childhood memory? He's about ten feet higher than the kid on a mobile throne like some sort of king on eighteen wheels.

But that's all over. Truckers are now back to being fat racists who piss in Snapple bottles. And they're an endangered species, not only because Elon Musk is going to make them obsolete with driverless trucks but because of their awful diet.

If you go into a truck stop, not only can you get the worst food you could ingest—hot and instantly available for pennies—but you can find lots of kitchen appliances that run off a cigarette lighter. I didn't know anyone needed a waffle maker on the road, but I guess they do. A George Foreman sandwich press that could run off a cigarette lighter is not something that God intended, but here it is. Truck stops have snacks that are so full of chemicals, they'll last longer on the shelf than anyone buying them will last on the planet, and shit that proves you're an American, like a "God, Guts, Guns" T-shirt. As if we didn't know you're an American because you're morbidly obese driving a Kenworth hauling logs. All that plus truck-stop hookers.

A quick tangent on hookers...

First off, we keep changing the language to make it sound better. "Whore" gave way to "hooker," which gave way to "prostitute," but now we've moved on to "sex worker." Like "waiter" became "server" and "stewardess" and "steward" became "flight attendant," I actually think this is a downgrade. If my daughter were to choose that livelihood, I'd rather her be a "prostitute" than a "sex worker." The latter sounds very unfulfilling. "Sex worker" makes it seem like she clocks in down at the sex factory or goes to her cubicle at the Sex Corporation. Taking it in the ass from nine to five until Mr. Sexly pulls the chain on the quittin'-time whistle.

Anyway, I don't wish for my daughter to be a whore. But if she were to pursue that career path, I would want her to end up on the top rung of the prostitute ladder. In the prostitute pecking order, the top ones are flown to Monaco for the F1 race. If you're one of those, you are world-class ass. You're getting flown privately to another continent. On the next rung down, you're getting flown in for the Super Bowl. You're still getting flown in, but you stay in the continental U.S. Then next is regional work. You come in for Mardi Gras, but you live in the South already. After that, you're down to basic call girl in a big city—Vegas, New York, L.A. You might travel from a different part of the city or from the outer suburbs, but at least you're not in your own neighborhood. Then it's any major city as a streetwalker. You're walking your beat. You don't have a long commute, but at least you live in a city. Next is runaway streetwalker. You're traveling, but it's more like you're fleeing. You're going from town to town making ends meet by prostituting yourself in motels.

The truck-stop hooker is at the bottom of the prostitute pyramid. It doesn't get lower than that. You're not traveling anywhere, even though your clients are; you don't get to ply your trade in a decent city or even a decent hotel. You're sleeping in your car outside a Flying J waiting for your next client. He's hauling cargo and also a bad case of crabs, and after he gives you some he's on the road again.

But back to the 350-pound topic at hand. We are in a unique moment in time when the fat people are the poor people. Never before in the history of civilization have the poorest been the fattest. Being "Rubenesque" used to be a sign of wealth. You had the money to eat and didn't have to toil in fields. Now it's a sign that you sit on your can all day watching *Judge Judy* and eating Ring Dings. It would be nice if we could get back to the fat cats actually being fat. We should want rich people to be fat so they can handle their own medical bills. Right now the people clogging the ERs with problems related to their clogged arteries are doing it on the public dime. They're driving up health care costs, insurance premiums, and COVID deaths (and thus related government overreach). Meanwhile, Jeff Bezos, Elon Musk, and Twitter's Jack Dorsey are the healthiest guys on the planet. We need to flip this script and have them be morbidly obese, so they'll die sooner and leave a library and an endowment behind. Right now, Trucker Bob is going to be the first one to drive his big rig off this mortal coil, and all he'll leave behind is an ass print on your in-laws' couch.

So, as far as your brother-in-law, I say just wait for the weight to catch up with him. Those basement stairs can only hold so much tonnage. He's only got a couple of successful runs on those stairs before he heads to the great convoy in the sky. ∎

. . . .

I run a business that employs independent contractors. I'm a male in my thirties, and most of my contractors are older males. I have few female contractors; one is someone I just so happened to have started sleeping with over a year ago. Casual is turning into serious, and we're trying to decide if we should make our relationship public. It's been over a year, and nobody else in our work circle knows about it. Curious if workplace relationships are still an issue in 2021?

Larry, 35, Arizona

No one may know about it, but when you reveal it everyone will say, "Oh, I knew something was going on." It's not true, but they'll say it. This doesn't happen when someone comes out of the closet. No one comes out to their coworkers and one responds, "I knew you sucked dick!"

And it will be the women more than the men who try to claim retroactive knowledge. They look at not knowing as a shortcoming; otherwise they'd have to admit that "women's intuition" is a bunch of bullshit. The men will decide based on how your girlfriend looks whether it's a good idea or not to pretend they knew. If she's a pig, they're not going to say, "I knew it." They're going to act cool, maybe even congratulate you, and then talk shit about you behind your back. But if she's hot, they'll act as if they knew so they can try to get details out of you that they can beat off to later.

But to answer your question, I never understood the problem with dating coworkers. They're your social circle. How are you going to avoid it entirely, unless there's some sort of exchange program? Which I think we should create. It'd be like arranged marriages between two Indian villages. You offer up eligible singles from your company, and the HVAC company down the hall does the same. The CEOs or owners could get together and be like, "I've got a 'seven,' a 'four,' and a 'three.' What do you have?" We could obviously broaden the scope beyond just the local office park. We have apps now that could point the way. We'd need to come up with a combination of Tinder and Indeed. Do you think there's a market for Tindeed? Imagine the résumés: "Types sixty words per minute. Proficient in Mac, PC, and Chrome-based applications. Turn-ons are guys who love dogs and aren't afraid to cry. Swipe right for more information and selfies." ■

I've just ended a fifteen-year relationship and, upon reflection, it's very clear I have never had healthy boundaries for myself—and I desperately want to improve this. I don't believe anyone in my family has any either! Shhhhhhhhhh-hhhhhhhhhhocker! I am wondering what you recommend as steps to create healthy boundaries for myself as well as how to grow them for my three-year-old.

Lisa, 43, California

Well, let me ask you this: How much do you weigh? What's your bra size? Does your child have a disability? DM me with the answers before you keep reading. I've got to figure out if you really do have poor boundaries.

If you actually attempted to DM me, then yes, you have shitty, shitty boundaries.

You should always work on boundaries, but don't overcompensate. We as a society shouldn't be able to tell if you're cultivating healthy boundaries. If somebody asks to cut in front of you in line because they're running late, that's not the time to exercise your boundaries. That's low-hanging fruit. It's easy to exercise stronger boundaries with a stranger in a Trader Joe's parking lot when they pull into the space you were trying to turn into. The hard work is doing it with friends and family. Good luck. ■

My wife is hot, makes great money, but is lazy. Any advice to help deal with my ever-present conflicted state?

Rick, 39, Kansas

If she makes great money, you're ahead of the game, no matter how lazy she is. This is as good as you can get, Rick. Hang on. If she makes great money and is also a dynamo around the house, that's going to be your worst nightmare; she's going to shove that in your face. But you can throw money, in this case her money, at this problem. Her income compensates for her laziness. She doesn't cook? You spend her money at a restaurant. She doesn't clean? Spend her money on a maid. She doesn't put out? Spend her money…wait, use your own money for that. ■

My family of four (two teen daughters) is taking a Disney vacation this year. We'll be staying in a standard studio hotel with two queen beds. What's the protocol if the wife and I want to get busy? Hang the "Do Not Disturb" sign on the door and throw the deadbolt? Send them a text so they stay away? Or do I just need to keep my snake in its cage for the week? Looking for guidance.

Victor, 54, Ohio

You probably want your kids thinking you have a healthy sex life. But you never want them to see it or hear it. That's traumatizing. Even just talking about sex with your parents is awful.

When I was nine, I lived with my dad in his second apartment after moving from a bungalow in Laurel Canyon. It was one of those shitty row apartments with paper-thin walls. We had one long hallway wall that we shared with another unit. I was lying in bed one evening, and the entire night I could hear this woman getting plowed and just making horrible sounds. It still haunts me to this day; it's why I can't bring pleasure to a woman. It was blood-curdling. All night she was screaming, "Oh God!!!!" and making horrific groans and howls. I went to my father, because at age nine you have no context for that kind of moaning and groaning. I thought she had the stomach flu. I was telling my dad we needed to call the paramedics. In that moment I saw his face, the twisted grimace of "Oh shit, am I going to have to have this [or in my dad's case, any] conversation with my nine-year-old?" and knew what was happening. I was just old enough to do the math on my neighbor's getting the bejesus fucked out of her. At six or seven, you innocently ask questions. At twelve or thirteen, you know better. But in between, you're seeing the person's awkward face and doing that math as they uncomfortably explain to a tween how to fuck.

So your kids are older than I was when I learned about the birds and the bees via the sounds from Apartment B. They already know, and they don't want to know. So there's going to be a "Don't ask, don't tell" policy for this. You could sneak back to the room while the girls are waiting in line for the teacups so you and the Mrs. can slide between the sheets and go on Mr. Toad's Wild Ride. But have your plan worked out with the wife. Otherwise you're going to be on Main Street USA saying, "Honey, I forgot the sunblock…come back to the room and help me find it," and not being on the same page, she'll say, "It's 8:30 at night," and your cover for getting under the covers and getting blown will be blown. ∎

....

I've been married for about two years, and as it turns out, the person I married has completely changed. Or, they did a good job of hiding their true personality, and now that we're married he's letting all his terrible habits out. He is immature, petty, resistant to constructive criticism, extremely narcissistic, and overall childish. I am the exact opposite! I come from a strict family, and living with him is like listening to nails on a chalkboard every day. Of course, I just had a very handsome baby boy who I love very much, but my plan to leave is now put on the back burner. Help me, Ace Man! What should I do? Try to stick it out for the baby, or take my precious boy and run?

Ilona, 38, New Haven, Connecticut

In my estimation, people don't change, especially if they don't think anything is wrong with them. The people who need to change the most are the ones least likely to do it.

I say take your kid and hit the road. I could plot a very detailed plan of what the next few years are going to look like for you, or you could just save time and watch the opening to the '70s sitcom *Alice*.

That said, I'm no couple's therapist, but you can't just announce you're the opposite of your husband and that you were blindsided by this. People don't just change that quickly, and they're usually not that good at hiding who they really are. So as you hit the road for a new life, stop at a therapist's office along the way and figure out what red flags you missed. ■

....

My fiancé and I live in a two-bedroom condo. We have separate bedrooms but are thinking of moving into a small house. I am a light sleeper and enjoy the freedom of my own bed. If we end up in a one-bedroom house, what should I do? Lucy-and-Ricky-style twins? Bunk beds? Or sleep on the couch? Please help!

Lee, 38, Livermore, California

You've come to the right person for advice on this one. Kris Carolla, my mom, was the pioneer of this in the '70s. My stepdad, John, had his own room, which was also our den. So you'd sit on the edge of his bed to watch TV. At least while we were watching *Maude* from his bed, we knew there was no way he and my mom had ever had sex on that thing.

And when I was still making my way as a carpenter, I built a bed for a well-known restaurateur and another one for his live-in boyfriend. I remember being confused about it at the time. Were they not getting along? I later realized what a genius move this was. Whether it's about sex frequency, open relationships, or sleeping arrangements, the gays are light-years ahead of us heteros. This must have added decades to the relationship.

First things first: The Lucy-and-Ricky plan won't work. You may eliminate the tossing-and-turning vibrations, but snoring travels across that three-foot gap. It's weird that in the '40s and '50s there were two beds and one car; now there are two cars and one bed. Lucy didn't have her own car, but she had her own bed. Now it's weird if you don't each have a car, and just as weird if when friends come over you're still folding up the pullout couch. They're just going to assume you guys are heading for divorce.

Second, how much of this is about beating off versus being a "light sleeper"? To me that sounds like a dog whistle code for wanting your own room to rub one out before nodding off.

I bet you think I'm going to say save a little more and get a two-bedroom. That would be good advice but not so much on the funny side. So I say bunk beds. People look at marriage as a prison anyway. Why not go all-in? You might find it surprisingly exciting. Like one of those hotels with theme rooms. There is something about sex on a bunk bed that makes you feel like you're getting away with something. Like you're at summer camp, in jail, on a boat, or in a *Taboo*-esque stepsiblings porno.

There's another good part of the couple's bunk plan. Twice a month you have to have sex on the upper bunk. If one of you struggles to get up there or you're afraid it won't structurally hold while you pork, it's time to start losing some pounds. ■

....

What relationship advice would you give for a straight and conservative male that goes to a liberal school with the majority of the population being liberal? I find it hard to meet girls, and once they find out my politics, they tend to lose interest.

Alex, 20, Philadelphia

Lie about your politics and then enjoy your hate fuck. Make the libs cry...with ecstasy!

It's sad that we're so politically, socially, and culturally divided that we need to use code like the gays did back in the day. If you were into the fellas back when it was literally a crime, there were all kinds of signs you could exhibit that would let fellow Greco-active gents know where you stood (or kneeled). So I think, sadly, you're going to have to go underground a little bit and subtly let your political orientation show, and see if any gals are quietly feeling the same way.

A MAGA hat would be too obvious. That's a little too loud and too proud. But you could ask a prospective date, "Do you like college football?" or "Did you see the movie *Gran Torino*?" and her answer will give you some clues as to where she stands. Call the January 6 chaos at the Capitol a riot. If she corrects you by saying "insurrection," you're probably fishing in the wrong pond. But if you ask her on a date and then explain how the restaurant needs to see your vaccine cards, and she refuses or even just rolls her eyes, you've maybe found Ms. Right (wing).

The good news for you is that if you convince one of these liberal ladies to sign the school-authorized sexual consent form, it'll be great. All these chicks hate their dad, so the fucking will be frequent and freaky. ∎

....

I am in my second marriage and have been married for four years. I "dabbled" in some swinging with my ex-wife before we divorced, and it was great. How do I bring up swinging to my new wife?

Barry, 44, Boston

Well, the first marriage ended in divorce, so maybe swinging is not a recipe for relationship longevity.

The problem with bringing someone else into the bedroom is that it's a hard sell. You can't get around the math. It's like sitting in a restaurant and the chef comes to the table, and you tell him how delectable and incredible his cuisine is but then say, "Wouldn't it be great if we got something from the Cheesecake Factory? I love your stroganoff, it's the best, but wouldn't it be better if we got stroganoff from the Cheesecake Factory?"

I'm not well-versed in swinging. Do the other swingers come to your house, or do you go to their house? Or is it like the Super Bowl, where everyone plays at a neutral stadium?

I don't even know that I should keep using the word "swinging" to address this question. That's not how it's referred to today. Now we put all these cute terms on this type of stuff and act like it's evolved. "Swinging" conjures images of 1970s *Bob & Carol & Ted & Alice*–style key parties. There used to be a uniform in the '70s that let you know if someone was a swinger. He'd be in a burnt-orange dickie under a blazer, and the chick would be in a crisscross halter top that could easily be untied from around the neck, and she'd be smoking long brown More cigarettes. Playing Spot a Swinger was easy. Nowadays they all dress like plain-clothes cops or air marshals. But back in the day, you could spot the swingers because their medallions were swinging.

The terminology changed sometime in the '80s to "open marriage." What you're wanting to open is your legs for someone else's dick. Now people use the word "polyamory" because it sounds fancier. But it still just means you want to fuck different people.

It's the same way cult leaders speak: "If God lets you love all the fourteen-year-olds, why wouldn't you want to share that gift?" Or people at nudist camps: "It's so liberating." Yes, you can now play snooker with your balls dangling, unencumbered by the tyranny of underpants. We put coats of verbal veneer on this behavior to make it more palatable. You're not evolved or progressive. You're just a perv who wants to get some strange. Stop making yourself sound noble.

Will and Jada Pinkett Smith are a perfect example of this. I know more about their sex life than I do about my own. They bloviated on their *Red Table Talk* about monogamy being "a prison," thus implying any of us who aren't banging around are somehow lesser, unevolved beings. But we all accepted it. It's like jeans with holes in them. When a rich person wears them, you think how cool they are. But when a homeless guy wears them, you think how sad it is. When titans of the tech industry and celebrities come out as being polyamorous, we think it's evolved, but if it's the trailer trash on *Cops*, we're not as forgiving—though as a fan of that particular porn genre, I thank Will Smith and say it's nice to see a black man getting cuckolded for a change. I believe this is a step towards the equity that all the progressives are talking about. ■

....

What's your opinion on pulling out? Is this conditional, a function of being married or single, or just governed by personal preference? Asking for a friend...

Doug, 55, Rochester, New York

I don't have any strong thoughts about it. But it does give me an excuse to tell a funny story.

I used to listen to Dr. Ruth on the car radio many years ago. It was great because she was diminutive, had that German accent, and didn't seem like someone who'd be talking about venereal diseases and sixty-nining. And she'd talk to some of the dumbest people on the planet. No offense to any of you readers who have been radio show callers, but those are usually not the brightest bulbs. They'd get on there all nervous and say something stupid like, "Hello, Dr. Ruth. You're a big fan of mine." And the call would always start, "Dan, Line 3, what's your problem? Dan? Hello? Caller Dan?" because the guy had said his name was Fred because he wanted to talk about how bad his wife's pussy stank, and in the nine minutes he was on hold he forgot he'd given a fake name.

I did *Loveline* for ten years and always marveled at how dumb our callers were. But one Dr. Ruth caller took the cake. In my decades of doing that show, my KLSX syndicated morning show, and my podcast, I've never had a caller this dumb. It was so memorable, I know exactly where I was when I heard it. I was driving my truck on the Ventura Freeway in North Hollywood, getting off the Coldwater Boulevard exit. It was 1985. The caller said, "Dr. Ruth, me and my girl, we've been having sex a lot. And we're not using protection. She's not on the pill, and I'm not using condoms. She's not getting pregnant, but I'm worried she could because we're not using protection." And Dr. Ruth asked, "Vell, do you pull out?" The guy paused for a five-Mississippi count, which is an eon of dead air in radio, and finally says, "Well, yeah. When I'm done."

Did this guy think Dr. Ruth was asking if he went to work with his girlfriend still on his dick? It's kind of hard to get through the door of the Napa Auto Parts with your girl still riding your honker. How do you go out to eat? Do you just take a sweatshirt and drape it over your dick in between you and walk sideways into the restaurant? ■

....

Are you into butt stuff? Did any of your girlfriends ever request it?

Jim, 43, Dedham, Massachusetts

Can't say I am or that they have. I've talked to plenty of dudes over the years on *Loveline* who were overly obsessed with getting a little back door loving. I always felt like it wasn't worth the trouble. The brown eye you get to put your dick in is not worth the stink eye you get from your old lady for the rest of your marriage. And call me old-fashioned, but when it comes to the ass play, I wonder: When did everyone get bored with fucking? Has a blowjob lost its luster?

But I do have some questions about ass play myself, specifically anal beads.

I did a *Man Show* bit a million years ago where I toured a sex toy factory, and the guy conducting the tour gave me a lecture about Ben Wa balls. He was very hung up on me not calling them that. I'm not sure why. I don't know if it's a brand name like Q-tips, and everything else has to be called cotton swabs. I had to look it up. I was trying to figure out why they were called that, but there doesn't seem to be a consensus. All I know is "Ben Wa balls" sounds like a punt returner out of San Jose State, or a pastry at Mardi Gras, especially if you spell it with French flair, Benoix Balls.

How does one give anal beads to the person whose ass you'd like them in? The presentation has to be awkward. "Oh, honey, you got me a necklace for Valentine's." "Well...umm..." "I don't see a clasp. How do I put them around my neck?"

And getting them in there has got to be a time-consuming process. Is there some sort of quick-loading clip you can shove up your ass? The anal bead equivalent of a magazine going into a Glock, as opposed to loading up a Smith & Wesson six-shooter with individual bullets or getting the ramrod out to stuff bird shot into the muzzle of a flintlock musket? I imagine otherwise it's like loading a PEZ dispenser. They keep popping out as you try to put the next one in.

Do you leave one dangling out? I feel like you need a lead. It's like when the string that goes through the hood of your sweatshirt gets sucked up into the hole and you spend an hour fishing it out. You need that knot at the end so it won't get absorbed. Is it like that with anal beads?

And when you do pull them out, do you do it slowly or is it like starting an outboard motor? Do you just rip it like you're firing up the two-stroke lawnmower? ■

. . . .

I'm new to the single life. My friends, who are generally much younger than me, are telling me to go online. I'm hesitant but feel it's probably good for a few stories. Here's my dilemma. I look pretty good for my age. Young at heart but an old soul. If I date in my age range, there could be some real snoozers. But if I date younger, we might not share cultural touch points (The Love Boat!). I'm financially self-sufficient. I don't need a sugar daddy, but I don't wanna be a sugar momma! What to do?! If I target a wider age range, should I put my age on my profile? Do men care?

Jian, 57, Houston

Once you pass your forty-fifth birthday, it's not just your soul that's old. It's your titties too. And I wouldn't worry about the sugar daddy part. That ship sails too about the time your soul gets past its "fresh until" date.

Remember, it's not about an age; it's about an attitude. As far as someone's getting your references and cultural touch points, it's not about age; it's about interest. My mom is eighty-eight and doesn't know anything. It's about having your eyes and ears open. It's about being interested.

But your question prompts a comment about the double standard women are always complaining about. Yes, as you age, men want to fuck you less. But you always seem to forget that when you're nineteen, supersuccessful people want to buy you cars. That doesn't happen to nineteen-year-old dudes. You might still be in junior college taking pottery classes, but forty-six-year-old Warren Beatty wants to eat your pussy and buy you a diamond bracelet. You just skip to the part where you're in your fifties and can't find a good man, forgetting that when you're nineteen and hot you can have all the good men you want, even if they're married, while no women are interested in a nineteen-year-old dude with no money, like I was. ∎

With porn being so ubiquitous, and having the ability to satiate people's desires for sex and relationships, do you think this will impact the world's population in the future?
Mike, 47, Las Vegas

I think it already has. Birth rates are down. The media makes it about millennials not wanting to bring kids into this horrible world, with all its political strife and global warming. Fuck that. It's because they have VR porn on their Oculus. (How has no one created porn-specific VR goggles called "Cockulus"?) It's all digital now. No one wants to go analogue with their log.

And totally realistic sex robots are starting to come off the assembly line, which is really going to destroy us. Let's face it, neither sex is wild about the other sex. We just want the orgasm. If we can streamline the whole process and not continue to populate the earth, we could get this global-warming problem sorted out lickety-split. But then again, these robots probably take some pretty hefty batteries. And the developed countries are going to be the first to be able to afford them, so our population will be going down. Meanwhile, Africa, India, and China are going to amass even bigger populations, declare war on us, and overrun us in a day.

But since we're talking sex bots: First off, let's do away with the name "sex bot." We can keep the bot part. But the sex part is a tell. If the wife discovers the box that says "sex bot" in the trash, you're screwed.

And where would you hide the sex bot? Back in the day, you could stash a couple of tattered *Playboys* between the mattress and box spring. Where would you stash a sex robot? You could do the whole hide-it-in-plain-sight thing, where it's just out and you can say, "If I were fucking her, do you think I'd just leave her in the living room?" I think the designers of these things also need to give them another skill, so we have plausible deniability. "Did you get one of those new sex bots?" "Oh, you mean my automated dog walker…who I occasionally fuck."

And if all else fails, you can put it on the roof with a shotgun to scare off looters. ∎

I'm a fifty-nine-year-old attractive, intelligent, funny, and fit woman who has been single for the majority of my life, except for a brief five-year marriage with a man with borderline personality disorder who had a girlfriend the entire relationship. Since high school, I've had many friends-with-benefits relationships with men, and some boyfriends that lasted briefly and then often morphed into friends with benefits or simply good friends. Without fail, every man has expressed in one way or another that he enjoys hanging out with me, being friends with me, and having sex with me, but for some reason he cannot explain why he doesn't want to date me.

Over the years, I've heard you (and other men) characterize men and women in a particular way, and I always fit the male type more than the female type. For example, I'm practical and logical more than emotional; I am orderly; I hate being late; I never lose things; I hate shopping; I'm great with finances and budgeting; I like to look nice but spend minutes, not hours, with showering, hair, and makeup; and I don't believe I engage in "chick think." Sure, I like to talk a lot and analyze things more than most men, but overall I've never been a girly-girl. At this point, you're probably thinking I look and act really butch/dyke-like, but I can assure you I'm short, cute, and feminine.

I started noticing that most men I've dated always talked about their crazy ex, and then eventually went back to said crazy ex or moved on to another woman they later called crazy. I asked my most recent ex-boyfriend if in fact men like crazy women, and he admitted that was sort of true. I am starting to come to the conclusion that I am too rational and even-keeled for most men's taste, and as much as they say they wish women would act more like men, they actually love the insanity.

What do you think of this theory, and what's a girl to do? Any advice would be much appreciated.

Judy, 59, Bergen County, New Jersey

I don't think men like crazy women. They like hot women, who are all crazy. Hot beats crazy every time. That's like asking, "Do rich guys like temperamental sports cars?" No, but they want to drive Lamborghinis, which are temperamental. They want a Lamborghini that's as reliable as a Camry. But the similarity between European sports cars and hot chicks is simple—all men want to get inside them, and some men have more patience for dealing with the bad wiring.

I think there's something deeper here. The phenomenon is that straight guys aren't flexible sexually. They don't hook up with dudes periodically. There's not a lot of wiggle room like women have. No straight guy has ever uttered, "Man, every time I drink tequila I start hooking up with my buddies." That's behavior that chicks can get away with, and sometimes get paid for. So, it's pretty much carved into straight dudes' DNA that they want to be with women. Maybe there's something going on psychologically if a straight dude hooks up with a hetero woman who has the psychological qualities of a man, making him feel psychologically gay. He doesn't think of that person as a potential mate. She doesn't have a dick and balls, but all the other qualities are male so he loses his sense of attraction. She doesn't fit the template of a potential partner. If the vibes or pheromones a woman is pushing out are that she's super pragmatic and organized and loves fantasy football, men are going to fuck her for a little while but won't see her as a mate, and will eventually move on. ■

Growing up in an age when porn was impossible to find and we had to rely on our imagination and the occasional **National Geographic** *topless native, deposits into the spank bank were infinitely necessary. My account included the obvious, like Marsha Brady, Mary Ann and Ginger, Barbara Eden, all guest beauties on* **The Love Boat** *and* **Buck Rodgers** *(don't sleep on Pamela Hensley/Princess Ardala). But every now and then an uncharacteristically plain chick like the one who played Mary Hartman on* **Mary Hartman, Mary Hartman** *would get deposited into my account. (Oh,*

those pigtails and overbite!) Did you have any embarrass-
ing inspirations in your spank bank, or was it just me?

Robart, 58, Colorado

The furthest I would stray from the full fantasy girlfriend would be Kate Jackson from *Charlie's Angels*. My Mount Rushmore of women I wanted to mount more had Cheryl Ladd, Linda Carter, and Adrienne Barbeau from *Maude*. I didn't see the logic in being attracted to the more obtainable or realistic women on TV, since it was unthinkable that anyone on TV would be attracted to me.

Thinking, *I'm going to go for Mary Ann instead of Ginger*, would be like me saying, "I'm going to strap a bottle rocket to my ass, but I'm not going to shoot for Mars; I'm just going to the moon." As long as we're fantasizing, I'm going with the "ten." My self-esteem is nonexistent, but it's still not poor enough to settle in my masturbation fantasies. ∎

• •

Why do you think it is that no one ever admits to being in
a relationship with a "five," and yet the majority of people
are dating or married to a five? Is it that people just don't
understand the bell curve?

Kevin, 43, Minnesota

First off, no man in his right mind is going to call his girlfriend or wife a "five," no matter how true it might be. Simply put, he wants to get blown again sometime this century. Second, he doesn't want to admit to himself that he's either settled for a "five" or that that's as good as he could get. The same goes for the chick. She might not want to admit that to herself either, because what does that say about her? I do have a feeling that most women would be more honest about the aesthetic number of their boyfriend or husband, but would then throw in a caveat, like her "five" makes good money, is good with kids, loves dogs, and so on.

Which leads to a larger point. We need to base the number on more than just physicality. And yes, that will fuck up the math. But it's not just about how good the person looks in a bathing suit. It's about a sense of humor. Employment. Good with pets. Good with kids. Number of previous relationships. It's an average. Think of it like a FICO score for getting laid. It's a FUCKO score. Guys who think they are "sevens" or "eights" will spend their life looking for an "eight" or a "nine" without realizing that they are driving a forklift and are behind on their child support payments, which knocks that number down to three and a half as far as women are concerned. Guys are more visually driven and will keep the number a little more looks-based, but it can still take a hit based on how a woman reacts to stuff. She'll get some bonus points for a good sense of humor, but if she turns into a hysterical wench when you don't text back immediately, her number is going to get a major reduction.

But that average then has to fit within a bracket. There are "tens," and there are *"tens."* Gisele Bündchen is a *ten*. She looks spectacular in a bikini and makes fifty-three million dollars a year. So she's definitely going to date someone high-caliber—an actor or an athlete. But she's not going to date Paul Giamatti or Tony Siragusa. She's going to be with Tom Brady and his seven Super Bowl rings. And she's never going to be with someone who is physically a "ten" but works at Red Robin.

You want to date above your number but only a notch or two. If you take too great a leap outside of your number, then he or she is going to have better options than you, and when they see you in your bathrobe eating Fruity Pebbles and watching *Columbo*, they're going to realize they can do better. Figure out what your total average number is. If you determine you're a "seven," then go to the "eight" pool and try to draw from there. Punch above your weight, but don't go chasing a "ten." That's a fool's errand.

It's not going to last. At the same time, don't go down to the "four" pool. That pool's for fools. ■

Dear Adam,

Should you answer (and if so, how) your wife if she says, "If I ever agreed to a threesome. which one of my friends would you choose?"

—Ray Romano

She's got you painted into a corner. This is the wife's version of the cop asking, "Have you been drinking tonight?" There is no acceptable response. A cop is not going to believe "I just had a beer after work" in the same way that your wife is not going to believe "No, honey. I only have eyes for you."

Try to avoid the question. But if she insists, then you have to answer, "I'm not going to tell you which of your friends I'd like to have a threesome with. That's just going to get me in trouble. So I'll tell you the one I wouldn't want to have a threesome with. Cynthia. She gives horrible head."

I was thinking about your particular gilded cage, Ray. You starred in a show called *Everybody Loves Raymond*, but you've been making love to the same woman for *thirty-five years*. Everybody loves Raymond, but you can't love them back.

If she asks again, just tell the truth. Like the great Danny Glover said in *Lethal Weapon*, "I'm getting too old for this shit." It's true. You age out of threesomes. At a certain point, there's a higher likelihood of you throwing your back out during the threesome than bringing one of the women to orgasm. Figure out what that age is. That's your Mason-Dixon Line, your over/under for having someone over and someone under you. Let's face it, Ray, we're both on the wrong side of that hill. Time to retire from the threesome game. ■

Chapter 4

Social Distortion

I don't have a degree in political science or sociology. I don't have a degree at all. There are girls currently living under Taliban rule who have a better education than I got. But having done carpet cleaning and earthquake rehab, and having grown up with ineffectual to incompetent parents, I think I'm overqualified to answer questions about cleaning up messes, fixing broken foundations, and dealing with lackluster leaders.

In general, American culture has been shaped and homogenized by nearly 250 years of appropriating and assimilating the cultures of all who have come to this great land. What are your thoughts on how modern shaming of cultural appropriation will impact the future of American culture?

Ron, 47, St. Louis

It's going to hit Halloween the hardest. There will be no more white guys dressing up as Pancho Villa and no more Mexican guys dressing up like the captain on *The Love Boat*.

The most insidious part of the culture war that we're currently waging is not what's going to be said, but what's *not* going to be said. All the jokes, all the ideas, all the remedies to problems that might involve a culture that's different from that of the comedian, sociologist, or economist that could make a positive difference or make someone laugh will be nipped in the bud. I ran into Sarah Silverman backstage at The Comedy Store last year. She repeated a joke of mine that had to do with Black people, saying she thought it was a brilliant joke. I've used it in another book, so I'll skip right to the punchline: "How are the world's fastest people the world's slowest pedestrians?"

She said it made her laugh but then added, "Too bad you can't do that joke."

That was a real watershed moment for me. A free-thinking, R-rated, brassy, ballsy comedian warning me not to do a joke because it was about a culture that wasn't my own. I, of course, have done the joke a hundred times since. A hundred and one if you count this retelling. But the people who never stop talking about an honest dialogue are simultaneously stifling any dialogue that could be remotely regarded as thought-provoking or engaging in terms of cultural differences.

If you're a white guy who opens a taco stand, you're a racist because you're appropriating a culture. If you're a white chick with dreads, you're a racist because you're appropriating a culture. But ironically, if you're a white guy and you display American culture—trucker cap, American flag flapping behind your pickup truck—you're also deemed a racist. What the people who constantly bitch about appropriation are saying to white people is, "You get no culture."

When did respect for a culture and wanting to participate in its arts, cuisine, and dress become a bad thing? Without cultural appropriation, we wouldn't have The Rolling Stones, The Beatles, Eminem, or even Paul Simon's shitty "world music" era. Without cultural appropriation, we wouldn't have Korean tacos. Do you want to live in that world?

There was a news story last year about a local news anchor and weatherman who put on disco outfits because the temperature was "in the '70s." These disco duds featured Afro wigs. Well, of course some professor had to get her panties in a bunch and say that it perpetuated systemic racism, and got the weatherman suspended. The news director for the station got fired. There were plenty of white guys in the '70s who were rocking the Afro. It was a tribute. Even one Jim Carolla had the 'fro.

He even had a pick with the Black Power fist on it. Now, they probably didn't do a lot of Afro picks with the Confederate flag on them, so that was probably the only one he could find. And what my grandmother, who is whiter than Jimmy Buffett's balls (the one part he doesn't constantly tan), is wearing can only be described as a dashiki. It looks like what Don King wore at the Rumble in the Jungle.

Seriously, she looks like she's stole her outfit from the wardrobe department of *Black Panther*.

Who is one of the most beloved figures of our childhood and adolescence? Who has had a huge pop culture resurgence in the past several years? Bob Fucking Ross. No honky has ever rocked the 'fro as well as Bob Ross, and no one has ever been whiter. And it wasn't a "happy little" 'fro either. It was big and badass. Are we going to accuse Bob Ross of 'fropropriation?

And there's an extra irony. We simultaneously stand against cultural appropriation but applaud mixed-race couples. If you're a blond woman married to a black guy in L.A., you're the toast of the town. But isn't that the ultimate form of appropriation?

Or being biracial but identifying as one race or the other. Can't President Obama and Colin Kaepernick be accused of a form of appropriation? Both Kaep's and Obama's dads took off on them. So why identify as the race of the guy who fled from raising you and not the race of the mother who did? (Or in Kaepernick's case, the white couple who adopted him when he was just a few weeks old.) When it comes to racial identity, I think the tie goes to the raiser. But Kaepernick is really leaning into it. It's all in the hair. His mom has straight blond hair. Google pictures of Kaepernick in college. He looked Syrian. But in 2017, when he was named *GQ*'s Man of the Year, he had a 'fro so big it went onto the back cover. He looked like the lead from the Hair Bear Bunch. And last year on his Netflix show, he wore a full Black Panther outfit (Vietnam-protest Black Panther, not Marvel-movie *Black Panther*). He wore a black leather jacket and a black turtleneck, and had a 'fro that could cause a solar eclipse. He looked like Malcolm XXL. How is that not cultural appropriation for someone raised by a white couple in Fond du Lac, Wisconsin?

Have you ever seen those articles about what American children are going to look like in the future? They basically show that we're essentially going to look like we all came from a South

American village. In the future, everyone will be the color of Mariah Carey and be "trendsexual," a new sexuality that applies to whatever is in the zeitgeist at the time. With all the emphasis on interracial couples that you see in advertising these days, I don't know how we're going to have a culture to appropriate in fifty years. Everything will be homogenized.

I get what's in it for the race hustlers, the politicians, and CNN. But I don't know why everyone else buys into it. You should be no prouder of your race than you are of your Zodiac sign. It was basically something that was assigned to you at birth, through no fault or achievement of your own. Explaining that you're a proud female Latinx is like saying you're a proud Virgo. It just makes me think you're a crackpot and that I don't want to hang out with you. The one place in America that is still fully segregated by race is prison. You want to be in "the yard?" There's an extreme version of what socialist AOC wants, and it's called Cuba. Well, the extreme version of what she and her stans want is called San Quentin. Is that something to strive for? We'd like to go halfway there, but that's not how it works. How about we don't even head in that direction at all?

Our current obsession with race can't possibly have a good ending. It's like we're trying to create a bunch of smaller countries within our country. It used to be a melting pot. Now it's the McDLT. (Google it.) ∎

If you didn't have to keep up on the news and politics for the podcast/work, would you?

Thomas, 28, Salt Lake City

Yes, because I find them to be an interesting examination of the human condition. Plus, I'm obsessed with people's ability to lie on camera. There's no more truth on a weekly airing of *Meet the Press* than on the average episode of *Catfish*.

That said, going on the road a lot more since the sane states started lifting COVID restrictions has meant I'm not keeping up with as much as I did previously. Last year when I went to Alaska for five days, I really noticed the absence of news. It was nice.

All the religions have a sabbath. As big an atheist as I am, I do realize that religions know what they're doing. The sabbath is a pretty good idea. There's a reason there's a day of rest. Unfortunately, our society insists on a twenty-four-hour news cycle and working weekends. So you're going to have to impose your own agnostic sabbath on yourself. You can't be trusted with the amount of information coming at you.

You could experiment with the news like you do with drinking beer or eating refined sugar. No one has ever gotten off booze or fast food for a week and not felt better. I would argue in today's climate, news is more harmful than alcohol, internet porn, or any other thing you would give up for Lent. The average American would feel somewhat better after giving up booze or cigarettes or sugar. But they'd feel a thousand times better giving up the news for a week. It would be tantamount to getting out of a bad relationship. You might not notice it, but when you run into people you haven't seen in a while, they say, "You look so much happier."

My kids were getting ready to leave for a Florida vacation with their mom at the height of the pandemic. On the eve of the trip, the news ran a story about a fourteen-year-old boy who'd been hospitalized because of COVID. They showed a picture of him holding a basketball, and my wife saw my son and said, "Sonny's fourteen. And he's got a basketball!" and was immediately terrified that he'd meet the same fate. After you watch stories about shark attacks, the healthiest thing you can do is go for a swim in the ocean. Face the fear and realize you swallowed the drug CNN was pushing.

News was fine when it was news, but it's no longer a daily reporting of facts you might need, it's evidence in a case for or against a certain viewpoint. There really is no need to watch news anymore, because as soon as you hear the topic, you know exactly where each cable news network is going to come down, facts and stats be damned.

Look no further than the awkward confrontation between Dr. Sanjay Gupta and podcaster Joe Rogan over Rogan's taking ivermectin. I'm not for ivermectin, but I'm not against it either. You know why? Because I'm not a doctor. But an actual doctor in the form of Sanjay Gupta had strong opinions about it. As far as he was concerned, it was a dangerous medicine for horses and Rogan was an idiot for taking it. Not that Gupta actually believed it, but his network believed it and he didn't want to have a bad time at the CNN Christmas party, so he went along. Rogan took umbrage with the network's saying he was taking horse paste and pressed Gupta on it. Rogan being Rogan, he did not back down. Like me, he has his own platform and doesn't need to. He eventually got Gupta to admit that it *can* be used for horses but it also can be used for humans and has been prescribed billions of times. It may not be effective, but it is also not harmful.

Of course, after getting his ass kicked by Rogan, Gupta went back to safe confines of CNN and into the arms of Don Lemon and acted as if Rogan hadn't backed him into a corner, where he had to own that his network had lied. As I always say when I see shit like this on the news, the politician, actor, commentator, lawyer is either stupid or a liar. Well, Gupta's a doctor. He's clearly not stupid. You can be wrong but not be stupid. So what does that leave? And Don Lemon got on his fainting couch and acted offended that Joe Rogan had called bullshit on their bullshit.

This is not a hill to die on. CNN's take is that this medication is for horses. You can use a brush on horses, and my daughter can use a brush on her hair. I don't walk into her room and wrestle away her brush saying, "What are you doing?! This is for horses!" There's a brush that has a horse application and a brush that has a human application. There's a difference, you dipshits. Shouldn't one of the people with a degree in *journalism* (!!!!!!) raise their hand and say, "Maybe we should just move on from this one."

A network shouldn't have a position on this. Do masks work? Does ivermectin work? Does hydroxychloroquine work? Is there outdoor transmission of COVID? How many Black men are shot by police as compared to unarmed white men? How did officer Brian Sicknick die during the riot on January 6? These are all facts that a *reporter* could *report*. But nah. That doesn't fit the agenda, which is to scare the shit out of you. CNN should change its initials to PTSD, because it's freaking everyone out. Stop scare-mongering, you fucks! Or at the very least, after you get done "reporting" on a drug that is going to kill everyone or a "super-spreader" event that is going to kill everyone, do a follow-up fourteen days later and let us know the body count. But there's never a follow-up, because that's not your business model. CNN is the boy who cried Wolf Blitzer. ■

· ·

What are your thoughts about the drought and the way California has handled water-supply demands over the years?

Geoff, 61, Marshall, Texas

I've been living in California my entire life, and the drought is nothing new. I've been hearing about it since I was a kid. It was actually welcome news in the '70s to my mom, who didn't want to maintain a lawn. The drought was all she needed to turn what should have been a front lawn into a dust bowl.

This problem is one hundred years in the making. I have no idea why California doesn't have a desalinization plant or an aquifer to trap rainwater when we do get it. Just like the bullet train that was supposed to go from L.A. to Vegas when I was in high school, it has never come to fruition. What else do you need to know about politicians, legislatures, and city councils? If Richard Branson and Elon Musk were in charge of California, could you imagine massive forest fires every year and not enough water to put them out? This is 2022. We don't have enough water, and the government's solution is "stop using so much water." That's a politician's version of how to fix a problem. A businessperson's version of fixing the problem would be creating and trapping more water. An effective person when trapped on a desert island learns to hunt and fish, and our politicians sit by the shore and hope that shit washes up that they can eat.

Not that we aren't wasteful with water. We take way too many showers. California wouldn't allow it, but we should just collect all the water that is used in the bathroom sink, the shower, the kitchen, whatever runs off the roof in a rainstorm, even the dishwasher and use it for irrigation. What would be the difference?

We need to think about how to conserve and grow. Democratic politicians, especially the ones drunk on power in California, are about control. Ironically, the Democrats are being conservative. They're only thinking about how to get you to use less rather than figuring out how to get more. Southern California is a desert, but in Oregon and Washington it never stops raining. Can't we get a pipeline going? No, that will never happen. Californians like water, but they don't like pipelines. Californians won't vote for anything with the word "pipeline" in it.

I'm not exactly a Greenpeace hippie, but I understand nature. That's why I have artificial grass at my house. I got the kind that even has a little hint of yellow so it looks legitimate. And this is what the front of my warehouse where I produce my documentaries, display my cars, and get shit-faced on football Sundays looks like…

It looks like...well, a desert. Which Southern California and the whole Southwest essentially are. They've got it figured out in Phoenix. The on-ramps for the freeways there look like the front of my warehouse. Yet in L.A. we're trying to shoehorn in ivy and shrubbery where it's not natural. It's a very L.A. thing to do. It's like the peroxide blond with the fake tits or the short guy wearing cowboy boot lifts who's balding and has the jet black comb-over. In trying to look like something you're not, you're calling even more attention to how bad you appear.

Could you imagine a politician saying, "California is short on water and short on power. I'm going to build a nuclear and desalinization plant at Point Mugu. We'll have as much power and water as we need"? I would give that guy a rim job and would have to fight through the tears of joy to find his anus. The yentas in the state assembly (and I include the men in that term) would never let it happen. They would take years commissioning some kind of environmental impact report, and that would be that. And they'd have support. The environmentalists took a page from the playbook of the attorneys for TV networks. Just say no to everything and you'll never get fired. ■

....

Do you think the world would be a better place or worse without the internet?
Brian, 53, Aloha, Oregon

It would be a better place if the internet had never been invented, but if you're talking about taking the internet away, it wouldn't be. Too many people have gotten hooked on that http: heroin. There'd be a lot of suicides, and every person under the age of nineteen in America would be institutionalized for not being able to get all the information they want at all times.

The internet is like a calculator. In the hands of an Asian Cal State student, it's a tool. In the hands of some dumb shit at Arizona State cheating his way through finals, it's not. It can be used by a researcher or the right student to learn and create, or it can be used to punch shit in, get the right numbers, and regurgitate them without learning anything.

It's also removed the delayed-gratification part of life. You measure a young child's success by how well they can delay gratification. What is their impulse control? The internet has removed the foreplay from life, the steps needed to get something accomplished. It has turned libraries into travel agencies and Blockbuster Videos—remnants of a bygone era. I think this is why people don't have that ability anymore.

Now everyone is drunk on overnight Amazon deliveries. When I was a kid, if you ordered some piece of Chinese junk, it would take thirty days to be delivered. If you told my kids something they ordered was going to get to the house in thirty days instead of thirty minutes, they'd torch the place and probably commit hara-kiri.

I'm not completely against the internet. Yes, it can be used for drug trafficking on the dark web, posting fake news and rumors on social media, and encouraging sexual addiction. But it can also be utilized for noble causes, like me being up at one a.m. drunk and looking up bit players from *The Love Boat* and how they died. You know, research and education.

I think we could learn to use the internet better. I have two app ideas that can help.

First is a browser called Split Decision. Rather than providing top website hits based on views, it would take your search request and feed you two articles from opposing points of view. And you wouldn't be able to see the opposite one until you've completely read the first. You'd type in "Do masks work for COVID?" or "Was there Russian collusion in the election?" and it would force you to read both sides before you could ask your next question. It could even apply to customer reviews for products, movies, or restaurants. You'd have to look at both sides before you could do your next search.

The other app I'd create would address the internet's tendency to focus on the negative and generate outrage. People rarely go out of their way to post a positive Yelp or Amazon review. They just enjoy their meal or product. But if the toaster is broken or the soup is cold when it arrives at their house or table, they instantly jump online to post a negative review. I'd call the app Mirr'r. If you attempted to tweet or post about any corporation, celebrity, or politician and use the words "insulted," "offended," "attacked," or "outraged," your phone's AI would swap your screen with the forward-facing camera so you have to take a long look in the "mirror" and see the pussy that you are. ■

· ·

Is there any way for someone to be effective in politics without turning into a complete liar, idiot, and/or asshole?

Andrew, 34, Stilwell, Kansas

I think this is a chicken-and-egg situation. Do people turn into idiots, liars, and assholes when they become politicians, or are they idiots, liars, and assholes to begin with, and that's what attracts them to positions of power? Only an idiot would want to go into politics. Half the country wants you dead and thinks you're an idiot, an asshole, or a liar.

When you get to a certain age, you realize you're older than the cops that are pulling you over. Some twenty-six-year-old kid is saying, "What I'm gonna need you to do for me right now is step out of the vehicle real quick." At that moment, all the childhood images you had of cops being smart authority figures crumble and you realize they're just dudes. It's the same with politicians. They have a veneer of intelligence and authority, but as soon as you put them in front of a microphone and ask them to speak off the cuff, they stammer and stutter like someone asked to give a spontaneous toast at a wedding. It hits you that as a civilian, you're smarter than the people in charge. There are representatives I wouldn't trust to run the gift shop at the Capitol, never mind be elected to serve there. I don't think they could make change for a dollar, never mind make change in our country.

California's current and recently saved-from-recall governor Gavin Newsom is the leader in the clubhouse when it comes to this. Usually I break down politicians and public figures into two categories, "stupid or liar," but he hits the trifecta of liar, idiot, and asshole your question poses. So, let's break it down along those lines. I had Newsom on my podcast in 2013 when he was still lieutenant governor, so I have direct experience. (By the way, those of you who know how well I spell, just imagine how many attempts it took for me to get "lieutenant" correct as I go on this jag about what an imbecile Gavin Newsom is.)

Let's start with liar. I'm going to be generous and hope that he's just a liar, because if he actually believes the stuff he's saying, he needs to be put down like a rabid raccoon.

Newsom's big lie, the one that had even true-blue California Democrats like my friend Mark Geragos saying we needed to oust the guy, was when he got caught dining at The French Laundry while the rest of the state was still in lockdown. After he was busted, he said that it had been outdoors and socially distant. But then a picture came showing that the distance was about nine inches. The elbow room required to eat high-end cuisine was as much social distance as he and his dinner dates had. And it wasn't outdoors. It was an enclosed patio with a sliding door that was sporadically open. (When it was closed, it was because he and his party were reportedly being too loud and were annoying other patrons.)

Oh, and who were these other dinner guests? Family members that were in his "bubble?" Essential coworkers with whom he needed to communicate in person for the great needs of our state during a crisis? Or a bunch of medical industry lobbyists? I hope you guessed correctly. Yes, the same people who were telling us to stay home, who were arresting people for going to the beach, who were essentially suggesting that for Thanksgiving 2020 you should fire the mashed potatoes across the yard to your guests with a T-shirt cannon, and for Christmas you should shut down caroling because it involved too much exhaling, were doing the exact opposite of what they were preaching.

It shows that Newsom doesn't believe in the risks of COVID to half of the extent that he claims. If he really felt this were a deadly virus, he would act as accordingly. There were seven different families represented at that dinner, laughing and exhaling all over each other.

And then in 2022 when L.A. still had a mask mandate there were pictures of him at Sofi Stadium at the Rams playoff game, maskless, with his arm around Magic Johnson. And when he was called out on this he said he had his mask in his hand. You know, following the science. What would he do if he was a cop? "Where's your bulletproof vest?" "It's under my arm." Hey, Gavin, don't ever take up welding or asbestos removal.

To be fair to Newsom, at least his answer wasn't as asinine as L.A. Mayor Eric Garcetti who said he was holding his breath. Are you protecting yourself from COVID or did Magic fart? I gotta say, "I held my breath around the big black man" sounds border-line racist to me. I couldn't figure out how he thought we'd be so dumb to believe that he held his breath the entire time he was hanging with Magic, but after a while I got it. Garcetti constantly talks out of his ass so maybe he breathes out of it too.

Newsom makes you wear a mask, but he doesn't believe it. Think about this. Ben Shapiro wears a yarmulke. He believes it. He wears it in the shower, he wears it while he's in a lap pool, he wears it on a moped. Every time you see him he's wearing it. He doesn't use his yarmulke as a beer coaster and then when you walk in the room slap it on his head. He believes it. (I was think-ing about it. The yarmulke is about the same size as one of those worthless masks. You could just put a couple of rubber bands on it and slide it down every time you needed it to go into Canters Deli.

So yes, Gavin Newsom is a liar. While Californians were in lockdown, he was at The French Laundry and Sofi Stadium get-ting drunk...with power.

Moving on to idiot. Gavin Newsom is retarded. He's an imbe-cile. What if he looked like Patton Oswalt? It'd be "shut up, troll" and he'd never get another vote. But he looks like a guy who sells used teeth whitener, so we act like he knows what he's talking about. He's got great hair, but there's no brain underneath it. Dumb people who look good say dumb shit and expect you to act like it's smart. Like when hot blond models tell stories that go nowhere and never end. We listen because we want to fuck them. I think the only reason Newsom is governor is because of the number of women and gay men in the fair state of California (let's not forget he broke onto the scene as the mayor of San Francisco) who want to fuck or be fucked by him. When I had him on my podcast, I attempted to talk to him about traffic and his reply was that he'd seen a billboard he liked that read "You're not *in* traffic. You *are* traffic." This guy would make a great oncologist: "Hey, I read something on a bus bench: 'You don't *have* cancer. You *are* cancer.' Pretty good, right? Anyhoo, you have six months to live."

The high point of his low IQ was when he was pressed by a podcaster (not me, but someone after my own heart) on the exodus from California. He had the balls, but definitely not the brains, to say: "I think Governor Brown, former Governor Brown, said it best. 'Where the hell are you gonna go?'"

When the host, Kara Swisher, pushed back on this, asking if "Where the hell are you gonna go?" was the new California motto, Newsom replied: "I don't know. But he said it."

Then why did *you* say it, dipshit? Do you just randomly quote people without knowing why? When your waiter at The French Laundry asked for your order, did you say, "Four score and seven years ago"?

The situation really went into the stratosphere when he continued challenging the host's notion that people were indeed getting sick of the high cost of living, the wildfires, the homelessness, and other issues plaguing the Golden State.

"I have a friend who just went to Utah," Newsom said. "Beautiful. It may be the right thing for him. They've made a ton of money. They have the ability to take their kids out of public school into private school, and they're doing that. I imagine they're not going to turn their back forever on California."

That is a rebuttal. That's his rebuttal to a question about people leaving California. First he says, "Where are you gonna go?" That's arrogant and naïve regarding the appeal of other states to the overtaxed, overregulated citizens of his state. But then he immediately undercuts his own argument by coming up with an example of a friend who fled to Utah. This is the idiocy. His counter to the idea that people are leaving California is discussing someone he knows who left California. It seems like maybe he caught his mistake towards the end by saying they might come back. Yes, Gavin, they may have their ashes scattered off Big Sur. This would be like getting caught cheating by your wife and when she confronts you saying, "I love you, honey. I'd never hurt you. I *am* fucking my secretary. I might stop. Who knows?"

When his idiocy goes into policy, that's the worst. In 2020 he signed a new law saying that convicted criminals can choose their prison based on their self-identified gender. Allowing criminals to decide if they want to identify as male and spend seven to ten years getting ass-raped by Latin Kings, or identify as female and live out a *Caged Heat* fantasy—what could go wrong? And what's to stop someone saying they self-identify as the warden and letting themselves out?

If Newsom says, "I'm in the mood for deep-dish pizza," you should get New York thin crust, because everything that comes out of that guy's mouth is wrong. When the founding fathers wrote the Constitution, they were thinking about protecting us from kings and foreign aggressors. They never anticipated dipshit governors. They were looking for evil, not stupid. They could have never anticipated Newsom.

Let's end with asshole. Gavin Newsom's extreme and hypocritical lockdowns are like an evil stepdad telling his stepdaughter, "Curfew is when the streetlights come on." How long before she says, "Fuck it," climbs out the window, and blows her boyfriend in a parking lot?

Newsom doesn't give a shit. That's the point. Whether it's dining out at The French Laundry while his constituents get Grubhub delivered because his state health department is fear-mongering, or arrogantly assuming no one would dare leave his state because he's so great and he's in charge so it must be great, he exhibits total asshole behavior. This is how an apex predator works. He has no fear of reprisal because he's in a Democratic supermajority state. He escaped recall, and he'd get reelected again if he runs. At some point he'll try to take his white teeth to the White House. But he's an empty suit and a haircut. He's got platitudes and attitudes but no answers. And, despite being in the state that boasts the most "I speak truth to power" people, we've been lapping up the "tell us what to do" gruel and asking for seconds. The only thing that disgusts me more than Newsom's dictatorial leanings is our cowardice in confronting them. I was onstage with Representative Dan Crenshaw from Texas, who talked about the Gonzales flag. It has a cannon with a star above it and the words "Come and Take It" underneath. It's essentially a Texas "fuck you" to Mexico. I told Crenshaw that in California we have a flag too. It's a cockroach about to be crushed by a boot worn by Gavin Newsom, and it says "Please Tread on Me." ■

··

What's one thing the left should learn from the right? And what's one thing the right should learn from the left?

Robert, 32, Pennsylvania

The right could learn to be more effective. The left is getting their crazy shit through because they do a masterful job of controlling the language. Look no further than the trans issue. The left has turned a hyena into a leopard just by calling it one. And all the stooges in the news agree. No actual spots need to be painted on.

And the right could teach the left that their progressive eighteen-wheeler speeding down Woke Highway needs to tap the brakes every now and again. You can't say "defund the police" while murder rates are going up, or that requiring voters to show IDs is Jim Crow 2.0 when most Americans agree that cops and IDs at polling stations are a rational idea. The right can teach the progressives to be more pragmatic. Anytime Bernie Sanders wakes up with a boner and a new idea about how America should be, you don't need to embrace it. ∎

Should aliens make contact with Earth, who do we send on humanity's behalf?

Chad, 32, Ohio

Obviously Dwayne Johnson, a.k.a. "The Rock," jumps to mind. He'd send a message. The aliens would inevitably ask him why he'd been chosen, and he'd say, "I'm the lightest. I have the smallest upper body of all the humans. And they know I'm docile and wouldn't scare you."

And we could pair him with Joy Behar in case they were thinking about mating with us, so we could nip that one in the bud too. ∎

The juror system has worked fine for a while, during the time people were raised with some decency and respect. Are you OK putting your fate in the hands of twelve random people in this day and age? Should we have more stringent requirements for people asked to judge us?

Andrew, 38, Sacramento

The scariest part is that with a lot of these high-profile cases, the jurors are just going to vote guilty or innocent depending which way the sociopolitical winds are blowing so they can get out of jury duty and sleep in their bed that night. I do multiple shows weekly with Mark Geragos, who defended Michael Jackson, Chris Brown, and Scott Petersen, among thousands of others and thus clearly knows his way around a courtroom and jury selection. He said something about the Kyle Rittenhouse verdict last year. He predicted accurately that it was going to come in around three o'clock on a Friday, because jurors hate the idea of spending another weekend sequestered in a hotel, or of not being able to talk to their family about the proceedings that day if they are allowed to go home. He also cynically added that they just wanted one last catered meal.

As far as jurors go, I'll take dumb people over scared people every day. I'm positive that many jurors have cast a vote of guilty not because they thought the cop was guilty but because they didn't want their town to burn down or to have protestors outside their house. I'd hate to have my fate in the hands of people who have their fate in the hands of CNN's narrative.

We built a computer thirty years ago that beat a chess champion. Technology has gotten much better since then. We should be developing AI juries. We'd feed in all the official particulars of the case, and the AI would come up with the correct verdict. I'd be much more apt to trust artificial intelligence than the suspect intelligence of a supposed peer.

I know many of you are thinking, *Why would you trust a machine? Technology never works for you.* Yes, that's true. I have serious Siri issues, and Waze is working my nerves. But I wouldn't trust my family or half the guys you went to high school with either. Driving around L.A. and knowing my jury pool would be angry chain-smoking Armenians, producers' wives with too much plastic surgery, and twenty-year-old Latinas who work at smoothie places, I'd take my chances with JuryBot 3000. ∎

....

I've long been a fan of the adage "Don't feel like a victim and you won't be one."

With that mindset, how do think our society will be affected long-term, when so many are offended, either personally or on behalf of someone else? Or in other words, what are the long-term effects of an affected nation?

Daniel, 38, Ontario, Canada

I definitely covered the victim identity permeating our culture and the outrage on behalf of someone else in my last book. But a word you used got me thinking: "affected."

Last year a college basketball coach misspoke, saying something about a plantation, and someone ratted him out. The details are unimportant, because what I noticed is something in the mea culpa from the school. In their statement, they apologized to all those "affected." Back in the day, they would say sorry to all those "offended." But offended is on the person who's taking offense. Offense is in the eye of the offended. This change in vernacular is a sign, and a bad one. No one was affected. Nothing happened. They might have been *offended*, but they were not "affected." It's part of the exaggeration of, and elevation of, words to actions that the left has mastered. ■

....

Why is it that I can accept Caitlyn Jenner and not Elliot Page?

P.S. I'm pretty baked right now.

Rusty, 38, Brussels, Belgium

I'm not sure, Rusty. I'd actually think it would be the opposite. Ellen Page had less trans distance to travel. She, when she was still a she, was kind of tomboyish anyway. It was a sprint to the phallic finish line. Bruce Jenner becoming Caitlyn was a dick-cathlon.

But if you saw him in the short shorts and crop top in the Village People movie *Can't Stop the Music*, you might have been able to see which direction he was heading in.

I've hung out with Caitlyn; she's a car guy and participated in my Willy T. Ribbs documentary, *Uppity*. I've got nothing but nice things to say. I do wonder though: Do you think Bruce picked Caitlyn with a "C" as a "fuck you" to all the "K's" in the Kardashian clan?

Speaking of transition surgery, it reminds me of an idea I had that, if I were a penis-removal doctor, would ironically make me a dick. I'd prank the poor bastards coming in to have their hogs removed. I'd say, "This procedure takes eight to ten hours." Then when they removed the surgical gown and I saw their cock, I'd glance up from my clipboard and casually say, "Oh. Never mind. We can knock this out in an hour."

Anyway, Rusty, I have to assume you're a redhead. Nobody is actually named Rusty. The name Rusty has never been written on a birth certificate. Too bad you're in Belgium and not Britain, because then you could be Ginger instead, which is a solid nickname.

I was recently thinking about this and why guys are into redheaded women but redheaded guys are not attractive. Ginger hair is too thick. It doesn't drop like Tom Petty's mop, so there's not much you can do with it. It's too coarse. You can't comb it down, so you end up with a Ralph Malph Jew-fro. For some reason, maybe a lot of chemicals and flat irons, women can straighten their ginger hair and you can get your Jessica Chastains and Julianne Moores. Fire-red hair on porcelain-white skin is good-looking on a lady but disgusting on a dude. But as hairstyles changed over the years, there were more options for men. Coarse red hair ain't gonna sit down or straighten out. And you're fucked if you try to feather it. But do a quick google of Bears quarterback Andy "The Red Rifle" Dalton and you'll see just how far gingers have come.

If the only option for him were to have Clay Matthews's hair, or God forbid, the classic "Broadway Joe" Namath look, it would be a shitshow. ■

· ·

I'd like to ask how there's only one of the two major political parties in this country that considers itself patriotic. I wondered while watching Trump rallies why there were tons of American flags but at Biden rallies there were hardly any. It seems that someone wearing a flag pin on their lapel is considered a right-wing nut. It's confusing because we all live in the same country, and when I was in grade school and high school, patriotism was something both parties were proud of.

Joe, 46, Kansas City, Kansas

Yes, showing patriotism started eroding in the '60s when the hippies were burning flags along with their draft cards or bras. Flags and American pride became a symbol of The Man, and that generation won that round of the culture war. They went to Hollywood and Silicon Valley, and infected the populace with the "America is an evil empire" bullshit.

I interviewed the late, great Ed Asner on my podcast about a decade ago, and we got into a discussion of 9/11. About the time he started talking about how the towers had come down too fast and blaming George W. Bush, I realized that it wasn't that he actually believed it. He just hated America. I know these people. My grandmother was pretty much a communist and definitely hated the USA. Ironically, while she was railing against the government, she was getting paid by the VA.

It's one thing for actors and producers not to act patriotic. That's kind of expected. It's worse when it's people in the government. The peak of this is Representative Ilhan Omar. She's the angriest at America. For a refugee who owes a lot to this country, she sure hates it. No country has done more for someone than America has done for Ilhan Omar. But like the family member that you give money to and they resent you, she's got a giant chip on her hijab.

She had a rally at the height of the "defund the police" bullshit and talked about how the Minneapolis Police Department was "brutalizing us" and that we needed to "dismantle it" and "allow for something beautiful to rise." She said we needed to "reimagine what public safety looks like for us."

That's the problem with these people. They don't have any solutions. They just know they hate America and everything it stands for. All they know is they want to defund, dismantle, and reimagine things. But what would replace those things? A white privilege hotline? Who do you call when someone breaks into your house with a gun? A social worker or a therapist? Judd Hirsch from *Ordinary People* is going to come in, roll up the sleeves on his wool cardigan, and start kicking ass?

This is part of the "zero tolerance," "no child left behind," "one death is too many" bullshit that politicians spout. There's no viable version of these all-or-nothing policies. I toured the Lance snack cracker factory a million years ago and learned that a certain number of crackers are going to come off the conveyor belt damaged. It's called breakage. Every business that produces a product factors it in. So when you make pronouncements like those above, you then have to take the opposite tack that if our country has even one death from COVID and if one unarmed Black man is killed by a cop, then we have failed and are evil. I don't know what mythical no-racism, no-corruption, everybody-healthy-forever country the idiots here keep trying to compare us to, but I wish they would all move there.

We have to stop beating up our country. We live in a good country. America is generally good. That doesn't mean there's nothing to fix. Like a '99 Ford Explorer, it's generally a good vehicle. It breaks down sometimes and needs some maintenance, but it's generally good. You show me a Fiat from the '70s and I'll show you something that is constantly breaking down and needing to be towed. We're the Ford, not the Fiat.

And not only do America bashers want to think we're that finicky Fiat right now, but they never stop talking about how crappy we were in the past too. Even if they believed we were that reliable Ford, they'd never stop looking in the rearview mirror and talking about how crappy the Fords that rolled off the assembly line in the '20s were. This is why all the statues are coming down. They don't comport with the new woke standards of the day. Well, a Model T isn't roadworthy by today's standards, but in its day, it literally changed the world. Just like all the old white guys whose statues are getting torn down.

I'm not talking about Confederate generals. They were clearly on the wrong side of history. But while yes, Jefferson and Washington were slave owners, they also did some good things—like found the fucking country that allows people to bitch about their being slave owners without fear of government reprisal.

When the country, cooped up from COVID, lost its collective mind in 2020 and took to the streets after George Floyd was killed, any statue older than fifteen minutes was ripe for a teardown. There'd be dudes with dreads wielding skateboards and rope, pulling them down like they were statues of Saddam in 2003. (By the way, when did the skateboard become the new Swiss Army knife? Want to break a window and steal something during a riot? Skateboard. Get away with that stolen merchandise? Skateboard. Attack a cop or a civilian trying to stop you? Skateboard. I imagine Tony Hawk watching the news like Dr. Frankenstein with a single tear running down his cheek saying, "What have I done?")

And where's OSHA during all this? If you want to put a patio on your own home, you have to deal with months of permit bullshit. But if you want to take down a statue, just bring a skateboard and some rope and have at it; no one's going to stop you. It's too dangerous to bring my dog and a Frisbee to the beach, but you can topple Ulysses S. Grant and light him on fire and the cops will just watch. Nancy Pelosi was asked about this and she said, "People are going to do what they're gonna do." Really, bitch? Can I get that in writing for when I want to smoke a cigarette on the beach or put a second floor on my house?

You know who the real victims are? The horses. All these generals in the statues are on horseback. What did the horses ever do? A horse can't be racist. The worst they can do is carry the racist on their back to the lynching. Doesn't matter if it's Robert E. Lee or Teddy Roosevelt; the horse they're riding is getting removed too. Why haven't we heard from PETA on this one? They want to rename "the bullpen" in baseball because it marginalizes our bovine brethren, but horse statues getting dragged through the streets doesn't move their needle. I think we need a campaign, and I've got a perfect name: "*Do* Spare the Horses." Go ahead and take down Stonewall Jackson but leave his majestic steed. I'd like to imagine a future civilization studying our ruins, finding all of them and saying, "They were a violent, gluttonous, and greedy people. But man, they loved horses."

All this statue-tory rape isn't about the founding fathers; it's about what they fathered, America. (And in Jefferson's case a couple of mulatto kids.)

Before we leave this patriotic portion, let me tell a quick, uncomfortable story.

I get hit up to host events for military veterans all the time. I'm usually happy to oblige. In 2013, I was asked to participate in "One Night for the Love of Our Country" at the Ronald Reagan Presidential Library in Simi Valley, California.

It was for a good cause, but I wasn't getting paid, so I put in my usual North Hollywood High level of effort. I usually just show up and something comes to me. They hadn't asked in advance for me to do a specific set length or anything, just to host the event and introduce the participants. Kevin Costner's band, Modern West, was closing out the evening. This was on a Sunday night starting at eight o'clock. People were sitting at tables eating, or standing up to head to the open bar or the silent auction table. They were dressed up in suits, and the Reagan library is a big, open space. So big that it contains Reagan's decommissioned Air Force One. Not an ideal space for comedy. So it was probably for the best that I was going to wing it under the wings of the Gipper's presidential plane.

Just about the time I was supposed to head onstage and introduce the first speaker, I was standing at a table sipping some wine when someone tapped me on the shoulder and said, "OK, it's time for you to go up and start the evening." I've done this a million times, usually with a beer in my hand, but it was a classy night so I had some vino. But as I was about to walk onto the stage, the coordinator told me what I had to do first.

He said, "So you'll go up there and be joined by the color guard and lead everyone in the Pledge of Allegiance." What? That's the kind of thing you should give someone a heads-up on. I probably haven't said the Pledge of Allegiance in its entirety since middle school, and now I'm middle-aged. The coordinator might have wanted to put that in the email to my assistant weeks before when booking this.

Panic set in. I started muttering and mouthing it to myself to try to shake the rust off. "Indivisible? Invisible? Shit!"

My memory refreshed as well as possible, I was shoved onstage. The color guard was behind me, complete with flags and guns, and a room full of veterans and VIPs was in front of me.

I took a glance around and realized that there was no podium, no dais, not even a table. The closest flat surface was Kevin Costner's band's drum kit. There was no place to put down my glass of red wine. I had the mic in my left hand, being a lefty, and my goblet of pinot noir in the right. It was too late. So, I put my right hand, vino included, over my heart and mouthed along while the people who actually knew the pledge performed it.

After that nightmare was over, I did a few jokes and praised our brave men and women in uniform, then walked offstage, hoping to put all the awkwardness in the rear with the gear. But alas, like a moment out of *Curb Your Enthusiasm*, it wasn't meant to be.

The next speaker was a decorated veteran in uniform I've come to affectionately refer to as "Colonel Buzz Kill." He was the military equivalent of the woman who heads up Mothers Against Drunk Driving. He was literally the guy in charge of the rehab and addiction programs for veterans. The man who had founded the program for traumatized vets who turn to alcohol when they get back stateside had to follow the guy who had chugged beer on *The Man Show*. It was the worst billing order since Jimi Hendrix opened for The Monkees.

He glared at me as I left the stage, took the mic, and let me have it. "I don't know you. I don't know your work. I guess you think it's a joke to hold a glass of alcohol while saluting this country's wounded veterans. But I'll tell you something, I don't think it's funny." He said he was "disgusted" and tore me a new asshole for ten minutes.

The worst part was that I couldn't leave. It's not like I could commandeer Air Force One and fly the fuck out of there. I had to get back onstage, get the microphone from him, and bring out the next speaker. I made a half-hearted joke about how I hadn't known it was going to turn into an intervention, and I could hear Costner laugh up in the balcony. But that didn't quite puncture the tension. I still had to get on and off the stage a dozen more times, introducing other people while Colonel Buzz Kill glared at me sipping tap water. I had to hang out until Costner's band hit the stage in two hours, but it felt like nineteen.

What made it even more uncomfortable was that people kept coming up to me quietly all night and saying, "He doesn't speak for us. Thank you for coming out." And then, to cap it all off, I was informed that I couldn't even slink out of there early after introducing Costner and Modern West. I needed to stick around until the end, when they were going to present me and him with a commemorative SEAL Team 5 Zodiac boat paddle. I wanted to take the thing and beat myself unconscious with it. But I did end up developing a nice friendship with Costner, who thought I handled myself well, so it wasn't all bad.

So as far as patriotism goes, the Ace Man loves, respects, and knows how to salute the old red wine and blue. ∎

Do you think, as a species, we have no ability to solve long-term problems? Do we have no interest in solving problems that will make life better for our children and people in future generations but not necessarily us right now?

—Judd Apatow

Our approach to problems is the problem. It's no better encapsulated than building in California versus building in Texas. We need some low-cost housing to deal with the homeless crisis. In California, we've been having a million discussions about it, impaneling commissions to study the problem, having town hall meetings where "stakeholders" (that is, everyone with too much time on their hands) get to weigh in, completing environmental impact reports because there's some indigenous toad that mates in the proposed area, and hearing the inevitable "homeless advocates" pontificate. (By the way, how about homeless "experts" instead of advocates? I'm an advocate for my dog Phil, but I wouldn't consider myself an expert. I take him to the vet when something is wrong. Leaving it to experts is advocacy.)

So, in California we've been arguing endlessly about what to do, and nothing ever happens. Meanwhile in Texas, a condo goes up in twenty minutes.

We used to be able to make things like the Brooklyn Bridge or the Golden Gate Bridge. It was assumed that frogs were going to get displaced and some Irishmen were going to get killed along the way. Here's a true and telling fact. When the Empire State Building went up, construction moved so fast that the steel girders that came fresh out of a foundry in Pennsylvania and were trucked to New York, ferried across the river, and craned up into position were still warm. We used to do shit and do it fast.

California has always been on the cultural vanguard: music, fashion, film. California is always leading the way for the rest of the country in these areas. My fear now is that California is leading the way in bureaucracy and never-ending hand-wringing discussions, and the country is following suit. We discuss how systems are letting down our most vulnerable citizens. Well, things don't stay stable if you don't take action; they get worse. If you spend a bunch of time debating what to do with an old, slightly rusty truck, it's going to go to shit. "We should scuff it and prime it," someone says. Then someone else says, "Well, what kind of primer are you going to use? Maybe we should use an epoxy-based primer? Let's put together a blue-ribbon panel to discuss it for five years." The rust is going to get worse and get into the frame of the truck, and then you'll be past the primer point.

We have given too many people a voice in every conversation. We talk all about our incredible democracy, but you can't give every crackpot a say in every decision. We're discussing everything to death. California has been talking about a bullet train since I was a junior in high school. Now my kids are. For a full generation we've been talking about, but not getting, a piece of technology that Japan mastered twenty years after we nuked them.

This is why when people ask me when I'm going to leave California, I tell them that I have to see my kids through high school. But I am going to show up at their graduation in a U-Haul. ■

Chapter 5

Don't Be a Tool

Some of you may be familiar with my home improvement shows. For example, the beloved TLC show *The Adam Carolla Project*, on which I renovated my dad's house with a crew of misfits including my old friend Ray. Or the much-missed *To Catch a Contractor*, where me and Skip and Alison Bedell busted shady contractors and made them fix their shoddy work and clean up the disasters they left behind for families. And perhaps even the short-lived Spike TV show *Adam Carolla and Friends Build Stuff Live*.

But my bigger fans will know that before I ever met Jimmy Kimmel and went from boxing instructor to radio personality, I had already produced a home improvement show. It was just a call-in show for Eagle Rock cable access, but technically it was my first foray into answering home improvement questions. Back in 1993, I was giving people free advice on their home improvement and construction projects. So why not keep the tradition alive almost thirty years later?

....

I have been working in construction since the early 2000s, and it just seems like there was more Porta John poetry then. It seems like this is a dying art form. Do you know what may have caused this? And do you remember any good poems back in your day?

Josh, 39, Wisconsin

As I covered in my first book, *In Fifty Years We'll All Be Chicks*, my favorite construction site poetry was on the outside of a Porta Potty. Written in Magic Marker was the phrase "Mexican space shuttle," and above the toilet seat liners someone had written "Free cowboy hats."

The problem with Porta John poetry is that no one on a construction site can speak, never mind write, in English. Construction, like boxing, has always been the domain of the poor. It's the lower class who are willing—or rather, desperate enough—to suffer head trauma from fists or girders to make a few bucks. In the early part of the previous century, when the poor folk were Irish and Italian immigrants, they arrived with a rich literary history, like James Joyce for the Irish or Dante Alighieri for the Italians. Now it's Guatemalan and Nicaraguan guys. Not only are they struggling with the language, but they don't have a strong literary lineage. Think that's racist? Give me the top three Nicaraguan poets. I'll wait. Can't do it, can you? Being a Nicaraguan poet sounds like a euphemism for barfing in an alleyway.

That's only part of the problem. I have to give the bulk of the blame to smartphones. Instead of staring at the wall of the Porta Potty, now the guy dropping a deuce on the jobsite is sitting on the pot watching ESPN and getting the score of the local ball game. No one needs to read the wall as a time killer anymore. I know it's been said before, so forgive the cliché, but having an iPhone is like holding the inside of ten million Porta Pottys in the palm of your hand.

Or maybe someone just got practical. How many eyeballs are you getting inside the Porta Potty? If you want to make a profound political statement, like "Hilary Clinton's a cunt," and tag it on the inside of a Porta Potty, your reach is nine guys who can't read English. But if you tag the side of a cube van that's driving to that construction site, you're getting six thousand eyeballs a day. It's interesting. There's less graffiti in places where there used to be, like Porta Pottys. But now it's on the island at the self-serve gas station and on freeway signs and overpasses. Seems like the taggers have been taking some online marketing classes.

Plus, with the advent of Tinder and PornHub, there's no longer a need for scribbled phone numbers under "For a good time call."

Since you've got me thinking about Porta Pottys, I have a few other thoughts unrelated to graffiti. The Porta Potty doesn't get its due from the progressives. If you think about it, the Porta Potty is the first unisex bathroom. It doesn't discriminate. It's going to disgust people of whatever gender who are occupying it. Guys have to look into a slurry of piss and shit, but at least when they're taking a leak, they don't have to strain their quads attempting to hover over the toilet seat.

Then there's the ironically named honey wagon that comes to suck up the human fluid stew from the Porta Potty after fourteen hours of Cal Jam 2021. That is the greatest chasm between a name and what it actually represents—the ultimate euphemism. When the honey wagon would show up to the jobsites I was working on, I would think, *There's a guy with a worse job than mine.* That's saying something. I was breaking my back digging ditches, but at least I wasn't that sorry sonofabitch. I'd feel good for about five minutes. By the way, ladies, if you're dating one of these guys, don't ever cross him. If you ever get caught cheating, he is going to back that honey wagon up to your car, take out the hose, and empty it into your open sunroof. ∎

• •

What five to ten things should one look for when inspecting a house before purchasing? And in those, what would make you walk away from buying the home?

Karl, 55, New Braunfels, Texas

If I were a home inspector, as soon as I walked in I would look at the Realtor with a deadly serious face and say, "I have a bad feeling about this," just to screw with them.

The home inspection is a good idea, but honestly, if it's a good house anything they might find is fixable. You can replace windows and appliances. Electrical is a bigger deal, but it's still something a good electrician can get in there and upgrade or replace. Even problems with the foundation can be fixed. You can get under that shit and jack it up. And expect them to find out the chimney needs repointing. Every chimney needs repointing.

I would say you should look for the things that the inspector can't find. I have lived in five houses since cell phones became a ubiquitous part of our life. In *every one* of those houses, my phone calls would get dropped. When you're doing the inspection, walk through the house with your cell phone. Try to make a call. Call me. I'll provide that service to save you all the heartache. Try calling from the master bedroom and see how many bars you get. If I pick up the phone, you should pick up the house.

Second, you should go there at five p.m. on a Monday and see if Waze is taking everyone down your street as a shortcut to get around traffic. People typically check out open houses and do showings on Sunday morning or maybe early on a weekday. They're not there when the afternoon commute is on.

And on that note… ■

. . . .

Help! What can I do about my loud, drunk neighbors who are ruining my sanity at my newly renovated dream home?! A few years ago, I renovated a supercute old cottage in a good hood. A two-lot property for my dream garden. I put in a fair amount of dough and lots of sweat equity...but then two or three times a week: drunk-neighbor backyard parties, outdoor TV blasting, crappy bass-heavy stereo blasting, karaoke yelling, and cornhole bags banging...so loud my house actually vibrates. It's like living next to a biker bar. I'm employed, single, female, and too chickenshit to confront them! What would an asshole do?

Lyn Marie, 53, Florida

You should have checked out the house on a Saturday night when your asshole neighbors were partying. You were probably there on a Saturday or Sunday morning, when the crazy Mexican biker gang was sleeping off the night before. The loudest houses on a Saturday night are the quietest on a Sunday morning during the showing with the Realtor. But it's too late for you. This is more of a warning/tip to other readers. ∎

. . . .

Having had a career as a journeyman carpenter and being on a few home improvement shows on television, are there any DIY shows that you enjoy? This Old House? Holmes on Homes? The New Yankee Workshop?

Robert, 43, Huntertown, Indiana

I like all of those shows. You can tell those guys know what they're talking about. What I can't buy are the shows where couples renovate and flip houses. I'm getting divorced right now, and there's no doubt that the fights we had over replacing the dryer, painting the bathroom, and hiring and firing the gardener contributed to the demise of my marriage. If these renovating-couple reality show were actual reality, we'd be seeing actual couples strangle each other over peel-and-stick tile. The crew from *Dateline* could just film the show and transition seamlessly into a murder-in-a-small-town true-crime show.

What I especially don't get is the current obsession with tiny houses. When I was young, home shows were aspirational. There was *Lifestyles of the Rich and Famous* with Robin Leach touring Morgan Fairchild's estate and then offering everyone champagne wishes and caviar dreams. But now opulence is out of style, so we've got tiny houses, log cabins, treehouses, and vans. I blame Ikea. ■

. . . .

If Adam is all about efficiency and nonwaste, then why haven't we heard him wax on about installing a bidet in every bathroom at the warehouses, his homes, etc.?

Alex, 32, Florida

I don't have a full bidet, but I have the toilet seat that squirts. The Omigo. I love it. In fact, I don't leave home without it. I carry it around my neck like one of those travel pillows for sleeping on the plane.

I've been in love with these for years. I remember my first time, when I broke my behymen. It was at the Righa Royal hotel in New York (now renamed the Conrad). The whole thing is vaguely sexual. It's like a home rim job. Warm water on the asshole is always going to feel good. But if it feels great, you should have an honest conversation with your wife. If you find yourself using it without having taken a shit, it's time to stand up from the bidet and take a long look in the mirror. I wanted to get one for my son, but I don't know what the long-term effects are. I imagine a study in the future showing that 70 percent of men who used it for more than seven years turned gay.

I was so fascinated with it, Jimmy Kimmel later purchased one for me. The weird part was that it came with a wireless remote sporting a picture of a seal with a ball bouncing on its nose. Why? Tigers get to be "the tiger in your tank," or at least the spokesman for Frosted Flakes. Donkeys get to be Democrats, and elephants rep the Republicans. The lion gets to majestically announce the beginning of MGM films. But the seal gets relegated to being the mascot for an ass squirter. Seals need to get a better PR team.

It wasn't just the seal icon. It was the idea of the remote itself. To what end? (No pun intended.) Your TV needs a remote, because otherwise you'd need to get up to change the channel. The toilet seat doesn't need a remote. That'd be like having a remote for a car seat's recline feature. It's right there; it should just be a button that you reach down to use. There's no version of your needing a remote for the toilet when you are not on the toilet seat. You're not gonna wander off with your asshole covered in shit and then fire it off in another room. The only outcomes could be that your kid drops the remote in the toilet or you play a disgusting prank on your spouse after they come upstairs with the plunger to deal with the toilet you've clogged.

Plus, there are way too many buttons on the thing: jet pressure, temperature, air dry. You don't take advantage of them all because you're nervous. It's like when you're sitting in a rental car, you're uncomfortable pushing buttons because you might turn on the wipers or the emergency flashers. When you're on one of these seats, your pants are around your ankles and your asshole is exposed. You're in a very vulnerable position. You don't know if that button, especially if it's got a nonsensical logo like a seal, is going to shoot you in the ass with a nice warm jet of water, impale you with a Prussian helmet spike, or fire you off the toilet like a James Bond ejector seat.

And when you press the button, you have to wait five seconds. There's a crazy sense of anticipation. Is the water going to be too cold? It's like the Magic Mountain free-fall ride. There's always a slight, anxiety-building pause. Ironically, it makes you tighten your sphincter before the soothing warm water jet cleanses it.

One last thought: The bidet has been around in some form or another for centuries, but these modern toilet seat adapters were pioneered by the Japanese. It occurs to me that no culture needs it less. The Japanese subsist on a diet of a cucumber rolls and can boast a hairless ass. Armenians—that's who need bidets. They've got a diet rich in baklava and goat, and have a shag carpet for an ass. Every Armenian asshole looks like the guy Sacha Baron Cohen wrestled with in the first Borat movie. You know that footage you see of kids opening up fire hydrants in New York during the dog days of summer? That's what your average Armo needs his toilet armed with.

But as much as I love them, and to more directly answer your question, these seats promise in their ads that you'll never buy toilet paper again. I'm not sure about that. When you're done, you have a soaking-wet asshole with a little bit of poop on it. You don't save much toilet paper. Who is confident enough to drop a deuce, squirt themselves in the ass, pull up their britches, and go on with their day? If you eat ribs without a napkin, would you just dip your hands in water or would you still need a wipe? Hell no. There's always a wipe. So with these devices, the toilet paper essentially goes from being a cake spatula to being a squeegee. ■

What's the number-one thing to think about when building a new house? And also, what's something you have no idea you will want when it's complete that you'd be happy as hell you have?

—Eric Stonestreet

Don't get sold on adding a bunch of bells and whistles that you don't need. A lot of houses get touted for having whole-home vacuums. I've lived in a few houses with these. It sounds great in principle, but it's like the NuTone blenders that were built into countertops in the '50s. They never get used and eventually become an eyesore. Modern vacuums are small, lightweight, cordless, and more efficient than they've ever been. Pushing a Dyson around or letting your Roomba do the work completely undercuts the whole-home vac. You don't need to deal with hooking the hose up to the jack and dragging it around. Plus, the home vac's motor and catch basket take up the entire garage.

I'd say the thing that you don't know you want when you're building a house that you'll be so glad you put in, and which is very difficult to add to an existing home, is radiant flooring. When you get out of your shower, instead of stepping onto stone-cold tiles, you put your tootsies down on a warm piece of porcelain. You'll be so happy. You can put radiant heat under all kinds of flooring, not just stone, so on a winter morning when you get out of bed, your bare feet can hit hot hardwood.

Now, while I recommend having a heated floor in the bathroom, don't bother with a heated towel bar. It's overkill. Radiant flooring is to the bathroom as the heated seat is to your car. Once you have it, you can't imagine living without it. Especially if you live in an area with a cold climate. But the heated towel bar is akin to the heated steering wheel. You don't even remember to turn a heated steering wheel on half the time, and with the vents blowing hot air right at your hands, you don't even know if it's on. Your palms don't constitute that big a part of your body. Your ass, on the other hand, is a huge percentage of your body... well, not *your* ass, Eric. *One's* ass is a huge percent of one's body. That got awkward. I guess I just blew the invitation to your housewarming party, which will be extra warm if you take my heated-flooring tip. ■

Chapter 6

Alcoa Presents:
I Make the Call

I love sports. I love the grit. I love the meritocracy. I love the atmosphere of a good football Sunday with the guys. But I don't love what sports are becoming—a front in our never-ending culture war. I'm not just talking about taking a knee or renaming the Redskins. There are subtle ways in which the disaster we call our country is infecting our nation's pastimes. I can tell by your questions that you see it too.

....

If you could choose any Olympic sport to compete in, which one would it be?

Chris, 28, Northridge, California

I'd be in the four-man bobsled. But before I explain why, I have a question. Why is it that there's no three-man bobsled? You have the head-first single-man skeleton bobsled. Then you have the two-man version, and then they jump right to the four-man bobsled. What happened to a three-man version? Is it like how there's no thirteenth floor in high-rises? Just a superstition? It's like bra sizes. They have A cup, B cup, C cup, D cup, then double-D cup and triple-D cup before you get to the E cup. Why not just keep moving through the alphabet?

Anyway. I'd be in the four-man bobsled and, more specifically, I'd be one of the two middle guys. I think I could pull that off. I know what the guy in front is doing. He's steering. The guy in the rear is the brake man. But what about the other two guys in the middle? Are they just ballast? It seems to me their entire job is to run like hell, jump in, and then attempt to suck their own dick for sixty-one seconds. It's chug, chug, chug, suck, suck, suck, then pop up and find out if you got the gold.

Which reminds me, I'd like to make a change in the Olympics medal ceremony.

I believe in the sanctity of the gold, silver, bronze—a.k.a. first, second, and third place—winners being on the podium, and have ranted in *Daddy Stop Talking* (available wherever finer books are sold) about kids sports and the expansion of the podium into double-digit places. Eighth place is not a place. As a person who has placed fourth in a celebrity race, I have a passion for this topic. I've won some celebrity races, and it's exhilarating. And I made fourth in a race with twenty-two participants. There is no difference between fourth and twenty-second place. You don't fucking exist after third place; you're a ghost. I was just a bit off third place, and my ceremony was drinking a warm beer in the trailer. You get third place, someone puts a hat or a medal on you. You get fourth place, it's like you've never been born. That's how it should be.

My beef is with the podium height. This is my next mission, having succeeded in getting the NFL goalposts raised. (Yes, that was me. You're welcome.) In the Olympics, the silver and bronze podiums are the same height. Take a look. You might be on the podium, tearing up to your national anthem, but if the guy who placed after you is taller, it looks like he finished ahead of you. It's bullshit.

We've all seen the famous photo of the Black Power salute at the Mexico City Olympics in 1968. Everyone remembers that photo. One of those brothers came in third. There was some Australian honkey in second, and no one gives a fuck about him. Take a look.

Photo Credit by Bettmann via Getty Images

The bronze medalist, John Carlos, came in .04 seconds behind the Australian, Peter Norman, but because John Carlos was six foot four and Norman was five foot ten, it looked like the Black guy beat the white guy in a foot race—as is usually the case.

This is my platform, and it's about platforms. We need to raise the silver platform on the podium so that it's twice as high as the bronze. We can keep it simple: Third place would be one foot high, second place would be two feet high, and first place would be three feet high. Are you listening, International Olympic Committee? ∎

· ·

Boxing, wrestling, or football—which is the best to teach toughness and grit to a child?

Peter, 34, Vancouver, Washington

I will pick wrestling, because it's a sport I never participated in. Football is the best for teamwork, but I believe wrestling is the best to instill individual grit. But if I were going to sign up my son, who very much likes comedy, for either wrestling or football, I would ask him first: "Do you want to do stand-up or group improv?" If he picks group improv, football would be better, as it's a team sport, whereas wrestling is more like stand-up, as it's an individual sport.

Interesting side note: It is ironic that there are no funny Olympic-caliber wrestlers. There are former NFLers who have gone on to comedy success: Terry Crews, Alex Karras as Mongo in *Blazing Saddles*, Bubba Smith in the *Police Academy* movies, and, of course, O. J. Simpson being hilarious as Nordberg in the *Naked Gun* movies and as "guy putting on gloves" during his murder trial. But no Olympic wrestlers have gone on to comedy. Brock Lesnar doesn't strike me as the life of the party.

Anyway, this is male-focused. Wrestling will teach a young man grit. But the same dynamics that teach a boy toughness, like getting screamed at by coaches and learning to suck weight before a tournament, will result in an eating disorder if you swap in a girl and gymnastics.

That said, wrestling is still a little gay. It's got the word "Greco" right in it. The singlet is up there with chaps as far as gay appeal. If anyone ever made a suede singlet, it would be some sort of magical cape that would render gay anyone who donned it, like the homosexual version of the mask in *The Mask*. And back in ancient Greece, all wrestling was done in the nude. It wasn't like you could swing into the New Navy and get a tunic. Maybe wrestling was invented as an elaborate ruse to figure out who in town was gay. First guy to get a boner might win the match but lose in the court of public opinion.

Wrestling is also interesting in that it's the only sport where if you put the word "professional" in front of it, it becomes fake. The word "professional" usually makes everything better. Even bowling gains creditability when you put "professional" in front of it. Without the word "professional" preceding it, the bowler you picture is your brother-in-law or Homer Simpson. But if you shorten it to just "pro" it gets confusing. Because as far as race and status go, there is no bigger chasm than that between a pro bowler and a Pro Bowl-er. ∎

. . . .

Would you rather have the career/life you have now, or have attended college on a football scholarship, made it to the show, and had a respectable but unremarkable career playing four or five seasons on a team that made it to the payoffs a few times but never to a Super Bowl? (This scenario also assumes you have the same intellect/business acumen, so you were prudent with your earnings and so went on to own a few domestic car dealerships or fast-food franchises, or maybe some unpainted-furniture stores you could pass on to Sonny someday.)

Jon, 48, Princeton, New Jersey

When I was growing up, I kind of heard of everyone who played in the league, because it wasn't that old. There were only three TV networks, and I knew every cast member on *The Love Boat*. Now there are seven thousand streaming channels, and someone within a twelve-foot radius of you right now has been on TV. Now there are so many guys you've never heard of—thousands who have cycled out of the league—that it feels much less impressive. You turn on the news and some former NFL player is being brought up on domestic violence charges, and you've never even heard of the guy. But how many people can claim to have hosted *The Man Show* and had the number-one podcast in the country? Just Joe Rogan. ■

· ·

It seems the technology is more than sufficient to electronically call balls and strikes more accurately than human umpires. Almost all televised broadcasts use a form of this superimposed on the screen. Why is Major League Baseball not taking advantage of the technology?

Michael, 56, Chandler, Arizona

Baseball is steeped in tradition. In 1839, bats were wood, gloves were leather, and players were white. There was even a player named Whitey (Ford). Smash-cut to today and it's almost the same thing, minus the white part. The sport and the equipment haven't changed one iota. We could have a carbon-composite bat and a glove composed of whatever Jeff Bezos's jumpsuit is made of, but we don't. One day some intrepid individual is going to pioneer the Kevlar glove, and that guy will go down in history as the Jackie Robinson of baseball.

If MLB went with the automated strike zone, it would eliminate the only exciting part of baseball, which is the old fat white guy wearing tennis shoes running out to home plate to kick dirt at the other old fat white guy about the wrong call. ■

• •

Should we let biological males who claim to identify as females compete against biological females in their respective sports?

Christopher, 53, Enumclaw, Washington

Yes. Initially they should be able to compete, but if they dominate then we're going to have to even the playing field. If you are a fair to middling weightlifter as a male and you transition to female and dominate, no one would like that. It's about fairness and competition. That's what we love about sports. They're the last meritocracies left in our ever-declining country.

Before you decide that what I'm about to say is just bigoted, transphobic, misogynistic hate speech from me and other knuckle-dragging Tucker Carlson–loving goons, ask yourself why you never hear a peep about women becoming men and competing. How come the so-called transphobes don't care about that? You never hear them complaining about a biological woman becoming a man and going into powerlifting, because that doesn't present an unfair advantage. It's just about parity. We don't want shit like what happened in Connecticut, where the top two high school sprinters who broke all the records were born male but were competing against girls.

Anyway, back to my bigoted, transphobic, misogynistic hate speech. First, there should be some shaming. Biological men who identify as female and compete in women's sports should have to be called geldings. Second, we need to even the playing field when ladies who weren't born ladies are dominating in any sport. If you're a fan of GT racing like I am, you know they allowed twin turbos. Those cars started dominating, so they started restricting airflow to the turbos and added weight to those cars to achieve parity. I think there should be some version of this for the guy who wants to cut off his dick and run with the ladies. On that note, removing your dick and balls is already an advantage. That's what we call unsprung weight in the car racing game.

I propose we keep adding weight to the titties of the former males until it evens out. Not only would this achieve parity, but ratings would be through the roof. I know I would want to watch more track meets if a nice pair of D cups was jiggling though the hundred-meter dash. And it seems like if men want to be women, they'd want to be voluptuous. Now, I'm not talking about forced saline or silicone breast implants. I'm not a weirdo. Just get a sandbag bra and keep adding weight.

Speaking of sports and gender, I had to laugh recently when I got an email from Sonny's school. The note was about COVID protocols or something like that, but at the bottom, under the administrator's name, it listed his pronouns: "He/Him/His." First off, you had me at "he." I can do the math on "him" and "his." Does anyone list "he" as the main pronoun but then "her" or, even more confusingly, "their" after it? No one is ever going to say, "What does he want for her birthday? I don't know what to get they."

But the thing that made me laugh was a quarter-inch below the virtue-signaling pronoun breakdown. It said, "Home of the Spartans." The Spartans—the most vicious all-male fighting force in history. I've seen *300*. Gerard Butler didn't need to declare his pronouns. You couldn't get further from the concept of pronoun announcements, which I'll just shorten to "pronouncements," than the Spartans. ■

· ·

Do you think we will ever see any more dual MLB/NFL players, like Bo Jackson, Deion Sanders, and Brian Jordan?

Mark, 55, Suwanee, Georgia

I think we're living in a time of expertise and specialization. We're in the era of having to commit to a sport early, with all the requisite youth camps and personal coaching. The money is so lucrative in one sport or the other that you don't need to moonlight. So the days of Jim Thorpe or Babe Didrikson are a bygone era, although the amount of time between Jim Thorpe/Babe Didrikson and Bo Jackson is about the same as between Jackson and now, which is bizarre to think about.

Michael Jordan was also famously—or rather, infamously—a two-sport athlete. Showing that it pays to specialize.

Plus, athletes all have their mental trials and tribulations. I'm not sure athletes today would be able to handle two sports. In 1992, Deion Sanders famously started in a one p.m. game against the Dolphins while playing for the Atlanta Falcons, and then immediately boarded a flight to Pittsburg and hopped a helicopter to Three Rivers Stadium to join the Braves for game five of the NLCS against the Pirates. Can you imagine any of the prima donnas in either league doing that today? (By the way, the Falcons and the Braves both lost that day, so thanks for nothing, Neon Deion.)

I can't help but think how ironic it would be if famous biathletes Jackson and Sanders were the other kind of bi, like "I can't decide on a sport and I can't decide between a penis and a pussy." They are the least likely two humans to be bi, but I'm sure if they were, they'd crush ass in every sense of the word.

All of that said, I think we have to give the tip of the cap to Dock Ellis as the greatest two-sport athlete of all time, having achieved greatness in both MLB and LSD. ■

Football officials seem to have figured out how to use their microphones to announce penalties, booth reviews, etc. Why does MLB refuse to have umpires take a few seconds to inform the crowd of replay decisions and uncommon rulings on the field, such as balks, infield-fly decisions when the ball is dropped and/or runners advance, interference calls, and even ejection of players and coaches after on-field altercations? My guess is the union won't allow it.

Keith, 55, Springfield, Illinois

Perhaps it's because the Bataan Death March that is your average MLB game doesn't need any more flour added to its stew. Baseball games drag on enough as it is. Do you really think stopping the game so some doughy white dude can let us know about a balk is going to make it more exciting? Here's how bad baseball is: The majority of white kids choose to play *fantasy* football rather than *actual* baseball.

And I've complained in previous books and hundreds of podcasts about how long the baseball season is. I say baseball should take a page from pornography's playbook. Porn jumps right to the playoffs. Baseball needs to skip the foreplay. America's pastime is past its prime. Slowing it down ain't gonna help.

You were instrumental in getting goalposts extended. What's the next major change you'd like to see in sports, structurally or otherwise?

—"Cousin Sal" Iacono

Thanks, Sal. As a former long snapper, I know the importance of an excellent setup. You've just put me in a perfect position to punt-ificate on my genius ideas on how to improve the NFL if I were Commissioner Carolla.

D-Exchange

I would immediately institute a D-exchange program. There are guys named D'Andre in the NFL. We don't need the "D." You had me at Andre. I know you're a brother just from the name "Andre." We don't need to guild the black lily. I'm pretty sure the only white Andre's last name was "the Giant." But there are black guys in the NFL with incredibly white-sounding names. For example, Chad Johnson. Chad is either a guy who does landscaping and doesn't pay child support or the lead singer from Nickelback. Chad needs D'Andre's "D." D'Chad Ochocino would be a strong NFL name. Now, I will allow you to go with Chadwick. That would work, and you wouldn't have to steal a "D." There are guys like Melvin Gordon and Alvin Kamara who desperately need "D's." "Melvin" and "Alvin" sound like Jewish dudes who ripped off Black guys for the publishing rights to their Motown hits in the early '60s.

The best example is Todd Gurly. He needs to be D'Todd. A guy named Todd is a Dave Matthews fan who wears Birkenstocks to a PTA meeting, not a Meek Mill fan who wears cleats as a running back for the Rams. Maybe we could just move the extra second "D" at the end of "Todd" and he could become D'Tod Gurly. That'd be acceptable to this podcaster.

Number 30 for the Cleveland Browns is D'Ernest Johnson. That's a perfect application of the "D." Without that letter, we don't have a running back in Cleveland in the 2020s; we have a pharmacist in Kansas in the 1920s. One is trying to win the Super Bowl, and one was trying to survive the Dust Bowl.

But I still think it should be an exchange. There is precedent for this. Sometimes a player will get traded and want to keep his number, but the place kicker on the new team will already have it, and the traded guy will work it into his contract or pay the kicker to give it up. Jeff Feagles sold his number 10 to Plaxico Buress—another guy who definitely doesn't need a "D" in front of his name. The cost? A new kitchen. I don't feel we're far enough away from slavery that white guys can be extorting Black guys for granite countertops to get their number.

So if we can sell numbers, I think we can sell "D's." And I know exactly who needs to give up his "D" and hand it over to Todd Gurly. D'Brickashaw Ferguson has the most extraneous "D" in the history of the NFL. There are not many Brickashaws selling insurance in the Midwest. You had me at "Brickashaw."

By the way, Sal, speaking of "D's" and the NFL, if you ever joined the league you'd have to change your name to D'Generate Gambler.

Challenge Flags

Most people do not recall the story of Orlando "Zeus" Brown. In 1999 he was a Cleveland Brown and was temporarily blinded in his right eye by a penalty flag thrown by referee Jeff Triplette. It cost Brown the next three NFL seasons due to healing and rehab, and he subsequently sued for two hundred million dollars in damages (reportedly walking away with somewhere between fifteen and twenty-five million dollars). First off, the NFL should have seen this coming. You've got an older guy who hasn't run forty yards in forty years chugging downfield trying to keep up with guys in the prime of their career, and you expect him to be able to pull a yellow flag weighted with ball bearings out of their belt and throw it and not hit someone? I'm surprised this hasn't happened dozens of times by now.

Of all the things that can take you out of the league—ACL tear, CTE, off-season drugs, gang issues—this talent gets taken out in the same way that caused us to ban lawn darts.

This can never happen again, not on my watch. Solution? Four words: Monkey. On. A. Sheep. That would be delightful. Who hasn't seen that footage of a monkey riding a sheep at a rodeo in a little cowboy outfit? He'd ride out with the flag. It would be the best part of the game.

Football Color

We've all seen multiple plays over the years where it's a crucial fourth and inches, there's a scrum, and the refs have to decide where the ball is downed—which could make the difference. The problem is that it's impossible to see the ball in the pile of humanity, because it blends in with the skin color of that pile of humanity. The huge forearm carrying it is as brown as the ball. During the days of "Crazylegs" Hirsch, Frank Gifford, or Dave "the Ghost" Casper, that ball popped. But in today's NFL, the ball should be Kool-Aid red, traffic cone orange, or maybe the blue you'd see in the Israeli flag, or even have the Star of David itself. Not like a lot of Semites are toting the rock. Either way, the thing has to stand out. The color of the pigskin can't be the same color as the players' skin.

Streakers

Once or twice a season, some asshole runs out onto the field and delays the game, and the cameras have to cut away. The networks won't cover it for the same reason you don't negotiate with terrorists. It encourages more of it. So, we end up getting a long cutaway of a coach's fat face.

Instead of looking at the line coach's grimacing mug for that minute, we should use the same policy I declared years ago should apply to *Peanuts* creator Charles Schulz when he had no cartoon to put in the paper that week. Use that valuable real estate to show a picture of a missing kid. So the next time some drunken yahoo tries to streak across the field, we'll kill the audio so we're not all doing the theater of the mind listening to the crowd groan and cheer as the guy bobs and weaves and eventually gets tackled by security. And for the visual, we'll throw up a picture of a missing kid and play Soul Asylum's "Runaway Train."

Or we could lean into it. If the problem with showing streaking on camera is that it would encourage more of it, then let's make the consequences harsher. In my NFL, we'll go full *Planet of the Apes* with guys in complete gorilla costumes on horseback running him down with a net, and we'll pipe in the score from the movie. Maybe each team's mascot could take a run at the streaker. I'd like to see these guys getting kicked by a Colt or rammed by a Ram, getting speared by a Chief or shot with a musket by a Patriot, getting his eyes scratched out by a Falcon or an Eagle, and getting shit on by a Brown.

No Female Referees

If my experience with women is any indicator of what will happen, a female referee will make a bad call, the officials will review the tape and see that the player's foot really was inbound, and she'll say, "I know what I know," and take it to her grave. All of you married men know there are no overturned calls in your house.

Touchdown Celebrations

In 2017 the NFL did a training video for new players about appropriate and inappropriate celebrating. We all know how effective training videos are. Looking at the past few seasons, I'm not sure that this worked. I'm not sure a list of do's and don'ts really landed. Inappropriate celebrating should be decided on the same way Supreme Court Justice Potter Stewart said of pornography in 1964, "I know it when I see it." If you're celebrating, that's fine. If you're taunting the other team, then I'm pulling the hankie. If you're just celebrating, then go nuts (unless you're doing something like dry-humping the goalpost with the other team's logo). But if it gets into low-class mocking or taunting the other team, I'm pulling the TD.

My bigger beef is with the unnecessary celebrations. If you block a punt, that is cause for celebration. But every minor defensive play is getting a fucking parade nowadays. In the middle of the second quarter when the defense falls on a loose ball, the entire defense has to rush to the end zone to take a picture. You're down by thirteen and you fell on a loose ball on the fifty-yard line. You do not need all eleven players to rush to the end zone and take a selfie. The play wasn't that great. And then you'll hear later in the game, "It's the fourth quarter, and Tom Brady has the ball. There's a minute and a half left, and in Brady's hands that's a lifetime. And this defense looks gassed. They've been playing hard for four quarters, but they're having trouble getting to the QB." Yeah, because they made five needless sprints to the other end zone for an unnecessary group pic. As a coach, you've got to get the message to your team that unwarranted wind sprints are not the greatest idea.

What moment are those players even capturing? Most NFL games are recorded. Not sure if they're aware of that, but their standard-issue play was chronicled for all time. Also, at minimum, only two guys should be heading down there: the one who punched it out and the one who fell on it. The cornerback was running in the opposite direction. If he'd never been born, you'd still have that fumble. Why the fuck is he in the picture?

Then there are reversed calls. During the Chiefs versus Bills game in 2021 in the fourth quarter, the Chiefs were down twenty to thirty-one. The Bills quarterback threw from the one-yard line, and the Chiefs picked off the pass at the forty-yard line. The entire Chiefs defense scrambled to the end zone to take their yearbook photo and failed to notice there was a flag on the play. After running ninety-eight yards to the opposite end zone to preen, they had to hustle back. You've got to look for the flag. I feel like there's a flag on every other play these days. If you're going to waste time taking group selfies, wait until you're sure the play is going to stand so you won't have to do the walk of shame back to the line of scrimmage.

In college games when the defensive back picks off a ball and gets to the sidelines, his teammates take a medallion the size of Flavor Flav's clock and knight the guy with it. He picked off a deflected pass. That's his fucking job. He wasn't at Dunkirk.

MVP Trophy

This one flies in the face of my last point a bit, but that was about unnecessary praise for day-to-day plays. If you get to exalted MVP status in the Super Bowl, you deserve more than your standard-issue trophy. If you get into that rarified air, you've gotten pedestrian trophies and plaques all your life. It would get lost in your trophy case.

So I think it shouldn't be a trophy. It should be a scepter. It should be presented in a case lined with blue crushed velvet. The winner could use it to lead a parade or anoint new head coaches like the queen of England bestowing knighthood. Most scepters in movies can shoot lightning that vaporizes an enemy. Well, I'm not crazy. I know that's just fantasyland, but maybe we could install a little cattle prod at the top for tasing people. Imagine if Gronk got ahold of an electric scepter. That would provide newsworthy moments for a lifetime.

Super Bowl Sunday

I have to give credit where it's due on this one. If you're this far into a list of NFL tweaks and aren't bored and annoyed, you probably know who the aforementioned "Cousin Sal" is. I was on his podcast a few years back, and he said that the Super Bowl should be on a Saturday. I agree and would implement this as commissioner. We'd still have the alliteration working for us— "Super Bowl Saturday" sounds just as good. It's two weeks away from the playoff, so what's the difference between thirteen days off and fourteen days off? But most important, about fourteen million people call in sick on the Monday after the Super Bowl. Especially on the East Coast. That thing ends around midnight for those folks by the time they get through all the trophy presentations. I think most people hosting Super Bowl parties also would like the next day off to clean up. And I can definitely make the argument that, as far as alcohol and greasy-food consumption are concerned, I dig in much harder during the Super Bowl than on Christmas, Thanksgiving, or even New Year's Eve, which has a day off afterward built in. I don't have any numbers to back this up, but I'd bet that when your team (or the team you bet on) wins the Super Bowl, you're much more likely to go into work the next day and brag. So the opposite must be true. Give the losing team's fans a day off to lick their wounds and puke out their hangovers. Everyone wins.

Goalposts

It's long established that yours truly was the driving force behind the raising of the goalposts. So I know things are slow to evolve in this area. Think about the fact that the goalposts were right at the goal line for over a century, causing any number of traumatic brain injuries, and that we had ball turret gunners and the Empire State Building before we figured out how to put the uprights on one post. It's astounding. The goalpost was shaped like an "H" until the '80s.

But I have another notion that could enhance the game. We should add one more pole right up the middle of the uprights, and if the kicker nails it, it is good for eight points. It would get knocked down and fireworks would shoot out of the other two uprights. It would be amazing. Instead of going for a Hail Mary with seconds left and not making it, you set up for a field goal, and you could probably get a kicker who could drill it.

We also need to address stadium design as it relates to this. I'm not sure how, but we need to control airflow. I would like the two flags at the top of the goalposts to communicate a little better. There are two ribbons up there to show the speed and the direction of the wind. They're only eighteen and a half feet apart, yet one will look like it's in the middle of Hurricane Katrina and the other will be DOA. One is having a seizure and flapping like one of those inflatable guys outside the car wash, while a mere six yards away its twin brother is flaccid. My NFL would get on top of this ribbon situation. As commissioner, I'd commission a blue-ribbon ribbon commission.

Dreadlocks

I don't want to wade into the racial hot water of outright banning dreadlocks, but let's say I'd actively discourage it. I don't get it. I hate the heat because of where I grew up, and part of my hatred of it is the extra burden my Jew-fro adds to that misery index. I cannot for the life of me understand the brothers who are carrying around ten pounds of dreads while doing two-a-days in the Florida heat. If I were in the NFL, the second I got signed I would bust out the Wahl trimmer and go full Kojak. Why are dreads as a fashion statement so important? In a game where every ounce matters for running speed, why would you add three pounds of weight to essentially create a handle that the opposition can use to take you down?

Plus, nothing holds funk like dreadlocks. My nostrils are still suffering from the residual stink of George Clinton when he appeared on *Loveline* back in June 1996. In an NFL with a lot of drug testing, why would you wear a hairstyle that lets everyone know by its odor that you smoked weed in the past three days? It makes no sense. You've got an eight-pack, you are completely cut, and you're fresh off a twenty-six-million-dollar deal to play in the NFL. And you live in Florida. Why do you think you won't get your dick sucked unless your hair looks like the Predator's?

So, my rule would be that dreadlocks are now fair game. If you're an offensive lineman, you can hang on to Jadeveon Clowney's dreads like a subway handle, without getting a call.

Throwback Nights

I've got to give the tip of the cowboy hat (you'll get that reference a paragraph from now) to NFL Network talent and my old *Man Show* and KLSX morning show compatriot Dave Dameshek for this one, but I concur 100 percent. The NFL has been doing the "throwback" uniform thing since the '90s. But why should it apply only to the men on the field? Dave proposed to Wade Phillips, then defensive coordinator for the L.A. Rams, that on throwback night he should don the cowboy hat, boots, and duster of his father, Bum Phillips. (For those of you who are too young to remember Bum Phillips, let me lay it out for you. He dressed like McCloud. I'm sure that cleared it up.) And to Dave, I say kudos on an excellent idea, and where was stuff like that when we were paying you to write on *The Man Show*? Yes, the coaches should have to wear the attire of the coaches of whatever throwback era has been chosen. Imagine today's coaches in Tom Landry's hat, Don Shula's short-sleeve shirt and Sansabelt slacks, or Abe Gibron's far-too-tight shorts. It'd be great when the Bum-Phillips-for-the-night had to take off the ten-gallon hat because that's where he was keeping the red challenge flag. Or he could throw the whole hat with the challenge flag on it, like Oddjob from *Goldfinger*.

But as I told Dave, we need to take it a step further. We have throwback uniforms and throwback coaches. We need throwback entertainment. We've gotten used to the big fireworks-laden, choreographed halftime shows with Lady Gaga, Justin Timberlake, The Rolling Stones, Beyoncé, and Katy Perry. But it wasn't always like that. It wasn't until 1991 that New Kids on the Block broke the grip of marching bands and schmaltzy wholesome entertainment during halftime. Up with People performed three times during the '80s. And in 1987, George Burns and Mickey Rooney did a salute to Hollywood's one hundredth anniversary with the USC marching band.

But in the lesser games, they used to have sideshows. They'd have local high school flag twirlers and guys trying to break blocks of ice with their head. I would definitely sit and watch that instead of taking a piss break and hitting BetOnline. And I'd sure as shit enjoy it more than The Weeknd.

The crowd and stadium should have to go throwback as well. Smoking would be allowed, and everyone would be drinking pull-tab Stroh's beer and wearing horn-rimmed glasses and thin ties like the guys at Mission Control in Houston during the moon landing. And the teams would have to be ethnically the same as in that era. Sorry, brothers, but it's 1968 today and we've gotta have all-white skill-position players.

The CFL

I don't know that as NFL commissioner I'd have the ability to enforce this, but there should be one team in the Canadian Football League that is made up entirely of ex–NFL players, called the Sloppy Seconds.

Reversed Calls

We all know there are a lot of controversial plays and bullshit reviews in the NFL. I'm particularly incensed at the ever-changing definition of a catch.

You see this play all the time. The receiver goes up, catches the ball with both hands, tucks it under one arm, lands on both feet, and is immediately cleaned out by the defensive back. The ball is knocked loose, goes airborne again, and the catch is declared not a catch because the receiver didn't make "a football move." What the fuck does that even mean? One could argue that the ultimate "football move" is that the football stopped moving when it got to the receiver. It's a simple thought experiment. If the defensive back hadn't been born, would the receiver still have the ball? If the answer is yes, then it was a catch.

But this is the kind of play that gets reviewed and doesn't get overturned, because the ref who made the call on the field wants to save face when he pulls it out from under the hood and costs teams challenges. I have a perfect solution to these calls that get blown on the field. I have been talking about this since 2012, and that sound you just heard is NFL journalist Rich Eisen cumming because he is in love with this idea.

The fact that these calls start on the field influences their not getting overturned. Dr. Drew would call it confirmation bias. We need someone neutral, someone who has not been watching the game and doesn't even know what's going on or even what city he is in. So next time this happens, it's time to—as the great Quentin Tarantino wrote in the script for *Pulp Fiction*—"bring out the gimp." He'd live chained up in a basement in the bowels of the stadium only to be brought out to settle these calls. We'd play that surf saxophone song from that delightful anal rape scene in Zed's pawn shop. He'd have handlers like the buffalo that University of Colorado has, except they'd be scantily clad and flogging him with his own leash the whole way to the replay hood. We'd unzip the eye holes on his mask, and the gimp would wince at the stadium lights or the sun, having not been in daylight for weeks. Then we'd put him under the hood to make the call with unbiased eyes. This would be the best part of any game. Guys would be running back from the bathroom with their pants around their ankles as soon as they heard "Bring out the gimp" on the stadium loudspeaker.

Each stadium would have its own gimp, but the outfit would be standard black studded leather so there would be no hometown bias. I'm not opposed to the leather gimp outfit's having a logo for sponsorship opportunities. "The replay gimp brought to you by Pepsi" has a nice ring to it. Now obviously, if the gimp's call were to go against the home team, there'd be booing—and the subsequent whippings by the handlers/dominatrixes would get even harder. They'd kick him back into his dungeon below the stadium, where he would be given fresh water and clean sawdust as signs of a job well done. ■

••

Ace, I know you're friends with Geragos, who helped Kaep sue the NFL, but what are your thoughts on the new, woke NFL?
Matt, 36, Pelham, New Hampshire

I lamented the ruination of the Oscars in my last book, when I declared them "all woke and no joke" after they went hostless following the Kevin Hart noncontroversy about homophobic tweets. But recently they've come for my beloved NFL, and now it's personal. It's like that famous Martin Niemöller poem, "First they came for the socialists, and I did not speak out—because I was not a socialist..." yada yada yada. Well, first they came for the Oscars...now they've come for the NFL. Except I have been speaking out the whole time because I'm not a pussy coward.

It hit me last year watching a Sunday game and listening to Troy Aikman and Joe Buck call a game bereft of the jokes, ball-busting, and humor that used be part of every broadcast. It's a far cry from the glory days, or rather nights, of Monday Night Football—Keith Jackson and, later, the aforementioned Alex Karras, and of course Howard Cosell and "Dandy" Don Meredith. Dandy Don was to classic Monday Night Football what Jerry Reed was to *Smokey and the Bandit*. He wasn't quite qualified to be there, but you can't imagine it without him. He'd be dressed like a cowboy, smoking in the booth, and one team would be down thirteen points with forty-one seconds left, and he'd bust into the old country tune "The Party's Over."

Of course, Howard Cosell would be blotto. They were all shit-faced by the second quarter. It was a simpler time. Alcohol was, as Homer Simpson so aptly says, "the cause of and solution to all of life's problems." Back then you'd say, "I'm a little chilly," and someone would hand you a flask. If you were cold or achy, even if it was just bunions, it didn't matter whether you were driving a school bus full of special-needs kids—or retards, cretins, and Mongoloids, as they would have been called back then—someone would hand you a vermouth. And this predated climate-controlled booths. Those guys were bundled up just as much as the rest of the freezing crowd at Lambeau Field. No wonder the Monday Night Football crew was creating some serious Tuesday-morning hangovers.

Later you had the larger-than-life character of John Madden, who would draw sweat marks on Nate Newton's ass with the Telestrator, and the sometimes intentionally and sometimes unintentionally funny Terry Bradshaw was good too.

Which is why it's sad to see what's become of Joe Buck. Joe Buck is a funny guy. We've had him on the podcast a couple of times. He's got the makings of a stand-up comedian—deadpan delivery, broad knowledge of the subject, an eye for details that others might miss. But that talent gets left at the door of the announcer's booth because there's an inherent problem with jokes. There is a winner and a loser. There is someone making fun of and someone being made fun of. And that doesn't fly in our new "everyone is awesome," "no one gets their feelings hurt" culture. By definition, you can't joke anymore. If Joe Buck just came by your house for Sunday football, the over-under on the number of jokes he'd crack would be 117, which is the same number of beers I'd crack. But during a broadcast, it's deafening comedic silence. No one is going near any jokes. They don't want to run afoul of the woke police and risk losing their big contracts and gaining a social media shitstorm.

The guys watching on Sunday or Monday night are drinking Bud Light and wiping buffalo wing residue on their sweatpants. These are not shrinking violets and humanities professors. They're not going to be offended. This is the NFL tying their own cleat laces together, hurting their own product to solve a problem no one had. They've taken our football commentators and side-lined their senses of humor.

I was especially depressed when Cris Collinsworth broke my first rule—never apologize—in 2020. On one broadcast, he talked about Steeler fans and how the female fans seemed particularly interested.

"Everybody's a fan—in particular, the ladies that I met," he said. "They have really specific questions about the game, and I'm like, 'Wow.' You're just blown away by how strong the fans are here in this town."

What a monster. I'm sorry if you had to put this book down and do some self-care. Thank God he cleaned it up later that day.

"Today on our broadcast I made reference to a couple of women that I met in Pittsburgh who so impressed me with their football knowledge that I wanted to tell their story on the air…. I know the way I phrased it insulted many," he said. "I'm so sorry. What I intended as a compliment to the fans of Pittsburgh became an insult. I'm sick about insulting any fan, but especially female fans and journalists. I know firsthand how much harder they have to work than any of us in this industry. I was wrong, and I deeply apologize."

He didn't just apologize, he *deeply* apologized. For what, I don't know. When did we start twisting compliments into hate speech? He's attempting to say that women, who are not traditionally football fans, are surprising him. He's saying he is hearing women roar. Shouldn't that be a good thing? Not in today's NFL. Like the statisticians and directors during the broadcasts, someone got in his ear and told him he had to apologize. Who was hurt by this? Anyone who would be offended and thus boycott the NFL—its broadcasts and merchandise—isn't enough of a fan to be offended about being called a surprisingly big fan by a middle-aged dude.

The insidious part is that the Collinsworths and Bucks of the world have stopped talking. The color in the color commentary has become a flat gray primer. By the way, how long before we can't even use the phrase "color commentary" because it's too close to "colored"? I'd put money down right now that that title goes the way of the dodo before Super Bowl LVIII.

And since you mentioned Kaepernick in your question, Matt, let me address that quickly. The taking of the knee was a waste of energy and time. It was a futile gesture calling attention to a nonissue—namely, "systemic racism." There is a huge difference between living in a racist country and living in a country with racists. Of course there are racists. And there may be racists in positions of power. But to say that the country in and of itself is founded on racism is a straw man. We've all heard the saying "Seeing is believing." Well, in this case, believing is seeing. Kaepernick and everyone taking a knee with him—and now also everyone forced to sit through "antiracism" training in the post–George Floyd era (I'll save my twenty-page rant about *White Fragility* for another chapter)—are seeing racism everywhere because they believe it's everywhere.

Kaep had a Netflix show last year, on which he showed images of young Black men doing the NFL Scouting Combine and then compared it to a slave auction. Powerful. Except that it's complete bullshit. Plenty of white guys do the NFL Combine. And the comparison is also not apt in the sense that if these young men get through the Combine, unlike a slave auction, they get paid millions of dollars to tote the rock as opposed to whipped while picking cotton for free. Subtle difference; I could see how Kaep missed that. Plus if a slave tore an ACL they wouldn't spend a ton of time and money trying to rehab it to get back in/on the field.

Who made Kaepernick the arbiter of what is and isn't racist? In 2019, things became absurd when Nike was forced to pull from its lineup a shoe that featured the Betsy Ross flag, because Kaepernick found it offensive. The thirteen stars represented the thirteen colonies, which were founded during the slavery era. I'm sure all the civil rights leaders he looks up to who got sprayed with fire hoses, beaten with clubs, and attacked by German shepherds for using the wrong drinking fountain or sitting in the wrong part of the bus were relieved that we'd moved on to shoe-based offenses. Maybe there's not as much racism as you posit, Kaep, if our sole focus is the soles of shoes.

There used to be a game show in the '50s and '60s called *Make Me Laugh*. They'd take an old celebrity like Dick York, and comedians would have sixty seconds to try to break him up. I think Kaepernick's next move should be a game show called *Make It Racist*. I'd host. We'd open a curtain to reveal an innocuous item, and Colin Kaepernick would have sixty seconds to turn it into a racist attack. For example, I'd uncover a coffee mug, and he'd have a minute on the clock to say that African slaves were used in the coffee trade in the 1700s. Or I'd unveil a snow globe with Santa's village in it, and he'd stammer but eventually get out that in the Netherlands, Santa's elves are black. (Weird but true, by the way. Google it.) Eventually I'd just hand him my microphone, and he'd say the foam cover looked like an Afro.

Are you reading this, Netflix? Let's make this show happen. It'd be huge. Until Kaepernick realized that Netflix begins with an N and…you know what? I think I'll just stop there. ∎

Chapter 7

If It Doesn't Fit,
I Must Answer It

N ot all of your questions fit neatly into a category. If you thought you were going to stump the Ace Man with random out-of-the-box questions, you were mistaken. Like the food selection and the asses of the patrons at a Golden Corral buffet, my knowledge, advice, and opinions are vast and wide.

. . . .

What is up with paintball enthusiasts?

Matthew, 49, Dallas

I think paintball is appealing because it's a simulation of battle without the danger. I understand that not everyone gets to have sex, so there are real dolls and Fleshlights to simulate sex, but that's because we like sex. We have Beyond Burgers that simulate beef. Everyone loves brownies, so Weight Watchers does their best version.

What I don't understand is how as a civilization, we all agree that war is the worst thing that can happen to a nation or an individual, yet half the video games and all the paintball and laser tag games simulate battle.

What is this attraction to simulating something we find repugnant? Nobody likes a root canal, so there's no VR root canal. They don't make stick-on herpes sores. There are no Joy Behar impersonators.

I think we are so out of real problems that we try to simulate problems to light up that part of our brain that needs to be fed. Maybe that's what nightmares are for—to give us something to be afraid of in a world of airbags and air conditioning. For anyone under eighty and not morbidly obese, that was COVID-19. It wasn't actually necessary to fear it, but people dove head-first into that panic porn.

Paintball is one of the most aptly named activities. It's right up there with "toaster oven," "fireplace" and "sleeping bag." The name paintball is like if Stratego were called Plastic Pieces Game. It's totally on the nose. But I have a few suggestions for more dynamic names.

- Warpaint
- Splat Combat
- PAINball
- I'm on a Government Watchlist so I Can't Get a Real Gun Ball
- Get Away from My Shrew of a Wife for a Few Hours Ball

Paintball is definitely one of those hobbies the wife is pissed about. She's crunching the numbers on that year's taxes and sees that her dipshit husband spent seventeen grand on paintballs and canisters. Plus, WeatherTech doesn't make enough protective car junk to keep her minivan's interior from looking like the exterior of Janis Joplin's Porsche.

I also have a few suggestions for how to improve the game itself. People could save a lot of money on paintballs and really up the ante if they just had a hybrid game called frozen paintball. They could reuse the balls, and no one would have to rely on the honor system, because there'd be a welt system.

We also need more interesting courses. It always just looks like open fields with pallets, large wooden cable reel spools, and maybe some old junker cars for cover. We need to step it up and have themes: the "urban warehouse SWAT team" version, the "Bin Laden compound" version, the "school shooter" version, the "disgruntled employee shooting up a post office" version...except in these versions the high schoolers and coworkers get to shoot back.

And we need to get some good PR going. We need to get paintball back into the zeitgeist. I'm imagining a movie with an elite paintball team that wins the championship five years running. They get called in for a secret mission. SEAL Team 6 has gone down in a chopper, and our heroes need to infiltrate the compound while appearing to be simple civilian tourists. Think Ben Stiller action comedy. It'd be *Argo* meets *Black Hawk Down* meets *Dodgeball*.

And finally, you know how in the NBA three-point shootout there's a red, white, and blue "money" ball that's worth more points? I say we do that. Raise the stakes a little. Each paintball soldier gets one ball that counts more than the rest. But it's not worth more because it's larger or a special color. It's because it's filled with donkey semen. ■

••

Were you breastfed? (•) (•)
Jamie, 44, Monterey, California

I don't know, and I'm sure as fuck not going to ask. That's an intimate conversation. I remember distinctly as a kid hating the taste of milk and having apple juice in my bottle, which was essentially sugar water, which may explain my posture. In all likelihood I wasn't, because that would have meant my mom would have had to hold me. If there was a breastfeeding stand in the 1960s so she could provide me with milk without affection or contact it was maybe a possibility. ■

....

Please excuse the deep question, but I must know... Intercourse with a clone of yourself—gay or not gay?

Jason, 47, Springfield, Missouri

If it's a guy, it's got to be gay. If it's a chick, then it's hot. It's like the porn with the twin sisters without that pesky incest element. But if you did have a clone, there would be so many better uses for that clone—like it could have sex with the wife that you no longer want to bang.

And what if everyone likes the clone better than you? What if your clone got a film into Sundance but you didn't?

I feel like most people would squander their clones. Six months after most of the guys I went to high school with got one, it would be in the garage in its underpants, underweight and walking in a circle. People would neglect their clones like a pet that a kid begs for, gets, and then within a year doesn't give a shit about and leaves their parents to take care of. They'd be disposable. Most clones, at least in America, would have Howard Hughes fingernails and be maintained as well as a Baltimore public school.

Which is why I think a better use of a clone is a fight club where the owners/cloners could wager on themselves but not actually feel the sting of another man's fist. Or we could even hunt ourselves. Man, after all, is the deadliest prey. But we would have one up on ourselves because, like Patton shouting to Rommel in that movie that he'd read the magnificent bastard's book, we'd know all of our next moves because we are us. The hunter *is* the hunted.

Man, I feel like I'm on ayahuasca right now.

But this would never work. Every time you hear a news story about cloning a bull or sheep, it's a disaster. You always end up with a shitty version of the original. Maybe that's why our society is fucked. Maybe one day we'll walk into the Malibu Soho House and see the original versions of ourselves writing poetry and having smart cocktails, and it will all make sense.

Before I move on, do yourself a favor and watch the *Man Show* bit where I clone myself. It was the last one I ever filmed. ∎

If you could sock one person in the face, without repercussions, who would it be and why?

Brent, 47, Nebraska

That Asian doctor who got dragged off the United Airlines plane in 2017. Fuck that pussy. ∎

Why do we still have tollbooths?

Steve, 45, Seattle

Because we got rid of the job known as elevator operator and we need a place for the dumbest kid in your high school to work. Adult loser jobs of the past were covered with a snappy uniform. When you're wearing an ascot and the crest of the hotel you work, it disguises the fact that you're an idiot whose only skill is pressing a button. That job has gone the way of the dodo, but bathroom attendants in strip clubs still have a pretty dapper uniform.

Think about the ice cream man of yesteryear. He had a white starched shirt and a tie. He was the Good Humor man, bow tie and all. That uniform made him look legit, as did the truck. Now take a look at this picture on the next page I took of the twins when they were younger.

First off, it's not even a truck. It's a van with a camper top. It's covered in rust and faded, sun-blasted paint. This unroadworthy vehicle is piloted by a sixty-year-old chain-smoking Armenian guy while a warbly off-key rendition of "Ring Around the Rosie" plays like the soundtrack to Stephen King's *It*. The sign on the back reads "Stop for Children." Yes, stop for children, much like you would say, "I'm going to stop for Chipotle on the way home." This is an abduction van. It's stopping to snatch up kids.

Imagine the blizzard of documents necessary to open a restaurant in L.A. How many checks and how much red tape need to be cut to obtain whatever licenses one needs to distribute food to children in Los Angeles County. Do you think this guy has the proper paperwork? This has been going on for decades in L.A. These are the only ice cream trucks my kids have ever known. But now the situation has reached a new level of absurdity. In a post-COVID world, how do ice cream trucks even exist? Outdoor dining was verboten at one point. One of the few restaurants that dared to defy The Man, Tinhorn Flats in Burbank, got shut down. The city built a fence around it so citizens couldn't commit the heinous act of eating a cheeseburger outside. The fence looked like the Berlin Wall before it came down. But where is that kind of energy when it comes to these *E. coli* distribution vehicles? The people who were telling us to disinfect our groceries and who were keeping kids out of school don't have time for that. Why? Same reason as with the aforementioned leaf blowers. Whitey ain't driving these things, so it's bad optics—and there's no money to ring from the guy making half a penny profit on SpongeBob SquarePants popsicles, which have disturbingly melted and then refrozen so that SpongeBob looks like the dude from *Mask*.

But back to your question, Steve. I say we use tollbooths to house the homeless. The homeless would get a warm booth that would be bigger than their tent under the freeway, they would get off the street, and they would get to apply a well-honed skill: putting their hand out and asking for change. ∎

. . . .

Have you ever owned a pair of button-fly jeans?

Adam, 44, Michigan

One of the first purchases I made with the first paycheck I got was a pair of Levi's 501s. After a life with Toughskins and J.C. Penny Super Denim, it was a proud day when I could afford my own pair of button flys. But here's how bad my luck is: I still managed to get my dick caught in the zipper.

We need to bring back the button fly. It's hard to be fat in those jeans. We wouldn't have the obesity problem we currently do if everyone had to struggle daily to get those buttons hooked up, unlike with the endlessly forgiving zipper.

I'm surprised we still wear jeans. It's a testament to how far they've come. It used to be that you'd have to break them in. You had to wear them and wash them over and over to get them to fit right. Back in the day, new blue jeans were stiff and sort of shiny.

Now they're all infused with stretch fabric, so they feel more like yoga pants than the tent canvas Levi Strauss made them out of. We went from Levi Strauss to Lululemon and from Buddy Holly to DJ Khaled.

Another thing that has changed about Levi's jeans is the big leather-like label patch on the back. I think Levi's phased out these patches because the size was printed on them. If the waist size number is higher than the length number it's shaming. By the way, that patch was made of a wonder fabric. It wasn't quite leather. It was a miraculous cardboard that could survive two thousand washes. It would eventually come undone, and you could pull it off. You knew it was time for a new pair of jeans when the label gave out. Until your question, I didn't know what that patch material was. So I looked it up. In 1955, Levi's switched from actual leather to Jacron, a synthetic leather made of wood pulp. The patch went from steak to Salisbury steak. (By the way, Jacron sounds like a masturbating robot.)

Here's something else I'd never thought of until your question. Zippers and buttons have lived in harmony for a hundred years. But they could have been mortal enemies. Buttons were around for 1,500 years, and the zipper came along in 1917. My dad was born a mere ten years after the zipper was patented. It was new technology back then, and you'd think it would do to the buttons that Napoleon and Henry the Eighth used on their pantaloons what the internet has done to travel agents, the fax machine, and print journalism.

Yet they live in harmony together. Open your average closet. Zippers and buttons live side by side. We could learn a lesson from them.

I'm Adam Carolla, and once again, I'm asking for your vote. ∎

· ·

Why is everyone who gets murdered always "beautiful, lit up the room, vibrant, etc.," not to mention "they had their whole life ahead of them"? Duh?

Becky, 68, Fayetteville, Georgia

I swear if I turned up dead, my mom would say, "Some people thought he was funny."

We should be more precise when we say, "They had their whole life ahead of them." The average life expectancy for a male in the U.S. is seventy-nine years. So when someone dies, it would be more accurate to say, "It's such a shame. He had 13.5 percent of his life ahead of him."

How we as a society deal with the death of public figures is interesting. In September 2021, we lost one of the greats, my friend Norm Macdonald. And it seemed like there was a lot more mourning than for some previous celebrities who died. It was the same with Eddie Van Halen the year before. It seems to me we treat these people like commodities. Essentially, we ask, "Did we have any more use for you?" We weren't done with Norm. We weren't done with Eddie. They had so much more to give. I would still want them to crank out an album or do another special. We were done with Anna Nicole Smith. It's sad, but tell me I'm wrong.

We're all narcissists when it comes to mourning. We can't help but think, *What does this mean for me?* If a Southwest Airlines pilot has a heart attack and dies, we're not that interested, but if it happens in the cockpit and we're on that flight, we're insanely interested.

Your impact on the world and your value as a human are both on display when you have kids. Mine are already setting up accounts on Bringatrailer.com to sell off my Newman collection, and the name Menendez keeps popping up in the autofill on their web browser.

I think eulogies should be made by impartial third parties. That would keep you on the straight and narrow. Anyone in the family is going to sugarcoat the dearly departed's personal character a little bit. They'll remember the good times—the Christmas mornings and the baseball games—but they'll leave out the drunken arguments and coffee mugs thrown across the room. The neutral outsider would be able to keep it real. Instead of "a beloved brother and a talented musician who was cut down in his prime," it'd be "a wannabe rapper gangbanger who was shot during a bodega robbery."

I think I could set up this service. I'll get some comedians and commentators who aren't afraid to speak the truth. They would go through the deceased's Facebook page and Google search history, and interview their neighbors. That would give us an accurate picture for the funeral. I'd call the speech a "Fuck You-logy." ■

· ·

If you had the opportunity, would you go to space?

Kyle, 50, Plaistow, New Hampshire

There's a lot of space-tourism talk right now. I think it'd be like feeling your first titty. You anticipate it so much, but when you finally get the experience, it's about what you expected.

I think I would go, and I'm sure my family would be happy to see me go. What's an appropriate response from your spouse if you get the opportunity to go into space? You don't want them to be like, "Yeah, let me pack your bag." You don't want them to be too eager to get you off the planet. At the same time, you don't want them to forbid it and ruin your dream. There should be an appropriate amount of hand-wringing.

But space travel is progressing fast. When my kids are my age, they might be able to enjoy a premium version of it. We'll see if they'll be able to afford it. There are three players in the private space-travel game: Jeff Bezos, Elon Musk, and Richard Branson. But these are all rich guys creating space flights for rich guys. A Southwest-style carrier has to come and undercut them. It won't be long before we'll have dudes in cutoff shorts and flip-flops punching out space-flight attendants and my grandson will be complaining about the Fiesta Mix the crew hands out. I've even got the name for this discount carrier, a little nugget for you *Star Trek* nerds: Final Frontier Airlines.

Because that's eventually what it will devolve into. We should still be amazed with plane travel. A journey that used to take months and likely result in death from hypothermia now costs eighty-three dollars and is considered a burden. I can imagine a documentary on people complaining about travel throughout the centuries. It'd start with two cavemen bitching about the wheel and how it was easier to just walk across the continent. Then it would cut to some centurions whining about how their chariot can't handle the potholes on the Appian Way. Then it would show the Wright brothers fighting with each other over who got top billing on the ads for the first plane.

And we all know where this is leading. What's the over-under for when the first porn in space will be shot? Ten years? Every technology that comes along gets integrated into porn at some point. The filming crew would have to drape the space station in Saran Wrap, like in the locker room after the World Series before the champagne gets sprayed. Fluids could be released during the porn filming that could short-out systems. Everyone would have to put goggles on. With all the floating semen, there's going to have to be some serious vetting. I imagine a NASA guy—who for some reason is dressed like the guys on the 1969 moon-landing ground-control team, with their crew cuts and thin ties—asking very earnestly of the porn star about to go into space: "I'm going to ask you a question, and I need an honest answer. Do you swallow?"

I have bad news for everyone. Bezos, Branson, and Musk are not dummies. They are some of the smartest people on the planet. They are privy to inside info, and they're all planning on living to be 140. All of a sudden, they went from wanting to make a shit-ton of money on Earth to losing a shit-ton of money trying to leave it. Why do you think that is? People have chalked it up to the ego trip. I think it's about a different kind of trip—a one-way trip. These are superwealthy, superconnected geniuses. They know our planet is fucked, and they are getting out while the getting is good. While we've all been distracted by their shooting a Tesla or William Shatner into space, they've been seeing different strains of COVID coming up, race riots, and the Chinese launching a nuclear-capable missile that can circumnavigate the globe in minutes. They want out, and they want out fast.

You know how sometimes you go to a concert and it's great, but you know getting out of the stadium parking lot is gonna be a nightmare, so you skip the encore and beat the rush? That's what these brilliant minds are doing. And I want in. I'm officially inviting myself on Musk's or Bezos's next flight. I'm not waiting for the latest virus to escape the Wuhan lab. We're eventually going to need to rebuild the population and society of whatever new planet we land on. And that new Earth will need laughter, which is why we're also bringing the ventriloquist Jeff Dunham. But I make a killer Denver omelet.

That said, Bezos's genius is mythology. Here's how you know: He got busted sending dick pics. That's not a genius move. That's something your brother-in-law who installs gutters would do. We treat Bezos like he's a soothsayer. He said recently that in the future, we'd colonize space and come back to Earth as tourists, like visiting Disneyland. I grew up in North Hollywood, but Disneyland in Anaheim was still out of reach. I might as well have asked to go to the pyramids. Can you imagine the future's version of the cheap fucks like my family trying to visit Earth from Space Colony #9? I couldn't get forty-one miles down the 5 freeway to see Space Mountain. "Sorry, kid," the future version of my family would say. "The shuttle is out of gas."

Bezos is smart, but he's not Nostradamus. He made his bones selling junk from China on the internet. I get that we should ask him for advice rather than the guy who skims your pool, but let's stop acting like he's Thomas Edison. He accurately predicted that lazy Americans would want cheap shit delivered to them rather than getting off their fat asses and going out to a store. Success doesn't always equal intelligence. The chick who invented Spanx is also supersuccessful, but we're not asking her for prognostications about the future of the planet. ∎

. . . .

Hey, Adam, tits or ass?
Jeff, 46, Roseville, California

I think it's well-documented that I'm a boob man. Nothing wrong with a nice ass, but tits take the top spot, literally and figuratively.

We have a weird relationship with the human body and the aesthetic of it. Why is it that we have a ranking system for some parts of the body but not others? It's like how we think dolphins are beautiful and jellyfish are gross, or squirrels are cute but rats are disgusting. Even within the human body we're attracted more to certain portions over others.

Certain parts of the most beautiful body in the world will still gross you out. I couldn't tell you the difference between Gisele Bündchen's anus and that of a Walmart greeter. It's about context. If you saw two eyeballs just sitting on a steel tray in a lab, you'd be grossed out. But put those eyeballs into Emma Stone's orbital sockets and they become beautiful. ∎

. . . .

Why do you think the ukulele never became as popular as the electric guitar?

Justin, 37, Valley Stream, New York

It's the size. Think about it. The guy I feel sorry for the most is the guy who plays the giant guitar in a mariachi band. He's always the shortest, fattest guy in the band. He did the guitar-size-to-groupie-number math. He looked at the guy playing the ukulele and thought, *He's got a miniature guitar and a handful of groupies.* Then he saw the guy playing the medium-size electric guitar and saw that he had a bunch of groupies. So this guy had the lightbulb go on over his sombrero and thought, *I know, I'll play a giant guitar.* Yet he ended up with the fat chick who worked the churro cart. ∎

. . . .

If time machines were real but you could only go on a one-way trip, would you go to the future or the past?

Robert, 32, Pennsylvania

I wish it were a two-way journey, because I would take my snot-nosed spoiled kids back to 1974 and have them be raised by my parents. I'd let them suffer in North Hollywood shitboxes for a year or two with no air conditioning—or hair conditioning, as my helmet head from that time can attest to—eating my mom's shitty health food or scrounging off friends whose parents had a pulse. Then I would bring them back to their palace with their Grubhub and their pool, so they'd have some goddamn appreciation. It would be like *It's a Wonderful Life* meets *Back to the Future* with a touch of *The Wizard of Oz.* There's no place like home, unless it was the Carolla home of my youth.

But your question mandates a one-way ticket. So I would go to 1978. I know that seems like a weird choice, but that time period was wasted on me. I was fourteen years old, so I couldn't really enjoy it. As I've long declared, the greatest period in our nation's history was pre-AIDS, mid-coke. I would love to be my current age and have my current wealth when getting coked up and fucking strangers was not only safe and accepted but encouraged. As the Bee Gees were imploring everyone, "What are you doing on your bed on your back? You should be dancing." I was roasting in the attic of my dad's shitty A-frame house. I was on my back because if I stood up, I'd hit my head on a roof rafter, and I had night fever but that was just from sweating my ass off sleeping up there at night. ■

What do you think is more embarrassing: getting dragged off of an airplane for being drunk, or being the guy that cums too fast in prison?

—Adam Ray

Why does it have to be one or the other? I can easily think of a scenario where we get diverted to Cleveland because I'm shit-faced in economy plus and getting handsy with the flight attendants. Then when we land, I'm greeted by police on the tarmac, get thrown in the drunk tank, and then cum too fast in a nonconsensual prison shower reach-around. Use your head, Adam. ■

What is the shittiest place you have ever been to, and why?

Dan, 54, Middletown, Delaware

The shittiest place I've ever been to was a real dump full of ugly idiots and fat whores. It was a tiny town just past nowhere. I can't remember the name of it, because I blocked it out of my memory. But I think it was called Middletown, Delaware. ■

Chapter 8

Deep Shit

Why are we here? What's life all about? Is God real? Where do you go when you die? These are questions that the greatest philosophers, poets, theologians, prophets, and gurus have struggled with for millennia. Aristotle, Buddha, Plato, Kierkegaard, Jesus. All hacks. Finally, someone has come along who can answer humanity's hardest questions—me, the Nietzsche of North Hollywood, the Socrates of SoCal, the Sartre of the San Fernando Valley. Seek answers below and ye shall find.

....

You stand before St. Peter at the Pearly Gates. He reviews the ledger. "Yes, looks good, I think you just squeaked in..." Suddenly, he pauses. "Oh, I didn't see this. I'm sorry, this sin is an automatic sentence to hell, Ace Man." What unforgivable sin did he see on your ledger?

Robby, 41, Bakersfield, California

Of the classic Ten Commandments, technically I didn't honor my father and mother, that's for damn sure. So that would probably do me in. And in the course of writing this book, never mind on my podcast, I certainly took the Lord's name in vain plenty of times. And I coveted the shit out of my neighbor's wife and oxen.

But with my luck, it would be some stupid prank I pulled when I was a dumb kid, like what happened at Humphrey Yogart, a frozen yogurt place in L.A. My friend and crush, Beth Ringwald, Molly Ringwald's sister, worked there. And like the desperate Dumpster diver that I was, me and my buddies would go there to coax her into sliding us some free soft serve. There were rules, though. If the manager was there, we'd have to turn around and head out. If there was a line, we had to kill time until the coast was clear. And there were limits. We had to settle for the lesser flavors, like raspberry or vanilla. Triple fudge was off the table. But it's not the sin of gluttony that I'm going to hell for. No. For some reason, we were wandering around there on a summer night after Humphrey Yogart had closed, just feral, unparented kids from the Valley getting into shit, when I noticed the mail slot. Like many things when I was young, dumb, and full of cum, I decided to stick my dork in it and take a leak. It wasn't revenge for Beth's not giving me free rocky road. It was just funny. They must have assumed it was some depraved junkie when they had to mop it up the next day, but it was, as was often the case with me and my buddies back then, just a case of pissing on stuff (and sometimes people) that shouldn't be pissed on and thinking it was hilarious.

Before we move on from this question, let's talk about moving on to the afterlife. I don't think heaven is all it's cracked up to be. Sure, you'd want to go to heaven and play ping-pong with Abe Lincoln and Warren Zevon, but after a while, Abe Lincoln wouldn't be Abe Lincoln; he'd just be that guy who sucks at ping-pong. You'd want to meet Marilyn Monroe, but after a while, you'd rather just look at her pictures because you'd see she could barely string together a thought. You'd feel uncomfortable watching the founding fathers dropping N-bombs in front of Jimi Hendrix, and as far as reuniting with your grandpa goes, you didn't want to go to his house when he was alive. ■

....

I have an irrational fear of death and loss of loved ones. It clouds my thoughts and keeps me from enjoying life. I know I'm being a puss, but how do you block out negative thoughts on your mortality, especially as a fellow atheist?

Jesse, 36, Lafayette, Louisiana

My advice is to get super busy. If you have a bunch of responsibilities, you wouldn't care if you died; it would almost be a relief. Think about it. Would you even want eternal life? That'd be like saying, "I wish I never had to sleep." After several hundred years, you'd be wishing you could kill yourself.

A lot of people are paranoid about going under sedation, but everyone who comes out of it says, "That was great. Thank God I wasn't awake for the root canal." You're there and then you're not. And when you're not is when the worst part happens. Death is like being in a dentist chair except that after they put you into twilight sleep, you never leave the office.

Speaking of anesthesia and mortality, everything reminds me of something, and this is no exception. A few years back I got my first colonoscopy. People say you're supposed to get it on your fiftieth birthday. I don't know if they mean that literally, but it is not the way to celebrate. Dr. Drew is a prostate cancer survivor and a big champion for getting screened, so he had been on my ass about having a periscope in my ass.

For the record, I'm all for it. Get screened, get tested, do it all. The process isn't bad in and of itself. You are completely unconscious during it. But the lead-up is not so pleasant, especially if you're me.

The day before is rough, because you have to drink a gallon of a seawater-like laxative. You'll shit your brains out the day before,

Deep Shit

but by the time you get down to the final hours before the procedure, what's coming out of you looks like it's from the land of sky blue waters. And you have to be driven in and picked up. You're going under sedation, and they don't want to be responsible for you plowing through a farmer's market on the way home.

As I was drifting off, the anesthesiologist said, "By the way, that was a nice spread on your Newman race cars in the *L.A. Times*." First off, the choice of the word "spread" as I'm about to be anally violated is maybe not the best. Get a thesaurus and don't remind me of my sore ass. Second, you son of a bitch, you're putting me under sedation. Finally, someone is asking me about something I give a shit about, and I'm going to fade to black before I can pontificate. Ask me about my kids and I might not need the sedative; I might just pass out. But my real babies, my Newmans, I could spend hours on.

That wasn't the first unfortunate word choice. Before the anesthesiologist did his thing, a nurse asked me if I had done the procedure before. When I told her I had not, she said: "Oh, first rodeo." There are many sports where your ass does not take the pounding that it does in professional bull riding. One could argue that it's the most sphincter-smashing sport. She could have said "your first bowling tournament," "your first swim meet," even "your first ski jump." Unless there has been some freak fencing accident, any Olympic sport would have conveyed less ass trauma than rodeo.

As far as tone-setting, it was not a top-to-bottom calming experience as I was waiting to have my bottom violated. While I was in the waiting area, there were eight guys whose average age was seventy-one. You don't do this procedure before fifty typically, and a percentage of that group were probably there for their second or third rodeo. There may have been a worried wife or two sprinkled into the mix. And yet what was blasting out of the speakers? Pharrell Williams's "Happy." It mirrored the mood of no

153

one in that room except the doctor who was going to cash a good insurance check for hacking through the jungle of my ass hair and exploring my colon canyon.

Oh but wait, it gets worse. Much worse. As if the jolly song from *Despicable Me* wasn't enough of a juxtaposition, after I briefly went out to the parking lot to dismiss my assistant and tell him to come back in a few hours to pick me up, I walked back in to hear…wait for it… "Livin' La Vida Loca." Fucking Ricky Martin. That's what was pumping for the retired guys who had just filled out their next-of-kin paperwork before going under.

I know what's going on. That song was chosen by the twenty-six-year-old Latina chicks at the reception. Read the room. Even if it wasn't all white guys, which it was, they were all born before The Beatles were on Ed Sullivan. And even if one of them just happened to be a huge Ricky Martin fan, the day you're going to get a hose up your ass to find out if you've got malignant polyps is probably not the time for such a peppy tune. I'm sorry, *mis mujeres*, but you're at work and you have to listen to what your customers want, not what you want. There is a device. That device has a knob. You can turn it and the music will magically change to something more palatable to the old honkies trying to forget what's about to happen to them. What if I really enjoyed listening to translated speeches from Mussolini? Should I be able to listen to that at the tire-balancing place that I work at?

And just because I'm me and it couldn't go any other way, when I got home I met up with my family, who had just returned from a vacation in Chicago. I declared that I hadn't eaten in twenty-four hours, had just had my rectum bored out like the Chunnel, and was in the mood for Mexican. I was voted down. I would have thrown a shit fit if I hadn't fully evacuated my bowels the entire day before. ∎

Hypothetical question: Would you rather get diagnosed with an illness and know you will die painlessly in two years, or unexpectedly die peacefully in your sleep in exactly twenty-four months?
Patrick, 46, Washington, D.C.

Excellent question. Everyone should take this test. There's an argument to be made for having the diagnosis in advance, so you can handle the legal stuff and get your affairs in order. And when I say "get your affairs in order" I mean have as many affairs as possible and order as much market-price lobster as you can handle.

You have to consider what the diagnosis is, though. I know you said "die painlessly," but is there deprivation along the way? Would I be confined to a hospital, or could I take that cruise around the world before I cruised off this mortal coil? That would change my calculus. If I knew I could carpe 730 diems before then, I would pick the first option, because knowing you're on borrowed time is what we all need to do. Because it's true. I had *Tuesdays with Morrie* author Mitch Albom on my podcast last year, and he quoted Morrie as saying, "Everyone knows they're going to die, but not everyone believes it." I think knowing our exact expiration date would have all of us embracing life more. If we knew we were going to die in two years, we'd all be doing what we want to do. We wouldn't be wasting our precious life in that postal sorting facility. We'd be starting that business or that band. We'd ask out that out-of-our-league girl at the end of the bar. We'd tell our sons we're proud of them and really enjoyed their podcasts, documentaries, and independent movies. (Sorry, got a little cathartic there.)

Fans of my podcast and even fans going back to *Loveline* and my syndicated morning radio show know I have a running list of things I want to do before I die. The classics are:

- Have my hands registered as weapons
- Get kicked out of a casino for winning
- Jump into a body of water with a knife between my teeth
- Have a cape removed onstage

Well, it's been over a decade since I codified that list in my first book, and it seems like it's time for an update. First, a few from my loyal listeners that made the cut:

- Get stitched up by a veterinarian late at night because there are no doctors around and I've been shot
- Be measured for a suit by multiple people while I talk business on the phone
- Wake up after emergency surgery and have the doctor tell me that the only reason I survived was due to my incredible physical condition before the accident
- Smash a guitar over someone's head
- Cut into my forearm to see if I'm a robot
- Make an "If you're watching this then I'm dead" video
- Empty the clip of an enormous machine gun, drop it, pull out a pistol, and keep shooting
- Evade police or bad guys by driving at high speed in reverse
- Start a conga line
- Smash through a locked chain-link fence in a stolen vehicle

All strong entries. Here are the best of my batch from the past ten years:

- Eat crab by a pool while in swim trunks and a loose robe while henchmen loom around. And then dismiss the goons while I talk to my lead guy about "taking care of our little problem."

- Step down as an elected official due to scandal. (By the way, farewell speeches are all too scripted, and you can tell that the speaker is burning with desire to start ranting about the media or opponents or even the voters. I think we should have a rule. When you give your farewell speech, you either need to wing it, or if you're going to read a speech, you have to do three shots of Jägermeister first.)
- Have a blind woman drag her hands down my face and announce that I'm beautiful.
- Retire a champ—not retire *as* a champ, but be the one who goes up against a champ in his last fight. Every now and again someone hangs around a bit too long, and they have one last fight where they need to go up against someone who is still good enough to be a challenge on their way out the door. Trevor Berbick had to retire Muhammad Ali. I want to be that guy; that's a good feather in your cap.
- Be at a high-end dinner party and get put on the spot to play the piano, then in an "Aw shucks, I'm a little rusty" way sheepishly go up to the baby grand and absolutely slay some Chopin.
- Hide out from my enemies in a swamp and breathe through a hollow reed.
- Sue someone for an unspecified amount. That means you've arrived. If your settlement is too good for the company or individual to allow you to broadcast it, you made out good.
- Throw wads of cash into a crowd to cause chaos while trying to escape from a bank robbery.
- Light two cigarettes—one for me, one for my fallen comrade.
- Answer my enemy's question "What are you gonna do?" by saying, "Something I should have done a long time ago."

The point is that life is too good to waste. So go out there and live. Live your life as if someone you haven't seen in a while is going to ask, "What are you up to?" You don't want to answer, "Binge-watching *90 Day Fiancé*." ■

· ·

A while ago, against my better judgment, I decided to experiment with ketamine at one of the local medical clinics. Long story short, I went deep down the "k-hole" and essentially experienced what I can only imagine death is like. I went to a place where nothing from my life mattered; work, money, family, fame, goals, politics, etc....all was vanity. Hard to describe, but I was reduced to merely a consciousness, but without direction, drive, or purpose. Now, even months later, the lingering feeling that everything in this world is temporary, vain, and insignificant is still with me.

My question is, how do I find purpose again with the shadow of "nothing really matters" hanging over my life?

Kurt, 41, Memphis

I'm pretty sure "Deep Down the K-hole" was the name of the Kim Kardashian sex tape.

Can you look at it as liberating? You could be free to live without the sense the rest of us have of ramifications and long-term effects. Now you're unencumbered. You can just be in every moment. You can truly live, because you've already died. You can take the best parts of the near-death experience and use them as your compass.

Near-death experiences are supposed to change your life. I would love to do a documentary in which I track down everyone who was on US Airways flight 1549, a.k.a. "The Miracle on the Hudson," and see if they've changed their life in any way. I would ask, "After 'Sully' Sullenberger saved your life by safely landing the plane after a double bird strike, did you take stock and lose some of your figurative baggage as your literal baggage sank into the river?" Their names are on a manifest. I bet I could pull this off. There was an eight-minute period when each one of them knew for certain they were going to die. And then they didn't. Did they act as if life were a miracle from then on, or did they go back and mistreat their stepson the next day? Sadly, as with a lot of lottery winners, I bet they immediately took it for granted.

Kurt, you were reduced down to your quintessence, consciousness, and then you came back to be able to have a human experience again. Don't waste it. ∎

I believe you have stated, in one way or another, that one of your greatest attributes is your curiosity about everything. From the outside looking in, it seems as if that would lend itself to you being more religiously agnostic, rather than decidedly atheistic. Are you still curious about there being a greater purpose? If not, then why?

Brant, 29, Greenville, South Carolina

I'm probably more agnostic than I used to be. I just call myself an atheist in case I run into Bill Maher at Seth McFarlane's Christmas party. ∎

I've always wondered this, but why don't more people kill themselves when they are out on bail? Especially guys awaiting sentencing for kid stuff, or know they are guilty, and the evidence is overwhelming.

Adam, 52, Minnesota

I've always asked that same question. They don't kill themselves at a high enough rate or flee at a high enough rate. I guess they figure there are so many prison suicides that they'll have a chance to do it there, and figure they'll take the roll of the dice on the trial and maybe get a hung jury—and if not, they can hang themselves. Hell, if Jeffrey Epstein can off himself in the joint, anyone can.

And I'm fine with this, for the record. These guys can kill themselves all they want. I'm a pragmatist. Think about how much it costs to house these guys. How much did keeping Charles Manson alive cost the State of California? You know how airlines doing a red-eye flight shut the lights as soon as you take off? That's so they don't have to deal with you. You're not going to be asking for Fiesta Mix when it's dark. We need a prison version of that. I think we should leave a belt and a Hefty bag in each cell.

I'm not trying to make the lives of pedophiles any easier, but I have two tips beyond the idea of killing yourself as soon as you can. If you are going to go to prison and your rap is child molestation, you have to shoot a cop while you're out on bail. Don't kill him; just make it a flesh wound—so when asked in prison why you're there, you can say you shot a cop. Everyone is going to find out why you're in the joint, and we all know what happens to kid diddlers in jail. They get the same treatment I got while "Livin' La Vida Loca" was playing, but without the anesthetic.

Second tip for all my pedophile fans. You never know when the chick you're talking to online is a teenage girl home alone or is actually the crew from *To Catch a Predator*. So before you show up to the trap house and have a one-on-one with Chris Hansen, pull up six houses down the block. Park your car and call Domino's. Send a pizza to the house. If the door opens and you see a boom mic, keep driving. It'll be the best $7.99 you ever spent. But if it's actually the teen girl you were sexting with, then it's a win-win: You've got your underage poon and a fresh, hot pizza.

I know some of you may be thinking that it's unfair that these criminals can escape the consequences by killing themselves and that they should have to suffer in a cell for the rest of their lives. I'm down with the suffering part; it's just paying for the cell that bothers me. And I do think they'd suffer. If you've seen the documentary *The Bridge* about the frequent suicides off the Golden Gate Bridge, you'd know that the few people who have survived that fall have said that they immediately regretted it after stepping off the edge. I would love to think that the last thought of every one of these suicidal shitbag criminals was, "I wish I hadn't done this." I think that's a fitting, and cheaper, punishment.

Here's a little story to prove my point. There was a troubled young man who attempted suicide in 1977. He was living in Hawaii and working as a security guard. He grew depressed because he was a deeply religious person and had had an affair. He tried to kill himself by connecting a hose to his car's exhaust and putting it through his car's window. Fortunately for him and unfortunately for the world, the plastic on Mark David Chapman's hose melted and he was left alive to shoot John Lennon. Wouldn't we all be happier if he had succeeded and weren't on this planet, and if his twelfth parole hearing weren't scheduled for one month after this book comes out? ■

Would you rather be remembered as funny or smart?

—Jay Leno

I think you're going off of a question I asked John Cleese on my podcast in 2019 that he was really stumped by. In essence, I said he clearly had a superior intellect and could have pointed it at a lot of professions—teacher, engineer, or attorney, for instance, which he was studying in college to become (actually, he was studying to become a "barrister" as they say on that side of the pond) when he founded Monty Python. And I asked if he had steered that gift for critical thinking toward comedy or if he just felt like a funny person. After a long pause, he responded: "What

an interesting question," and then talked about having a good balance of the logical mind and the creative mind. It's still one of the
best compliments I've ever gotten.

Cleese is kind of the poster child for that idea of being funny
and smart. But as far as how I would like people to view me, especially posthumously, I would go with funny, because being funny
makes you de facto smart. Being smart doesn't necessarily make
you funny. Funny covers both. Unless you're a prop comic.

This is a newer revelation in that I was always simultaneously considered the funniest and dumbest kid in every class I
was in. It seems bizarre now, but at the same time as I was the
class clown, I was also widely considered a moron by my teachers. Using funniness as a defense mechanism is pretty fucking
smart. But my teachers weren't armed with the ability to see that
I was quick-witted and dim-witted at the same time. I was the
quickest dimwit in the West. ■

· ·

*Is there a meaning to life? Since you are one of the small
number of atheists, I thought your perspective would be
refreshing.*

Jeff, 42, Illinois

Life having meaning is a First World problem. We have a West-
ern elitist definition of "the meaning of life." Do all the poor kids
living in drought, poverty, and famine wonder about the meaning
of life? Their meaning of life is life. It's survival. Simple as that.
So we can't say the meaning of life is fulfillment, creativity, or
wealth. Those are not possible for the woman carrying well water
in a gourd on her head.

For me, the meaning of life is reaching your potential. There
are the people who are aborted in the second trimester, and they
don't have a great chance to get a lot done on this planet. Then

there are eleven-year-olds who get hit by drunk drivers, and their potential is robbed. There are people born during a plague and never stand a chance. The meaning of life is what you do with what you can control. You can become a serial killer or, worse, a superdouchey neighbor. Or you could invent penicillin and make space travel affordable for the masses. The meaning of life is whatever you get out of the part you can control—how you play the hand that you're dealt and how much you squander.

Some people say that "children are the future." But not all of them are. A lot of them are going to grow up to suck from the government's teat and be chain-smoking litterers. I very much like the proactive take on the meaning of life, that it's in how you conduct yourself. I like to give the power back to the individual. The part where you just ponder doesn't do anything for me. I'd rather be with someone who was proactive than pro-pondering. I came from a family of ponderers. My father is a person who is very interested in the meaning of life. He's read a library's worth of philosophy books, but he's never actually gone out there and lived. My father would have had a hell of a lot more meaning in his life if he'd put down the Aristotle and put on some Adidas.

I have a theory: The more specific shoes you have had in your life, the more meaningful it was. If you had shoes specific to dancing or golf, you embraced life. Military dress shoes. Track cleats. Even bowling shoes. The more of those kinds of task-specific shoes you have had, the more fulfilling and meaningful your life has been. You want to go to your grave having a widely varied and well-worn shoe collection.

How long you live is not the measurement of a meaningful life. There are people who lived for ninety years but were never truly alive. How many laughs did you have? How many family vacations did you take? How many ball games did you go to with your kid? How many nights did you spend alone with your spouse drinking wine in front of a fire? It doesn't have to be BASE jumping in Yosemite. But there have to be pure moments when you are really, truly alive.

Speaking of all of the above—mortality, my family, and my family's laissez-faire approach to living—I'd like to close out this chapter with what might be the greatest and most telling story about them. When my maternal (not that she was maternal in any way) grandmother, Helen, was dying in the hospital, there was an incident. My mother was visiting and stepped away from her bedside briefly. My grandmother had put into place a DNR (Do Not Resuscitate) order. She did not want to be revived if she were dying. During the few moments when my mother left the room, Grandma left this life. The nurses and doctors rushed in and brought her back from the brink. The DNR hadn't been put on the door. In a "so Carolla that even a Carolla couldn't write it" moment, when I talked with my mother about her mother's being brought back to life while she was down the hall getting a cup of coffee, she looked down with sadness and said, "By the time we got back, it was too late." ∎

Chapter 9

Pop Goes the Culture

Growing up, my window to the world was a thirteen-inch black-and-white Zenith TV. Living in a household devoid of actual relationships, connections, and activities meant that my family was the Bradys. I learned the facts of life from *The Facts of Life*. I turned to the tube for guidance. Then, through sheer force of will, I fought my way into showbiz. So, as a viewer, listener, and producer of entertainment, I'm more than ready to answer your television, movie, and music questions.

....

As a kid, I loved the TV show Kung Fu. *I imagine your mom loved it too, as it never failed to show the wrongs done by the white man to a peaceful Chinese man in the Old West who spent his days walking the earth in search of enlightenment.*

Today, while that message still should hold up, David Carradine playing the mature Grasshopper role would be kinda "problematic," to say the least. Does that cancel out the overall message of white man = bad, China man = good, and peace over violence unless "he had it coming"?

Jim, 57, Chevy Chase, Maryland

Yes. White bigots in cowboy hats getting their asses kicked by an Asian guy would be more than welcome on television today, but Grasshopper would definitely have to be played by someone of Chinese descent. We're long past the days of John Wayne playing Genghis Khan in *The Conqueror* and Charlton Heston playing a Mexican in *Touch of Evil*. But we've taken it to an extreme; nowadays if you play someone who is gay you must be gay yourself, and if you play someone who is trans you must be trans, and if you play someone who is disabled you must be disabled, which kind of flies in the face of the whole "acting" part. Yet, if you are gay and play someone straight, no one would bat an eye. It might even go down as being "brave."

I think it's a dangerous path. By definition, acting is pretending. A good actor convinces us they are someone they're not. If they can convince us they're some*thing* that they're not, then that's the best of all worlds. I need only think about the rave reviews I got for my chameleon-like performance of a carpenter-turned-boxer in *The Hammer* and a burnt-out C-list comedian in *Road Hard* to know this is true. I think we can all agree on two things: that we're glad Robert Downey Jr. was in *Tropic Thunder*, and that Ben Kingsley deserved his Oscar for playing Gandhi.

Quick tangent on my dear friend Sir Ben Kingsley before I get back to the *Kung Fu* discussion. We were doing the upfronts for Spike TV in 2015. (For the uninitiated, upfronts are big presentations networks put on for advertisers to sell them on putting ads into their upcoming slate of shows and movies.) Sir Ben was there promoting a three-part sweeping Egyptian epic miniseries about the pharaoh Tutankhamun called *Tut*. I was promoting *Adam Carolla and Friends Build Stuff Live*.

A bunch of heavy hitters were there, like LL Cool J and Dwayne Johnson. Kingsley was just sitting alone in a corner backstage. No one was talking to him; I think they were all intimidated. So I decided to introduce myself, and being myself, I decided to do it in the most dickish way possible. I walked up and said, "Hi, I'm Adam Carolla. Listen. I know you're a movie actor and you probably haven't gotten a lot of stage time in front of a live audience, so this is probably a little intimidating for you. But I'm a comedian. I live onstage. So I know you've probably got some butterflies in your stomach. I remember my first few times when those stage lights hit me in the face and I saw the audience right in front of me. Again, you're a movie guy, so you're used to being able to blow a line and try it again. But there's no second takes when you're live in front of an audience. That's scary. So if you want any tips, I'm here for you."

To his credit, he played along and asked, "What should I do?" I told him he had to face his fears and face the audience. "A live audience is like a dog," I said. "They need to know you're in charge. They can smell fear. Don't blink a lot. That shows them you're scared. I can see it, but they don't need to." He half-heartedly continued playing along as I said, "Just remember the beats. Just work the beats. Tut. Egypt. Epic. Miniseries. You're gonna trip over your lines if you're nervous." Eventually the gag wore thin, and at the exact moment he got sick of it, and me, someone took this picture.

Back to *Kung Fu*. I love *Kung Fu*. My favorite part is when you hear that Asian flute. If you hear that pan flute, you'd better get out of Dodge, perhaps literally, because that means it's ass-kicking time. Grasshopper would walk into a saloon, get some dirty looks from the dusty cowboys, and announce that all he wants is water. Someone would say his kind isn't welcome. He would explain that all he wants is peace and then, within a few minutes, after getting called a Chinaman and thrown out of said saloon, he'd be back to crack some skulls underneath some ten-gallon hats. For a guy who says he doesn't want any trouble, he sure does a lot of ass-kicking.

It's kind of a metaphor for what women want. Chicks like a guy who says, "I come in peace," but their nipples get hard when that guy is throwing a spinning heel kick at someone else's forehead. He can come in peace, but if he can then turn around and do some ass-kicking, he can cum in her pussy.

My friend Jay Leno had a joke about how you always knew who the first guy to die on an episode of *Star Trek* would be, because he was the new crew member they'd just introduced on that episode. We all knew Ensign Smith wasn't going to make it to the next airing. In *Kung Fu*, the first guy to get kicked through the window of the saloon was the one who called Kwai Chang Caine a "Chinaman."

By the way, this was the Old West. Glass was rare and expensive. Yet so many people got thrown through saloon windows. Which got me thinking. I wonder if that's why saloons had those swinging half doors. The owner got so tired of replacing the windows after guys got tossed through them in rot-gut-whiskey-infused, poker-triggered brawls, he was just like, "Fuck it. I'm popping the hinge pins on this door, and I'm just going to have half a louvered shade." If I owned a saloon back then, that's what I'd do. It's like what I do with my dog when it's gonna throw up on the carpet: I try to get it to move to the hardwood or tile. If I were a saloon owner, I'd shepherd the brawlers towards the swinging doors and away from the windows.

Kung Fu wasn't just a huge TV show; it was a trend in the '70s. Everybody was kung fu fighting. Those cats were fast as lighting. In fact, it was a little bit frightening. But they fought with expert timing. The fact that I didn't have to look up those lyrics and you now have that song stuck in your head proves my point. "Kung Fu Fighting" by Carl Douglas was number one on the Billboard Top 100 in 1974. Clearly there were no cultural appropriation police back then. A Jamaican guy in a headband and whatever the male version of a kimono is singing about funky Chinamen in funky Chinatown wouldn't pass woke muster. But the popularity of kung fu led to a helpful stereotype. No one messed with Asians back then, because everyone assumed they were all karate experts. The Asians have tamped that down nowadays, and I think it's a mistake. When people thought all Asians could break blocks of ice with their forehead and go full Bruce Lee on your ass at any time, they didn't get fucked around with. Now that Asians have leaned into the math-genius, violin-playing, engineering-student stereotype, it's open season. It went from everyone thinking they had black belts to them being belted by Blacks.

A final thought on David Carradine and *Kung Fu*. In 2009, Carradine was found dead in a Bangkok hotel, hanging naked in a closet. After suicide was ruled out and his ex-wives spoke up about his sexual proclivities, it became clear that he was into autoerotic asphyxiation. This is tragic. I shouldn't know this about a legend. Photos of his dead body got leaked. This wouldn't have happened back in the day. If this had happened in the 1950s, someone would have chosen to give him his dignity. They would have dressed him in a red, white, and blue *gi*, folded his arms across his chest, put some nunchucks in his hands, and said, "We found him this way. He's kicking ass in heaven now." ∎

· ·

In TV and movies, why does throwing a bucket of water on someone who is unconscious always wake them up?

Jon, 47, Greenville, Mississippi

It may not be 100 percent effective, but at least it makes sense. If you were asleep or knocked out, the cold water might actually wake you up. I've done enough cold pool dunks to know that shit will wake you up and keep you up. It's energizing.

What doesn't make any sense is when someone is knocked unconscious on that piece-of-shit show *Gilligan's Island*. There were multiple episodes where a character got bonked on the head with a coconut, and rather than getting a traumatic brain injury they either got amnesia or, even more far-fetched, had a 180-degree personality change. Gilligan would get smart really fast after getting concussed with a coconut, or Mary Ann would forget who she was and start acting like Ginger. Comedy! And, without fail, the solution was a second TBI. Like banging on the side of an old TV to get it working again, they just needed to conk the brain back into place with a second whack by a coconut. You know, it's just good science. With all we've learned from the NFL's concussion scandals, it's hard to imagine that this was common fare on a major network TV show. The episode with the Harlem Globetrotters showing up on the island and playing basketball against a bunch of robots is more grounded in reality.

TV from when I grew up was full of tropes that didn't make sense but persisted. One trend that found its way into several different shows was the idea that dental work caused the character to pick up radio waves. No, I'm not making that up. Here's the actual IMDb summary for a *Partridge Family* episode titled "Old Scrapmouth":

Laurie gets the bad news that she needs braces just as she thinks Jerry, the boy across the street, might finally get up the nerve to ask her to go steady. However, if that wasn't bad enough, Reuben informs the Partridges that they have been booked to appear on a high profile talk show. Things then go from bad to worse when Laurie's braces somehow pick up radio signals during rehearsals and cause her to play a different tune than the band.

This is what passed for writing when we had only three networks. In the era of Netflix, Prime Video, AMC, HBO Max, Hulu, and all the other content providers, can you imagine this schlock getting past a first draft?

And then there's the episode of *The Love Boat* titled "Radioactive Isaac," where Isaac gets a tooth filling that picks up radio signals and interferes with his romantic pursuits. We all know that when you start picking up a radio station on your tooth filling, you can just change the station by twisting your ear like a knob. Again, this is basic stuff that every first-year medical student learns.

The action shows of the past had their fair share of clichés too. A fan of the podcast left us a voicemail wondering where all of the wrecking balls from '60s and '70s TV had gone. It seems like the cops were always chasing a bad guy, then got taken out by a wrecking ball. And any character being held hostage was bound to a chair in a building that was about to be hit with a wrecking ball. It was an apt and timely voicemail, because that weekend I had seen a still frame for an episode of *The Six Million Dollar Man* where he was holding a wrecking ball and pushing it back. On some shows, evil contractors used a wrecking ball to tear down orphanages. Now we have controlled demolition explosions. I'm sure the liability for wrecking balls was insane, and hundreds of filthy Irishmen were killed in wrecking ball accidents in the 1930s. Sadly, the only wrecking ball used nowadays is by Miley Cyrus.

Some of the TV tropes that never seem to die are less scientifically implausible and more sociologically implausible. Apparently, from the advent of television through the late '90s, everyone had a boss who would come over for dinner, and if things weren't just right, it'd be a disaster and possibly lead to the person's getting fired—or at the very least, losing some generically named big job like "the Johnson account." I've never once had a boss come over for dinner. In my early life working low-wage gigs, my foreman was too strung out on pain pills to show up at my one-bedroom for some Top Ramen. And the closest I ever got to dinner with my carpet-cleaning boss, Art Fuss, was getting yelled at by him for eating stolen cream puffs from a long overnight shift cleaning carpets at the Russian Tea Room. Later in life, I had dinner out with network executives, but they never came to my house. If you're having dinner with the boss, most likely he's paying and calling it a tax write-off. I am a boss and I've had dinner with employees, but I've never once gone to their home and been outraged that their dizzy dame of a wife burned the pot roast.

And, God forbid the dizzy dame was making a soufflé. That was another persistent sitcom cliché. The very important soufflé would always rise perfectly until some "comical" moment, when it would then deflate like a balloon, taking the baker's hopes and dreams of a good dinner party with it. I saw an episode of *The Brady Bunch* where Mike was very invested in his soufflé until Jan literally started tap dancing next to it. And there was an entirely separate episode where Alice is having trouble with multiple soufflés. Was there a '60s soufflé mandate? Was it part of LBJ's Great Society initiative? There was certainly no soufflé in the Carolla house. In order for the soufflé to rise, my mother's ass would have needed to rise off her mattress on the floor and head to the kitchen.

I've long said the fakest part of *Bewitched* was how much Samantha cared about her husband Darrin. Elizabeth Montgomery, who played Samantha, was a fox. But the hottest thing about her was that she was very concerned about her man. This doesn't exist today. I could easily suspend the disbelief that she was a witch and could teleport Dr. Bombay in to help her out. But I still can't buy that the ice bucket was full of fresh cubes every day when Darrin got home from work. ■

....

Whatever happened to television shows giving out the address to where, if you wanted, you could request a written transcript to the show you just watched? And what kind of person do you think actually wrote to them requesting a transcript?

Mike, 47, Las Vegas

I bet a lot of people did it just for the thrill of getting something heavy in the mail. Especially if you had to sign for it. Growing up, I didn't get anything that weighed more than three grams. Getting a postcard would have been a delight, had I known anyone who had a couple of shekels to rub together and travel. Now Amazon boxes are being dropped off every two minutes at my house. Ironically, the amount of carboard my kids get shipped to my house in the form of Amazon boxes is going to lead to our not having an Amazon rain forest.

As far as the transcript thing, there was quite a range. You'd watch a show, and they'd say you could request a written transcript. But then you'd switch to the ball game, and they'd yell at you that any recording without express written consent of Major League Baseball was a crime. One minute they're promising to send you a transcript, and the next they're threatening to prosecute you for taping the Padres game.

Why would you want a transcript? Thinking about the shitcoms I grew up with, I couldn't imagine wanting any of them written out. Do you really need to get the script for that episode of *Chico and the Man* to keep under your mattress? Shows back then were so dependent on the affectations of the actors and the catchphrases that I can't imagine they would translate well to the page. Try to imagine getting a script for *What's Happening?* in the mail and *reading* Dwayne say, "Hey, hey, hey," or getting a script for *Good Times* and seeing "Dy-no-*mite*" as a line of di-o-*logue* and howling with delight.

Fast-forward to today and talk shows. Could you imagine reading a transcript of *The View*? You wouldn't even know what it was. You'd have to conclude that the hosts are five of the dumbest people on the planet. You'd think it was a transcript from the waiting room of a methadone clinic.

It was probably some FCC rule that legally the networks had to provide a transcript for those who were hard of hearing. Which got me thinking about the sign language folks you see during every news conference. Why are we still signing in the age of closed captioning? I saw this a lot during all the press conferences with mayors and governors during the early part of the COVID pandemic. Mayor Bill de Blasio would be speaking, and someone, or some AI, would be furiously transcribing it onto the screen. Couldn't people just read what he was saying? Dr. Drew told me that American Sign Language is a different language than English, which I get, but that doesn't mean all deaf people are illiterate. I'm pretty sure they can still read. Hell, they can probably read better than me.

But these interpreters became celebrities themselves during the pandemic; some of them really throw themselves into their signing. It's a workout. I was afraid some of them were going to tear an ACL doing ASL. I guess it's because they don't always get the spotlight. Pandemics and hurricanes for sign language guys are like St. Paddy's Day for dwarves. ■

....

I'm a big fan of Comedy Central Roasts. Were there any jokes that you didn't do that you wanted to do? If so, what were they?

John, 43, Augusta, Missouri

I love watching a good roast, but I have to admit I don't love being on them. All the participants always end up taking a bunch of shrapnel as we sit on the dais, and we can't really fire back. As time has gone on, the easy jokes about my being gay with Jimmy Kimmel have given way to my being envious of Jimmy's success. Only one of those things is true. And back when I did my first two roasts—Hugh Hefner in 2001 (with Jimmy as the roast master) and Pamela Anderson in 2005—the producers didn't really have it dialed in the way they do now. We'd write a bunch of jokes, put them on three-by-five cards, and as the night progressed, Jeff Ross, Nick Di Paolo, or Lisa Lampanelli would do one of my premises and I'd have to chuck the card. Now producers vet the material to make sure nobody steps on anyone else's stuff.

But that's not really the issue. Saying you're good at comedy is like saying you're good at sports. Yes, you can be athletic and do well in baseball and football, but you're probably better at one or the other. It's the same with comedy. Some stand-ups are good in sketches and movies; some aren't. Some stand-ups do setup/punch-line jokes; others, like me, are more storytellers. Roasts involve a different kind of joke writing and delivery altogether, and I'll admit they're not exactly my sport. It's a different kind of pressure. In pure stand-up, if something isn't going well, you can do some crowd work. You can try new stuff or get creative on your feet. It's kind of like when you had to do a book report as a kid and it was like, "Well, I didn't really read the whole thing about Levi Strauss, but I think I got the gist of it." Except instead of Mrs. Wolk and some other unprepared kids as your audience and competition, you've got some of the sharpest minds in comedy, a bunch of celebrities, and millions of viewers judging you. You will be exposed. If you didn't do your due diligence, it's gonna show. There's no cramming for a roast. It tends to ruin the three weeks leading up to it, because you want to have a couple of drinks and watch SportsCenter but you've got this sword of Damocles hanging over your head. And you think there's a finish line three days before the event, when the jokes are locked in, but that's not necessarily the case. I saw this while writing for the two Oscars that Jimmy hosted. On the day of, someone drops out, some news event has ruined a joke, or something happens (like during the 2017 Academy Awards Jimmy hosted, when they named the wrong Best Picture winner) that requires some rewriting. So it's never really over until it's over.

A couple of memories from some earlier roasts:

Courtney Love, who was out of her gourd drunk on the stage, kept threatening to pull her top up and shoot the crowd a winger. When you're threatening to pull your top up and the crowd is yelling, "No!" that's a gut-check moment. When she was in Hole fifteen years earlier and threatening to pull her top up, everyone in the amphitheater cheered. It must be tough when you had a good twenty-year run of crowds shouting, "Show us your tits," and now they're holding their hands up over their eyes like they're looking at an eclipse.

I had many years off, until I got a call from my manager Mike August saying Alec Baldwin was going to be roasted and that I should cash in our friend chip and get on the panel. It was only about two weeks before the event, and I was hesitant. Again, roasting is not my sport (and even if it were, I was a little rusty from having not done it since George W. Bush was president and no one knew who or what a Kardashian was); plus, I didn't want to impose on Alec. It felt a bit gauche to ask him directly to put me on the show. If the producers wanted me, they would have reached out. But August insisted, and I shot an email to Alec and was surprised, though not exactly delighted, that he wanted me to join the dais.

I didn't have the kind of time I would have liked to prepare, but those roasts have writers. I used a little of their stuff with my own modifications, and then a writer I work with (he's typing this now) and I cranked out the following five minutes.

Sean Hayes, everybody. So funny. No, seriously, I love the gays. I've always kinda wondered what it would be like being blown by a guy. I imagine it'd be a lot like wearing Crocs. Sure, it feels great until you look down.

Here's how fucked up Hollywood is. Bruce Jenner announces he was transitioning and everybody applauds him. But when they find out he was Republican, they're outraged. Cut your dick off? Hero. Cut taxes? Hitler!

Ken Jeong.... We all saw your tiny dick in The Hangover. I haven't seen a dick that small since I took my nephew ice fishing.

Let's move from small dicks to big names.... Robert De Niro's here and Alec Baldwin's here, both amazing actors. But if I learned one thing from all the Harvey Weinstein stories, well, it's that pretty much anyone can act. What other profession works this way? "Want to be a commercial airline pilot? Hmm...let me think. OK, just blow that fat Jew. We'll have you up in the air by noon." This is your profession. You want to be a dental hygienist? Just watch that fat Jew beat off into a ficus plant.

Bob, I know you're going through a divorce. That's rough. It's hard to meet ladies, especially at your age. Might I suggest a new dating app for old fucks like yourself? It's called Carbon Dating. Don't worry—carbon is black. Robert just dates the sisters.

On to the man of the hour. We all love Alec's impressions— the impression of Trump, the impression his ring leaves in foreheads of photographers. So many classic lines over an amazing career. "Coffee's for closers." "You ask me if I have a god complex...I am God!" And who could forget "Welcome back to Match Game."

Alec, you're a great friend and a great actor. And if I can rant for a minute, you're a good sport with a great sense of humor...unlike the social justice warriors who are gonna tweet that all our jokes were "problematic." Blow me, you pussy fuck-sticks. This is a goddamn roast. Comedians need a place to be offensive without your bullshit fake outrage. You hashtag heroes. You already ruined the Oscars. You're all woke and no joke.

So, if you were offended by anything said tonight, please give a reach-around to your emotional support dog and shut the fuck up. This is our safe space, bitches!

But even if the cancel culture wins, Jeff Ross would still be the roast master...at the Arby's in Glendale.

That's the stuff that made air. But to your question, was there stuff left on the cutting room or writers' room floor? Yes. And here it is.

Sean Hayes, everybody. So funny. You remind us of a bygone era when gay people had a sense of humor.

How about the triumphant return of Will & Grace? What a comeback! Incidentally, Sean's nickname in high school was "Cum-Back."

Chris Redd is here tonight. Alec loves untalented brothers... he's got three of them. Chris, I was worried about you when I heard the unfunny Black dude left SNL. Thank God it was Leslie Jones.

We all know Alec from Match Game, but Caroline Rhea's on a new game show called Ding Dong. It's on the Ring Doorbell network. She orders Grub Hub, and the driver has to guess who the fuck she is. It's a cross between Cash Cab and suicide.

Hugh Hefner was the first roast I did, almost twenty years ago, in 2001. Back then I was a young man and Caitlin Jenner was a middle-aged man.

Robert De Niro's been in more Black women than the Ebola virus.

Let's not forget The Departed. *By the way, being de-parted is what happened to Caitlyn Jenner.*

And of course, Raging Bull. *De Niro gained sixty pounds to play Jake LaMotta when he was a fat, washed-up has-been in cheap nightclubs. You know, like Jeff Ross.*

Alec Baldwin. We've been friends since the '90s when I was on MTV, Alec was on TV in A Streetcar Named Desire, *and his wife Hilaria was on a changing table.*

Your brother Steven Baldwin is an obnoxious born-again Christian. Alec, I know you secretly wish he'd convert from "born again" to "dead already."

When did you turn into the white Steve Harvey?

Alec, your brothers aren't here, because you hate them; your colleagues aren't here, because they hate you; and your best friend isn't here, because he hung himself in a Manhattan prison cell. What are you going to miss more, the plane or the island?

Alec, I don't think this was a good idea. I'm bad luck for the ones I roast. My first was Hefner and he's dead. And the next was Pam Anderson, and her last paying gig was blowing Julian Assange.

It was a fun and surreal night. During the commercial break, Larry David came up to me and said he loved the Weinstein joke. I've been a big fan of his show *Curb Your Enthusiasm* for its entire run, so it was flattering.

Just to close it out, you want to know a roast joke that should have gotten cut but didn't? Before the Pam Anderson roast, I ran into the aforementioned Nick Di Paolo in the bathroom. He said, "You're half Mexican, right?" I said, "No. Half Italian." Twenty minutes later, Nick was onstage delivering this joke. "Adam Carolla is half Hispanic, which means not only is his last name Carolla; he was probably conceived in one." I guess it was too late to rewrite it.

Speaking of The RoastMaster General... ∎

Adam, if you could roast anyone from history, who would it be?

—Jeff Ross

I've thought a lot about this. I could just say Abraham Lincoln and write a bunch of jokes about how he was gay and Mary Todd was fat, or pick Thomas Jefferson and do some Sally Hemings jungle fever jokes, but I'm going to go a little outside the box.

It occurred to me that there was a roast of Donald Trump in 2011. At the time, we knew he was a celebrity, but no one would have considered him a historical figure. And I doubt that anyone at the time would have bet on his being president, and especially one so controversial that he'll be talked about for generations to come.

So I'm going to do a roast of someone from future history. At other roasts, the roastee is someone who is already famous and you're limited to jokes about shit they've done. I want to roast an infant. That way everything would be on the table. Who knows how famous that kid could be? I want to get in on the ground floor. Little Mason may seem cute now, but later, when he's a porn star Klansman arsonist, I'll be the only one who busted his chops while his crib was up on the dais. ∎

What happened to horns in rock music?? I remember listening to Loveline back in the day, and you used to get rocking to some Blood, Sweat & Tears. There was obviously Chicago, and then the whole ska movement with the Bosstones, Less Than Jake, Reel Big Fish, etc. We can probably glaze over the '80s and the era of synthesizer horns. But there's just something about the horns and guitars that seem to work magic. There was even a Tom Petty live album from 1985 where they had a horn section, and it sounds great. The other day I heard a version of "Hard to Handle" by The Black Crowes that had horns, and it was phenomenal. Maybe it's because playing in jazz band was the only thing that saved me from the hellhole known as high school many years ago that I was conditioned to a good horn section. But we need to bring this back. So what happened to the horns???

Mike, 34, Buffalo, New York

There's a very simple answer for you, Mike. Playing a horn doesn't get you laid anymore. There was a time where playing a horn made you the star. Think about the big band era. The guitar wasn't even a thing. It was a rhythm instrument. The guy who was the bandleader was always playing a horn, or even a clarinet. Glenn Miller played the trombone, and Benny Goodman was on the clarinet. Then saxophone took over, and blowing that instrument would get the player blown. But after The Beatles and the British invasion came in with the drums, bass, and guitar combo, that was it for horns being the pussy magnet, though the sax did have a brief resurgence in the '80s with "The Big Man" from The E Street Band and Rob Lowe in *St. Elmo's Fire*. Then in the '90s grunge era, even keyboards became passé, and people playing anything other than a busted-up Kurt Cobain–style pawnshop guitar didn't get any tail. Nowadays, I'm not even sure about that. I think if you want to get laid now, you have to do some freestyle rapping or, ugh, DJing. Playing instruments takes discipline and talent. Now you can call yourself a DJ, press the space bar on your MacBook Pro, then throw glowsticks around, and you're considered worthy of a BJ. So fucking depressing.

But yes, I am a horn rock aficionado. And, as such, I present to you my definitive top ten horn rock rankings. Honorable mention to Chicago before we dive in. It's hard to argue with "25 or 6 to 4" or "I'm a Man" in the horn rock department, but they are pretty conventional choices. My top ten runs a little less orthodox.

10. "Mexican Road Race"—I could have picked any Herb Alpert & The Tijuana Brass song, but this one stands out. Alpert's contribution to popular music should not be underestimated. Plus, the album cover for *Whipped Cream and Other Delights* made me a man.

9. "Polk Salad Annie"—Like many of his songs, Elvis didn't write this one, but he did the definitive version. This is jumpsuit-era Elvis at his karate-kicking best.

8. "Get It On"—Like a trumpeter plays "Reveille" in the morning to roust soldiers out of bed and to attention, the trumpet on this song by Chase is also a clarion call to "Get it on in the morning now."

7. "I Can See for Miles"—"But Adam," you say, "The Who's 'I Can See for Miles' certainly rocks, but there are no horns." True. But I'm talking about the Lord Sitar version. Put this book down right now, go to YouTube, find it, and thank me later.

6. "Dr. Worm"—I know I don't seem like the kind of person who would be into They Might Be Giants. You're right. They're definitely in the nerd rock category. But it's hard to argue with the horns and drums on this track.

5. "Tower of Strength"—Another hidden gem from someone you'd never have heard of if not for me. Gene McDaniels put this one out in 1961. Written by Burt Bacharach, it's a funny song about a guy wishing he had the strength to leave his woman. The verses feature a wobbly horn, signifying weakness, and the choruses about being a tower of strength have a driving, powerful horn section. It's really clever and well done.

4. "What Is Life?"—I've always had George Harrison as my favorite Beatle. His solo stuff is far superior to Lennon's and McCartney's post-Beatles work. And Ringo's two best solo outings—"Back Off Boogaloo" and "It Don't Come Easy" were produced and written by Harrison. Used so perfectly in *Goodfellas* during the coke run scene with the helicopters chasing Henry Hill, this has to be on your horn rock playlist. Like most of the songs on *All Things Must Pass*, this one is so good that the album's producer, Phil Spector, could in my mind have been allowed one murder. If you produce something with a wall of sound like this tune has, you get to snuff one cocktail waitress and skate.

3. "Army"—Fans of my podcast know of my love for Ben Folds Five. When you think of Ben, you obviously think of piano. He's a virtuoso. But the horns on this track are excellent.

2. "Vehicle"—Getting close to the end of the list, and it would not be complete without my *Jimmy Kimmel Live* entrance anthem. Most people think this is by Blood, Sweat & Tears, but it's by The Ides of March.

And...

1. "Lucretia MacEvil"—*This* is Blood, Sweat & Tears. No other song could take the top spot on my list. It's on the 1970s album *Blood, Sweat & Tears 3*. This is how good Blood, Sweat & Tears are. They don't even need to name their albums. They just number them in sequence. That's a power move by a powerful horn section. A perfect '70s horn-drenched rocker about an "evil woman child" and "backseat Delilah" who's "the talk of the sticks." I defy you to do better than that. ∎

It feels like you've done everything but a true crime podcast. If you had to, what unsolved mystery would you do a six-part deep-dive podcast about?

Pat, 46, Washington, D.C.

Not being the possessor of a vagina, I'm not really into the true crime genre, and I don't get the fascination with it. I'm just not into the cold-case thing. Half the time when the sleuths figure out who the murderers are, they're long dead, like The Zodiac Killer. A group of independent cold-case investigators think they figured out who he was in 2020. The only problem was that he died in 2018. Catching serial killers after they're dead is kind of disheartening. I know it's supposed to bring closure to the family, but I think I'd be disappointed if some retired detective came to me and said, "You know the man who took your precious daughter fourteen years ago, raped her, and left her in the woods? We found him. He died three years ago of natural causes." I want the family to be able to watch him fry in the electric chair, not just find out who he was so they can go blow a snot rocket on his grave.

By the way, cops, why are journalists and bored housewives with too much time on their hands doing your job? Every time I watch these *Dateline* true crime shows, there's a moment when the case goes cold for a while and the cops are sitting at their desks when the phone rings with a tip. That's the plan when the trail goes cold: head back to your desk and wait. Fictional cops on TV are always sliding across the hoods of their cop cars, kicking down warehouse doors, and shouting, "No time for backup!" Well, I'm going to create a show called *Plenty of Time for Backup* with cops sitting on their asses waiting for Patton Oswalt's dearly departed wife to do their job for them.

But to answer your question, Pat, if I had to do a long-form deep-dive podcast on a true crime, it would be on James Dean's car. To give you the bullet points, in case you're not aware: In 1955, James Dean was driving his 1955 550 Porsche Spyder along Route 46 in Cholame, California, with a mechanic friend. He was driving it to the track at Buttonwillow and was attempting to break in the engine on the way there before a race. A twenty-three-year-old named Donald Turnupseed was driving a 1950 Ford Tudor coupe and was attempting to make a left turn in front of Dean's car, which then collided into the Ford. Turnupseed didn't see the Spyder because it was a low, silver convertible, and he couldn't brake in time when he did see it. The impact flipped Dean's car multiple times; the car eventually landed in a gully. His friend was ejected and survived, but Dean was pinned inside with a broken neck. He died on the way to the hospital.

That car, the wreck of it, then made the rounds as James Dean's death car, as a way of instructing people on the dangers of driving tiny convertible sports cars. How this would be instructive, I have no idea. That Spyder was about a foot off the ground and had no roof. In 1955, anything that hit it would have been tons of solid steel. Dean didn't stand a chance.

Dean's insurance company took possession of the wreck. It then got sold a few times, eventually ending up in the hands of George Barris, who had originally customized it including the stenciling of "Little Bastard" on the side. ("Little Bastard" was reportedly an insult thrown at Dean by Warner Bros. president Jack Warner.) Barris was a designer and customizer who made iconic cars for TV and film, like the original Batmobile, the Monkee-mobile, and the Munsters-mobile.

He then took the engine and transmission out and sold them to two doctors, who put it in their Porsche and Lotus respectively in 1956 and went racing. The Porsche driver spun out of control, hit a tree, and died instantly while the Lotus driver also crashed but survived. Another person bought the two surviving tires from the original wreck, but when he attempted to use them, they blew simultaneously and sent his car hurtling into a ditch.

What remained of "Little Bastard" was in a locked container but was lost during shipping from Los Angles to Miami in 1960. That mystery has never been solved. The transaxle—a transmission and two axles attached to drum brakes—was sold at an auction in June 2021 for $387,000.

I dare you to tell me that story wouldn't make for a compelling pod. It's got a celebrity death at the center of it; there's a mystery element of where the car's remains disappeared to; there's the curse that killed one of the guys who bought a part of it and nearly killed another. There's the George Barris element. Fuck, it's even got a guy named Turnupseed.

Oh, and there's the amazing true-life character of Jay J. Armes. He was a private detective in the '70s whom Barris hired to search for the car. Here's why this is interesting. He had *no hands*, and his name was *Armes*. This is 100 percent true. Not only was he a private investigator, but he was also an actor who was in an episode of *Hawaii 5-0* titled "The Hookman." In 1972, he rescued Marlon Brando's son Christian after he was kidnapped by his mother and hidden in Baja California, Mexico. Armes became such a pop culture icon that an action figure was based on him. You could attach various guns, knives, grappling hooks, and even suction cups to where his hands would have been. I shit you not; this was a real thing. Go to YouTube and find the commercial for the Jay J. Armes action figure. I understand why you'd doubt me. If you were to try to describe all the above to someone with no context, they'd think you're on mescaline.

If the story on Dean's car doesn't pan out, my second choice for a true crime that I'd like to solve on a podcast would be figuring out how *RuPaul's Drag Race* has won twenty-four Emmys. ∎

....

I'd like your thoughts on the power move of striking a match on another man's face as often seen in older westerns. Good stuff, need more of it.

Charlie, 38, Tacoma, Washington

This falls into the same category of tropes that work only in movies—not in real life. Ads for "strike anywhere" matches make it seem like you can flick the match with your finger and it will burst into a flame. In movies, no one ever has to do it twice. Whether the striking surface is a nearby rock, the person's pant leg, or another dude's face, it works the first time every time. It never blows out, and there's never a breeze. But anyone who's ever tried to do this in real life knows that the eleventh time is the charm. ■

....

As an avid Love Boat *aficionado, which character would you like to be on the show?*

Robert, 43, Huntertown, IN

I do love me some *Love Boat*. I saw it as a teen in the '80s, but I was about as connected to it as a young Black man watching a speech by Ronald Reagan would be. I was like, "Who has their own luggage? And goes on a trip? On a boat?!" Never mind the fact that Joey Heatherton and Charo were on the ship too. The shit that happened on *The A-Team* was more relatable and believable to me than what was occurring on *The Love Boat*, because at least I had seen a van somewhere in the San Fernando Valley. I couldn't even conceive of how people secured passage on the boat. No one in my family had a credit card. Did people just go to the dock and hail the boat like a cab, and hope they had enough cash to go to Puerto Vallarta?

But I have a different appreciation for this show now. I watch it every night and talk about it with Dr. Drew on nearly every podcast we do. It's simultaneously a time capsule of the era and a throwback to an even earlier time. The hair is pure 1979, but the guest stars are from 1959 and the plotlines are from 1939. It's vaudevillian in the predictable plot twists, hackneyed one-liners, and "a beautiful woman like that wouldn't date me; I'm just a mechanic" sociological tropes. It really is like an archeological dig. I watch *The Love Boat* like British generals looked at the African tribes they were about to colonize.

To answer your question, Robert, I think I'll have to go with Dr. Bricker. He lives in a consequence-free world. He openly hits on passengers. All he does is pound highballs and chase poonanny around that ship. He greets them as soon as they're up the gangplank: "Hey, mind if I walk you to your cabin? I'll bring my stethoscope!"

He's the official ship's doctor. He's in uniform. Yet he routinely attempts to date-rape the female passengers. He'll give them drinks while he's drinking himself. If Dr. Adam Bricker were a real person, he'd give Dr. Larry Nassar a run for his money in a creep contest.

That's what's so telling about the era—not that date-raping doctors existed, but that showing this type of behavior on a major network was acceptable. The cruise line featured on *The Love Boat* was real. It was Princess Cruises. The show was shot on an actual ship. Princess obviously cut a licensing deal with the network—an integration, as we'd call it today—to use their property, branding, logo, and so on. That means they had script approval. There is no way that the executives of Princess Cruises would let an episode on the air where the entire crew came down with botulism at the buffet and the passengers had to take over. There were no episodes where the ship lost power or ran adrift on some jagged rocks near the shore. That would never pass muster. But there are numerous episodes where the ship's middle-aged doctor attempts to date-rape twenty-one-year-old passengers. ∎

· ·

*You watch a lot of vintage TV—*The Love Boat, Charlie's Angels, T.J. Hooker*—but I don't hear a lot of* Rockford Files *talk. It's well-written, funny, and self-deprecating. It's also a time capsule of Los Angeles from the late '70s. What are your thoughts on the show?*

Keith, 50, Las Vegas

I don't have a ton of thoughts on *The Rockford Files*. I don't watch it for the reasons you gave. Because it's good. When you study history, you study the wars, slavery, ethnic cleansing, and the like, but you don't really spend as much time on civilizations that were fair, equitable, and scandal-free. There's much more to be learned from bad than good. I already explained my anthropological study of *The Love Boat*. Whether it's music or architecture, the way you can tell it's good is if it's timeless. Bad stuff has an expiration date on it. It's time-stamped. You'll know exactly what was going on in any era if you watch a bad TV show or even a Budweiser commercial aired then. You'll know what was in the zeitgeist at the time. If you can place the year a song came out, it's always a horrible song. It's the same for fashion. Music that sounds like 1985 is shit. But there was good music from 1985 that didn't sound like that year.

You mention *T.J. Hooker*. This is a perfect example of this—the cars, the hairstyles, the Synsonics drums during chase sequences. *T.J. Hooker* is of its era. Adrian Zmed's hair alone lets you know what decade it was. But I have to admit, I do love me some *T.J. Hooker*. I feel guilty when I'm watching an episode I've seen eight times before, and my kids are in the next room and I haven't seen them that day. I grew up in L.A., so when I'm watching the show and see T.J. drive by Henry's Tacos and places that I walked by growing up, there's a novelty to it. I sip scotch, watch for landmarks from my childhood, and laugh about how the show's creators expect us to believe that the paunchy Shatner we saw wheezing as he ran down an alley ten seconds prior is the same person now launching himself over a Dumpster to tackle a perp—no stuntman here.

But since you asked about *The Rockford Files*, I will add that when I was growing up, my dad looked like Angel from that show, and my buddy Chris Boehm's dad looked like Jim Rockford. Here they are for your entertainment pleasure. ∎

Photo by Disney General Entertainment Content via Getty Images

· ·

What songs are the worst to hear while you are sober and the "singers" are drunk and having a great time?

Eric, 41, Delano, Minnesota

Why would you ever be sober at a karaoke bar? ■

· ·

I know you were a childhood friend of Nick Menza's but have never heard you comment on his band Megadeth. Have you ever listened to them, and if so, what are your thoughts?

Jimi, 44, Houston

Not really. I've never been into that genre of music. I don't dislike it as much as rap or DJing, because at least metal musicians play instruments. I was always kinda put off by the name Megadeth, but I do like a few Hoobastank songs, so I shouldn't be so judgmental about a band name.

I think I'm turned off by music that is trying to put out a message that is beyond the music. Whether it's glam rock or ghoul rock, when the image and the costumes become more important than the music or lyrics, that's a problem for me.

You could count KISS in this category, but they had some decent songs. Bands like GWAR, Insane Clown Posse, and Slipknot are what I'm talking about. The granddaddy of them all is Alice Cooper. But he bequeathed the "all style, no substance" throne to Marilyn Manson. Unfortunately, according to the news recently, it seems that Manson started listening to his own press. There are more than sixteen accusations of his being an actual abusive creepshow pervert in real life, not just for his image onstage. Several women have come out saying he forced them into sexual servitude; one even says that he forced her to wear a Nazi uniform and goose-step around his house. I couldn't even get my ex-wife to bring me an In-N-Out burger when she was at In-N-Out Burger. How does this talentless hack get hot chicks to dress up like der Führer?

Alice Cooper should have gotten ahold of him early in his career and staged an intervention. "Hey, Marilyn, or should I call you Brian? You know this is all an act, right? The horror movie makeup is just to convince dumb people you have talent when you don't. Take it off after the show, put on a collared shirt, check your stock portfolio, and go golfing like me." ∎

At a movie theater, which armrest is mine?

Christopher, 53, Enumclaw, Washington

I'm not sure how many theaters are doing the shared-armrest thing anymore. At all the theaters I've been to lately, each fully reclining chair has its own set of armrests. But if you're concerned, just put your drink in the cupholder you want to mark your territory. ∎

You have great taste in music. Other than your parents being too cheap to pay for the instrument or the lessons, why did you never learn an instrument? If you had the money when you were a teen, what instrument would you have learned?

Kevin, 43, Utah

As great as the guitar is, I love a good song with a piano lick. I've already mentioned my love for Ben Folds. And all my favorite musicians—Joe Jackson and Elvis Costello come to mind—incorporate the piano well. Ironically, my mom's house and even my grandparents' house had an upright saloon-style beater of a piano. I just never had enough discipline to learn. It's kind of a rich-man, poor-man situation. Hand-me-down pianos are something the rich and poor have in common, except the rich can afford to have theirs tuned, and the pianos don't have circular stains from the Mr. Pibb bottles that got left on them in 1978.

Here's how bereft of entertainment I was as a kid. Every now and again my cat, Norman, would walk across the keys, and that would delight me. I can't imagine that being a source of entertainment for my son—sitting around and waiting for the cat to jump up and tickle the ivories. ∎

. . . .

If you could go back in time and all you had was an iPad with no internet access but one movie downloaded on it to show our founding fathers what their country would look like in 250 years, what would you show them?

Graham, 41, Wheeler, Mississippi

I'm gonna have to break the rules and give the founding fathers a double feature, because there are two benchmark movies in the past fifteen years that illuminate what a shitshow our society was to become.

The first runner-up is *2012*. Not because I'd want to show them about climate change; I'd want to show them societal climate change. As you probably know, it's a disaster movie. The plot is that there's some problem with the planet's core, and the ice caps are going to melt rapidly and Earth is going to get flooded. As Noah did in the Old Testament, some arks get built. Secretly, the rich people knew this was going to happen and had built three giant arks, hiding them in the Himalayas. At a certain point, all the well-to-do people who paid for the arks got an email or a buzz on their special secret beepers and were told it was go time.

Enter John Cusack's character, Jackson Curtis, a down-and-out writer making ends meet as a limo driver. We are supposed to believe, from a shot of his driver's license, that he was born in 1979, making him thirty-three. Cusack was forty-three at the time and looked it. This is easily the least believable plot point in a very far-fetched script. I had a much easier time buying the fake science jargon about the Earth's core losing magnetism than that timeline tomfoolery.

Anyhow, the three arks are there to supposedly save the scientists, politicians, and other people from the flood and thus save humanity itself. When word gets out to the regular people, including thirtysomething Jackson Curtis, plebeians rush to get onto the arks. Oliver Platt's character makes a big speech about how everyone needs to stick to the plan, while Chiwetel Ejiofor's character says that if they let people die, they're going to lose their humanity.

This is my point. They make the Platt character the bad guy, but he's right. He's saying, "We have fifteen minutes and enough food for just the number of people on these arks. What do you want to do? Do you want to be responsible for the extinction of humanity?" The villain in the movie is explaining rationing to the hero of the movie. It's ridiculous.

I think this speaks to a larger political and cultural trend. We've lost our ability to understand sacrifice for the greater good, meritocracy, and capitalism. AOC would be rooting for the guy who literally wants to open the flood gates. Allowing everyone on the arks would defeat their purpose and effectiveness. The hero has no plan other than just letting everyone on. What about the rations? What about ballast? Aren't thousands of additional passengers going to sink the ark? The villain has a plan. It may be unpleasant, but it's a plan that looks at saving humanity for the long term, not feeling good in the short term. If there were several other unfilled arks, it would be a different story. But there's limited space, and the people who paid to build those life-saving vessels should get first crack at them, no?

I've long said that our society crossed the Rubicon on January 20, 2006. On that date, we officially became a sad sack of weak, fat pussies. Some blame the schools; others blame video games and social media. Not me. I think what we used to call a culture died with the premiere of *Little Miss Sunshine*. Since then, our society has been like the VW Microbus from that movie, breaking down and having to be push-started. That film led to the death of dads and the death of society. The cultures that do best, that have the lowest crime rates and the highest test scores, have intact, traditional families with a strong patriarch. This movie vilifies fatherhood and turns a person who should be viewed as a good dad into a demon. I have *many* thoughts about this watershit moment in cinema. Buckle up.

Let's start by examining the dinner table scene. Seven-year-old Olive is curious about her uncle's suicide attempt. The dad, played by Greg Kinnear, doesn't want to talk about it at the dinner table and immediately gets pushback from the family, especially his wife, who declares that they are a "pro-honesty" family. Olive is seven. Her parents were dedicated to telling her the truth, but she still believes in Santa Claus and the Tooth Fairy. If her dog died, they'd say it went to a farm. Not telling your kids everything is not a bad thing. As Kinnear's character protests, the family continues to push back: "She's going to find out anyway." So why don't we just boot up YouPorn and show her fisting videos? She's going to find out about them anyway.

Then there's the moment the junkie and sex-addict grandpa, played by Alan Arkin, drops some wisdom on his grandson about "fucking a lot of women." He's the *hero* of the movie. If you met this guy in real life, he'd be the scariest man alive. You'd never let him in your house. A grandfather sitting his grandson down to talk to him like this would immediately prompt a call to Child Protective Services. It's a good thing this movie came out in 2006. Could this scene possibly fly in the post-#MeToo world? Could a portrayal of a guy who got kicked out of a nursing home for selling drugs and sexually harassing people win an Oscar these days? Fuck no. But in 2007, Arkin nabbed the golden statue for Best Supporting Actor.

Let's not forget later in the movie, when the dad is driving and explaining his nine-step plan to make money. I don't know why his wife has to be such a cunt. She's rolling her eyes at him. Her man is trying to make money for her family. Yes, his plan has a low probability of success. But whether it's acting, writing a book, or starting a restaurant, there are no guarantees other than hard work and hustle. That should be respected. The entire time the dad is sharing his plan, the gay suicidal uncle is being sarcastic, as if his life has turned out great. They're in a VW Bus with a broken starter, the dad is pitching everyone an idea on how he's going to get them back on their feet, and everyone is rolling their eyes at him. I get that he doesn't have a great track record of success, but at least he's still trying.

And let's talk about maybe the most famous/infamous scene in the movie—the "ice cream breakfast." Little Olive wants to have waffles with ice cream for breakfast, and Dad has the audacity to try to talk her out of it. I thought you were the "pro-truth" family? Why is everyone looking at him like he's a maniac? "Don't eat ice cream for breakfast" is good advice anytime, but especially on your way to a competition that involves getting in a bathing suit. Isn't this the parents' job, to tell your kid, "Hey, this is breakfast, not dessert"? How many times as a kid did you hear, "You can't have that for breakfast"? Did it erode your self-esteem? Do you talk to your therapist about it weekly?

To put a cherry on the sundae that Olive shouldn't be eating, Grandpa tells her—again, she's a seven-year-old girl—that he likes a woman with meat on her bones. Again, the real-life guy would be in jail. Just to recap, before we move on to our next moment, suicide talk at the table is fine. That's just honesty. But nutrition talk is an attack.

Later in the movie, Grandpa teaches Olive to dance sexy for her competition, and as soon as she leaves the room, our hero snorts heroin. Not only would this character not fly in a post-#MeToo world, but we've made a mentor out of a degenerate drug addict. Would this scene and this character work in our opioid-epidemic world? Again, Arkin's Oscar-winning role was a guy who got kicked out of Shady Acres for selling heroin to other senior citizens. If we're going to give out an Academy Award for a horny junkie, Arkin should hand his Oscar to Val Kilmer for *The Doors*.

The following scene from *Little Miss Sunshine* doesn't outrage me as much as the previous ones for its societal implications, but it's still outrageously stupid. The son, Paul Dano's character, who for some reason has taken a vow of silence until he accomplishes his dream of becoming a fighter pilot, realizes he's colorblind. Wouldn't he have figured this out long before this moment on a road trip with his family as a teenager? He never had a vision exam at his pediatrician's office? He never got tested at school? And his gay, suicidal, Proust-scholar uncle is the one who tells him it means he'll never fly in the wild blue yonder? Not that he'd know it was blue. Why, all of a sudden, is the uncle an expert on the military and the requirements to be a fighter pilot?

First off, casting Dano was a weird choice. Dano is a scrawny emo guy. He looks like the fourth Ramone. That person in real life would have zero interest in being a fighter jock. He has Ringo's haircut from when The Beatles got off the Pan Am flight from London. If this were real life, the son would look like Bradley Cooper's character in *Wedding Crashers*. More important, in the real world, someone who wants to be a fighter pilot would agree with the dad about ice cream and discipline. He'd be talking about eating raw eggs and doing push-ups.

And I don't know why he took a vow of silence. I'm pretty sure you have to communicate as a fighter pilot—like, with other pilots, air traffic control, or your commanding officer. You actually have to communicate more than the average person. Letters become full words in that world—Baker, Charlie, Foxtrot, Whisky, Tango. He wigs out when he realizes how fucked his colorblindness has made him. He starts screaming, and they have to pull the Microbus over. Is this freak the one you want landing an F/A-18 Super Hornet on a carrier at night? The real-life version of this kid would be shooting up a school.

Along the way, the family stops at a convenience store, and the uncle runs into his ex. You might remember that he recently attempted suicide and is still sporting wrist bandages. It's summer in Arizona; everyone except him is wearing short-sleeve shirts. He's got a long-sleeve shirt on, with the cuffs inexplicably rolled up. Why? No reason other than to have this scene. Oh, before we leave this scene, let's not forget that pervert grandpa gives the uncle money for porn, telling him to get himself a "fag rag." Again, would this scene fly in 2022? You can bet your ass the woke Twitter mob that wasn't a thing in 2006 would have a lot to say today about the use of that f-word.

Finally, the climactic talent show scene. Olive goes out there and, like Grandpa taught her to, shakes her ass to Rick James's "Super Freak." The other girls in the show actually have a talent, but we're supposed to be rooting for the chunky granddaughter whose junkie grandfather taught her to twerk? It's a big societal problem when "being yourself" is more important than learning a skill or honing a talent.

With this movie, we didn't just jump the shark as a society, we went full Evel Knievel over fifteen sharks in front of Caesars Palace. It was the beginning of agendas trumping the truth. Whether the mom is arguing at the dinner table for an open discussion of suicide or shutting down good health and beauty competition advice at the dinner table, she is not pro-truth; she's pro-*her* truth. The dad is telling *the* truth. And it was the death of dads. Kinnear's character is a motivated disciplinarian. Just look around and ask yourself if we're not a little short on Kinnears in our society.

So, now that I've deconstructed and examined this film more thoroughly than the Warren Commission deconstructed and examined the Zapruder film, like a colorblind pilot, I'm going to bring this chapter in for a landing. ■

Chapter 10

Black Labs Matter

Fans of my podcast know I've got a big black Lab named Phil; I had a blond Lab named Molly and a German shepherd named after my beloved step-grandfather, Lotzi; and, going way back, I had a stray cat named Norman. I'm a pet lover. Except birds. Birds are evil and are for nutty bitches who try to replace the male companionship lost in their third divorce with a cockatoo. So I'm more than ready to give animal advice and answer canine queries.

....

I've worked with animal causes for most of my adult life and, like you, have bristled at the term "rescue." That said, over the past five years, I've been helping re-home potbelly pigs. Unlike with dogs, in many cases, these animals are in legit danger of being killed if they don't find a home. Can this be deemed "rescue" with a straight face? I'm torn.

Dan, 47, Gainesville, Florida

We need to get some clear definitions of "rescue," "victim," "hero," and other terms we've been throwing around. We went into overdrive on this during the early days of the COVID crisis. Operating a pallet jack at Sprouts during the pandemic does not make you a hero, and hearing Dave Chappelle make a joke about trans people in his act doesn't make you a victim.

And yes, "rescue" needs to be defined. I talked about this in my first book well over a decade ago. If something isn't on fire or taking on water, it can't be a rescue. SWAT-style rappelling gear and a smashed window must be involved. When authorities rescue kidnapped girls from cult leaders and African warlords, the cult leaders and warlords try to stop them; they don't give the rescuers free kibble and feature them on their Facebook page. Unless someone is trying to thwart you from rescuing the pig, it's not a rescue.

So no, I'm sorry, you cannot rescue a pig. Unless you're rescuing it from Martin's BBQ. ∎

What happened in the '70s that suddenly everybody had to write a song about some animal? With all the sneaky snakes, Jeremiah bullfrogs, three-legged dogs, wildfire horses, karate monkeys, white rabbits...it seems the '70s hit a beastly bump in the road musically, and I hated every minute of it! What are your thoughts?

Kevin, 59, Cape Girardeau, Missouri

My first thought is that singing about animals was definitely the dominion of the white man. The Godfather of Soul and Smokey Robinson didn't write songs about pets. The only Black man who ever sang about an animal was Michael Jackson crooning about a rat named Ben.

Which got me thinking about the song "Muskrat Love." We had a weird rodent run for a while. The Captain and Tennille were smart to jump on this. We had a fixation on furry critters in the '70s, and not just musically. It seemed like everyone had a hamster Habitrail (one more thing the Carollas weren't going to buy), and every other episode of a sitcom was about someone's rat escaping on the day when the boss was coming to dinner. "Muskrat Love" is a bizarre song about two rodents falling in love. What would that songwriter's internet history look like?

It seems like in the '70s, you could sing about life on the road as part of a rock band, banging sixteen-year-old runaways, or you could sing about a dog or a horse. That was it. Those were the only options. But it occurred to me that there are eight thousand songs about dogs, and zero about cats. Sure, there are lots of songs about cool cats, but that's in the jazz kind of way when you're talking about a person's being a cool cat. Actual felines never made their way into '70s songs the way dogs did. Mr. Bojangles had a dog that "up and died," and after twenty years he still grieves. By the way, we meet him "behind these county bars," a.k.a. jail, because "I drinks a bit." This is an emotionally unstable person. Yet the Nitty Gritty Dirt Band felt the need to immortalize him and his mutt in song.

And there was another person you wouldn't want watching your kids—Lobo, who was riding and living off the land with his pooch in "Me and You and a Dog Named Boo." People like him and Mr. Bojangles are drifters, but they have dogs. When I made that connection, I realized why there are no popular cat songs from the '70s. It's because cats don't travel. You're not thumbing across the country with your orange cat named Marmalade. Cats are always female, and when you travel with your dog he's always a male. Cats, like women, are a pain in the ass to travel with. A dog will just hop in the car and ride with its head out the window. A cat won't even hop on the couch with you if it doesn't want to, never mind into your custom van.

Tom T. Hall loved little baby ducks, old pickup trucks, coffee in a cup, and little fuzzy pups. Nary a word about cats. Even Cat Stevens didn't write a cat song. The closest we got was "two cats in the yard" from Crosby, Stills & Nash's "Our House." But those cats weren't even in the fucking house. They sure as shit weren't getting on the road to ramble. ■

I'm dating a girl whose dog is basically her boyfriend. It sleeps in the bed with us, and it has large male genitals. They aren't bigger than mine, thank God, but it's super close. This dog is getting all the loving attention that I feel I deserve because I pay for stuff. You feel me, Adam? How do I ask her to stop giving the dog the loving attention she should be giving me without sounding jealous, which I am?

—Kyle Dunnigan

I don't think simply asking her to stop would work. My guess is she'd become defensive and it would start an argument. I would suggest a more tactical approach that has never failed in any '70s sitcom I've ever watched. Instead of pushing the dog off the bed or shooing it out of the room whenever you want some alone time with your lady friend, point all your love and affection toward the dog. She'll quickly become jealous of your relationship with the dog, learn to resent him, and eventually say things like, "Can't we just spend one night together without the goddamn dog?"

Now, because this is all based on a sitcom premise, be prepared to slowly fall in love with the dog while you attempt this ruse and then to actually get upset when she forces the dog to sleep in a basket in the guest bedroom.

Like any bad sitcom from the '70s, this scene I've just painted needs a very on-the-nose name. I can see the *TV Guide* ad right now: "When an envious boyfriend fakes love for his girlfriend's dog to try to make her jealous, things get a little...ruff. This fall on CBS, Kyle Dunnigan stars in *Apartment K9*." ■

. . . .

How do you pick up your dog's poop when it shits twice and you only have one bag?

Steve, 71, Commack, New York

Little-known fact: This is why the great Bob Hope was never seen without a nine iron.

If you're on a trail or something, you can just kick it into the brush so some poor jogger doesn't get the treads of their trail-running shoes caked with canine caca. But if it's on a neighbor's lawn and there's a chance someone is home, then you have to do the same move as when a homeless guy asks you for change. You have to pat down your pockets as if you're looking for something, even though you know it isn't there, and then fake frustration. Then you go home, get a bag, and you and your dog come back with your tails between your legs. But if no one is around, just keep on walking.

Here's what you shouldn't do with your dog doo—put it in the neighbor's trash can. It would be more neighborly to kick it into their ivy. I'll make an exception if their trash can is on the curb, full, and soon to be removed by the garbage guy, or the robotic arm on the garbage guy's truck. But if the trash bin is empty, then you'd be putting your dog's shit in a receptacle that is going to get wheeled back up the driveway and sit next to their porch for a week. That means the smell of your dog's asshole will waft up every time they open the lid and remind them that you're an asshole. ∎

. . . .

If you were a dog, which celebrity would you want to own you?

Chris, 28, Los Angeles

Definitely not Lady Gaga. There's a chance I'd get kidnapped and the dude walking me would get shot.

I wouldn't even need to be with a celebrity. Every dog in America has a better life than I had as a kid. I saw a dog food commercial last year that talked about how dogs deserved "fresh food that belongs in the fridge right next to our food." When I was growing up, the idea of dog food being in the fridge next to our food was unthinkable, as that would imply there was food in our fridge or that I had a dog. It would have been confusing and gross to put the dog food in the fridge. That's a trope from a sitcom from the '60s.

I'm fine with feeding dogs fresh food instead of coagulated kibble. But the part of that dog food commercial where they put it in the fridge next to a big, and for some reason uncovered, bowl of cherries bothers me. It's a bridging of the gap between people and canines.

Treating dogs more like humans started with dogs not sleeping in the doghouse anymore. Dogs used to be outdoor pets. Now they sleep in a bed indoors. It occurs to me that husbands are more likely to be metaphorically in the doghouse after a fight with the old lady than that old lady's dog is to be in an actual doghouse.

Back in the day, there was the Chuck Wagon commercial where the wagon would come out of the TV and the dog would chase it around. This was high entertainment when I was a lad. That's the dog food commercial I'm used to.

But as far as being a celebrity's dog, I think I'd want to be my dog, Phil E. Cheesesteak. He's a big, lazy, 110-pound black Lab, and he's definitely got more power in my house than I do.

First off, he has more names than my parents gave me. We named him after Phil from *Modern Family*, but that got added on to. Here's how spoiled Phil is. He thinks his name is Treat. He doesn't respond when you call him by his actual name. Even if you do it in that low-growl voice you use when you're frustrated. But if you say "treat," he'll pop up like a jack-in-the-box. We eventually got to the point where we tried to outsmart him and start spelling it. Sonny was trying to do this the other day and asked if we should give Phil a T-R-E-A-T. He forgot that his old man is the product of L.A.U.S.D. and L.A.Z.Y. parents and had no idea what he was spelling. "What, Phil is trapped? He caught a trout? Hang on, let me get the phone so Siri can help us sort this out."

It's hard to get Phil to do anything. At a buck ten, he can park himself somewhere and you're not going to move him. I was walking him around the neighborhood not long ago on a hot day, and he hopped into a fountain in front of a church and started splashing around. It was like the opening of *Friends*, but with a fifty-year-old dude and a dog. A caretaker for the church (I wish it had been a priest or a nun in full uniform, because that would have made the scene even more absurd) came out and asked us to leave, and I couldn't get Phil out. He said, "Sir, we can't have your dog in our fountain." I pretty much resigned myself to the situation and said, "I wish I had a choice. He's in charge here." The church guy said, "Well, get him out," and I replied, "We're gonna need a crane."

It's hard enough to get him to move when he doesn't want to when he's awake, but when Phil is asleep, you'd have an easier time pushing a Camry with no wheels. Phil sleeps in Sonny's bed most of the time, but like the whore that he is, he does a lot of bed hopping. And he does not curl up at the foot of the bed. He stretches out and turns your portion of a queen-size bed into a summer camp cot.

He can sleep anywhere. Here are just two pictures of him sleeping where no one who's not in a coma could catch a couple of winks. The first is him snoozing next to someone digging out a tree stump.

I love this one. He's two feet away, dead asleep next to someone operating a Briggs & Stratton power wet saw. This is the loudest thing in the world, yet it means nothing to him. After seeing this, I had to wonder about the idea that dogs have better hearing than we do, because if I hear a mosquito in the next room, I'm up for the night. Phil could sleep through garbage-pickup day during the Blitz.

There's a certain Zen to Phil. So let me end this chapter with a little Phil-osophy. We should all be more like Phil.

Yes, he's lazy and he's dumb. So dumb that instead of getting out of a pool (or a church fountain) and shaking himself dry, Phil attempts that while he's still in the pool.

Maybe we're all too smart for our own good. With Phil's stupidity comes affability and trust. We got Phil as a pup around four months old. When he was about seven months old, we drove him to the vet who then proceeded to cut his nuts off. We didn't stop for soft-swirl ice cream; we didn't hit the In-N-Out Burger drive-through. We just went straight back to the house. He got home, recovered, and the next week I told him to get in the car. He didn't hesitate. He just started wagging his tail, essentially saying,

"Where're we going, boss?" If someone told me to get in a car and an hour later I came home without a nutsack, the next time you told me to get in the car, I'd have some questions. Most people who get their balls removed would have some hesitancy. If the guy who drove me to get castrated pulled up three days later and said, "Hop in the Denali," I'd turn and run.

Phil is the opposite of the guys who get foreskin restorations. Unlike those assholes who are in their midsixties and still have a fire burning for the mohel that butchered them in 1958, Phil isn't living in victimhood.

By the way, I recently learned that an adult male converting to Judaism is expected to get circumcised if he's not already. But there's a little bit of an out if you already had that procedure done in the hospital when you were born: A single drop of blood from your *schvantz* will suffice. I'm not down with this. Personally, I need all the girth I can get down there. Every drop counts. Now, I don't imagine they do the full bris and the cold whitefish platter for a forty-one-year-old male. He'll go into a doctor's office to get the blood drawn. A little negotiation has to go on behind that closed door: "Listen, Doc. There are two people in this room. One of them doesn't want to see my cock. The other doesn't want a needle jabbed in his cock. I've got seventy dollars in my pocket. Maybe we can look the other way on pricking the prick. Just take a drop of blood from behind the earlobe; no one will be the wiser. Come on. You people like money." (If you think that joke was anti-Semitic, why did you assume the doctor was Jewish?)

Phil is never on guard. If anyone he doesn't know comes over, he'll still wag his tail like the person is an old friend. He wants to greet them. He's not suspicious or standoffish. And he doesn't bark.

So, whether it's sleeping next to a wet saw or moving on after being emasculated, it would be nice if we could all pull a page from Phil's book and turn down our agitation meter—not be so reactive and get the fuck on with it. Maybe because dogs age in dog years, they know there's no time to waste on that shit. They have to enjoy life seven times more than we do. Wow. That was some deep (dog) shit. ■

Chapter 11

Taking Off the Kid Gloves

As anyone who listens to my podcast knows, I love my offspring. And by that, I mean I love *The* Offspring. They're one of my favorite bands. My kids, I'm lukewarm on. In fact, I'm lukewarm on kids in general. I think our society is fucking up kids six ways to Sunday, and they're returning the favor. I can tell by your questions that you're as concerned about the little shits as I am.

....

How do you get your adult children to move out of your house?

Pamela, 49, San Diego

When I was young, if I met someone who was seventeen and a half and didn't have their driver's license, I would call them a loser and make fun of them. My buddy Ray didn't get his license until he was eighteen. That was a long two years of verbal abuse by me that was repaid with physical abuse upon me. Kids nowadays don't care about getting their license. The same goes for moving out. There used to be a lot of pressure to get out of the house, but it's gone now. There doesn't seem to be a stigma anymore, and stigma was a prime motivator. Not much has changed in how kids live: They live somewhere free, raid the fridge, and sit on their dad's sofa and watch cable. That's how it was when I was a kid (minus the food and the cable). But the stigma has changed. Back then, if we met someone who wasn't going to college full time and was living at home, we considered that guy a loser. As soon as we could, all of us losers would pool our money, move in together, and put too many guys on the lease and on the futon.

It's much more acceptable to remain at home now. With Obama Care allowing kids to remain on their parents' insurance until age twenty-six, the government is sending the message that until their midtwenties, offspring are their parents' ward. That's got to be incentivizing a lot of "failures to launch."

The prolonged-adolescence thing has been going on for a while. People used to be veterans of WWII in their early twenties, or were driving tractors on the family farm at age eleven. Now everyone is refusing to grow up, and Peter Pan's got a gut and is consuming cannabis edibles in the basement of the house he grew up in. There should be a countdown clock. Once you sprout your first pube, you've got six years to get the fuck out.

We've learned that COVID doesn't affect kids, but we worry about them bringing it home to elderly grandparents, as if this is Italy in 1922. For the next pandemic, kids living with elderly grandparents could be a real thing. We may be making that come to fruition.

It's the parents fault too. The kids aren't growing up because the parents aren't getting old. A kid is twenty-two, and the parent is fifty-four going on twenty-six. Dad's not wearing a cardigan, smoking a cigar, and listening to Nat King Cole, Johnny Mathis, or Gary Lewis & the Playboys. He's wearing flip-flops and cargo shorts, and is excited that Foo Fighters just dropped a new album.

He doesn't act like Ward Cleaver and call his son "son" anymore; he calls him "buddy." My dad and stepmom were not my buddies. When I walked through the yard to go into the garage, I didn't even like seeing them through the window. I couldn't get away from my folks fast enough. Back in the day, parents smoked, smelled weird, hated everything you liked, and were the last people you wanted to hang out with. You were highly incentivized to hit the bricks. Now the dad is wearing every bracelet his daughter has ever made for him, is down with Kanye, and is playing Fortnite after eating a THC-infused gummy bear. Parents have become roommates with credit cards.

"Old" meant old when we were young. Realizing I was now older than Captain Stubing on *The Love Boat* hit me really hard last year. Even in the 1980s, "old" was old. Prepare to have your mind blown. Picture Ed Asner as Lou Grant on the first season of *Mary Tyler Moore*. He was a bald old man, right? He was forty-one. Tom Brady is forty-four.

It used to be that people wanted to get old. They took up smoking when they were fourteen. They faked being older so they could go fight in a war. Sixteen-year-olds were saying they were eighteen so they could go kill Krauts.

By the way, pardon the mildly unpatriotic tangent about the so-called Greatest Generation. No one ever talks about what horrible parents they had. These kids were barely out of the tenth grade and heading to Okinawa. Did that mean they loved their country or that they wanted to get the fuck away from their parents and their boring small town? This is a seldom-broached topic. I was watching all the 9/11 retrospectives last year, and it hit me that when a Marine being interviewed says something like, "I was sitting in my house in New Jersey and saw the second plane hit Tower Two. The next afternoon I went and signed up at the recruitment center," the interviewer then discusses what a hero he was, but never what a loser he was. The guy had no kids, wasn't married, and was home at 9:03 a.m. Why wasn't he at work?

Acting your old age in the past often came down to footwear. Being old meant you wore weird shoes. When I was growing up, there's no way a daughter or a son would wear their parents' shoes. Now every kid can rock their parents' checkered slip-on Vans. Think about *All in the Family* and how Edith and Archie Bunker dress in contrast to their kids, Gloria and Meathead. Archie wears leather shoes; Meathead wears Birkenstocks. Edith wears a paisley house dress, and Gloria wears bell bottoms. Now you turn on the TV and the *Real Housewives* chicks are dressed the same as their daughters.

So my advice, Pamela, is to get real old, real quick. Get rid of the Lululemons and start wearing support hose. Dress like Edith Bunker and use expressions like "good gravy!" Put out a bowl of ribbon candy and eat dinner at 4:30 p.m. The stigma around being an adult child living at home is not coming from outside the house, so it needs to come from within.

And work on a timeline. Act like a used car dealer. Sit your kid down and negotiate: "What's it going to take to get you out of this house today?" Pick a date and get them to commit to it. A technique I like to use, which has been completely unsuccessful with my family and employees but is still worth a shot, is to let them pick the date. They'll feel more empowered. Have them circle it on the calendar, and after that point, start charging for food and rent at market rates.

If that fails, you can pop the pins on your bedroom door and let them walk in to see you going down on your old man. That should be enough to get them out the door. ∎

. . . .

Is it inappropriate to teach a child that violence is some-times an answer, and moreover sometimes the best answer? Emphasis on "sometimes" here. I'm an asshole, not a monster.

Matthew, 34, Marcy, New York

Yes, violence is a necessary part of society as long as people are going to commit it randomly. If you knew that one restaurant catered only to people who had a concealed-carry permit and the other catered only to people who've just left an AOC rally, which restaurant are you going to rob? The ultimate example is terror-ists. Go kill them, or they'll do what they do and that's that. It would be nice if that wasn't how it worked. The big mistake is thinking unreasonable people can be reasoned with.

It's called the fight-or-flight instinct, not the flight-or-flight instinct. You need to have both options on the table at all times.

It's interesting that we're living in this time of apps, drones, and billionaires launching themselves into space, and on the news you still see Tucker Carlson getting confronted in a bait shop by someone telling him he's the worst person in the world, or some Black Lives Matter protester walking up to the table of a white couple dining outdoors and drinking the woman's beer. Would any of that happen to Mike Tyson? Fuck no. These "activ-ists" go after people they know won't fight back. It's always folks like former White House press secretary Sarah Huckabee Sand-ers who get picked on, not Charles Barkley. We're living in a time of lawyers and Ring doorbell cams, but we're still animals.

All there has to be is perceived violence. When my daughter, Natalia, was five she spit on Olga the nanny, who proceeded to smack her in the face. Olga went full George Patton on Natalia. When Olga informed me of this, I said, "Good." It was the take-no-shit attitude that I liked about her when we hired her. She told us she had worked for a family for three months before joining ours, and those parents had told her she couldn't say no to the kids. She had to quit. Natalia never spit on another human being again. And Olga never had to raise her hand to Natalia again. It's not like Natalia developed TMJ or her face turned into something like Sloth's from *The Goonies*. The sting lasted thirty seconds, but the message lasted a lifetime. ∎

What do you think of some sort of national service requirement (military, AmeriCorps, etc.) for every person before they turn twenty-five?

Eric, 56, California

I'm all for it. People think of service programs and the military as a way to help people go to college. I think everyone should get a job clearing brush for the forest service, picking up garbage on the beach, or emptying bedpans at the VA—not to earn their way into college but so they'll truly appreciate their jobs when they get into the workforce.

College doesn't teach you how to work. Work teaches you how to work. The most important attribute you can have as a young person is not being afraid of work. There's definitely something to doing physical labor to drive home the point that you want to get into the C-suite with some air conditioning. The biggest thing I got from doing tough blue-collar work was realizing that I didn't want to do that shit when I was forty. I think the work needs to be something physical. Go out, build up some calluses, and then go to college.

Plus, there's a lot of elitism in our country. The college-educated class looks down at everyone else as Walmart-shopping rubes clinging to their guns and Bibles. Getting out there and really working gives you some respect for and understanding of what real people do to pave the road you drove on to get to that Ivy League school. It also mixes up the races and the classes, so people get to know people from outside their bubble. One of the reasons we made such progress in race relations in the early '70s, as opposed to the early '60s, was the Vietnam War. The guy in the rice paddy next to you might have been a different race and from a different part of the country, but you were both in the shit.

The idea of working hard blue-collar jobs is not just about helping the elite understand the lower classes. When I was poor, I looked at rich people as if they were aliens. But a poor person from the inner city working next to a rich kid might realize that he or she could do the same job as the rich kid someday—a profound realization. When I started to turn a corner in my professional life was when I started connecting with successful people as a boxing instructor. Through that gig, I realized that they didn't have any tools in their toolbox that I didn't possess. And they were encouraging. Everyone thinks the answer for how to help poor people is to find one and give them $1,500. A much longer-lasting gift would be to help them learn that there are not as many differences in the toolboxes of rich and poor people as they think. ∎

I'm a parent of nine-year-old twin boys. When they were newborns and toddlers, people would say or ask the most intrusive ("Were they natural?"), obvious ("Are they twins?"), or ignorant ("Were they born at the same time?") questions about them. What are some of the dumbest questions or comments you've gotten about your twins?

Michael, 40, Dallas

My twins are a boy and a girl, and I still get asked if they're fraternal or identical. I always want to respond, "Yeah, one's got a cock and balls and the other has a coin slot. Other than that, they're completely identical. If you close your eyes, you couldn't tell them apart. Unless they spoke. But if you're deaf and have your eyes closed, they're completely identical. Unless you have hands and can feel them. Other than that, they're exactly the same."

I also get asked which one I like more. Of course, I'm not going to answer that question. Especially not in a book. But he knows who he is. ∎

· ·

We have one kid, an eight-year-old girl who wants a little sister. IVF hasn't worked, and we have had three miscarriages. Should we adopt?

Lew, 46, Texas

It really depends on what's going on in your life.

I was recently talking to a comedian on the podcast, a middle-aged woman who had adopted. She was talking about how she and all the other potential adopters had to put together profiles and packets for the woman giving up the child to choose from. It was like a dating profile, with hobbies, health, financials, and so on all laid out. There were pictures of her doing outdoor activities with her dogs, a résumé, and copies of diplomas. It occurred to me that if my biological mom had put together one of these packets, she would never have been selected. My dad too. My parents' packet would find no purchase. I'm not even sure what my mom could have put in her packet—a photo showing her sitting on a bean bag eating a TV dinner while listening to Helen Reddy and crying? No hiking, no mountain biking, no pets, no joy. Certainly, no other kids. My sister and I definitely wouldn't have made the cut. I had a helicopter mom. The problem was that she was the last helicopter out during the fall of Saigon.

This is a good thing for potential parents to think about. Think about yourself as being vetted by someone who can choose to send you their kin for the rest of their life. Think about your dossier being looked at by a stranger. Would they select you? Do you have your financial shit together? Are you healthy? Do you go on vacations, and did you go to college? So for you, Lew, I'd say maybe investigate the process a little and start putting together your packet. If you think the potential baby mama out there would give you the nod based on that, then go for it. But if you find that the eight-year-old you have never leaves the house because you're broke, you're living on Ramen noodles, and you're scheduled for gastric bypass surgery, maybe it's best to leave well enough alone. ∎

Now that I'm in my early fifties and I don't have a wife or kids, do you think it's too late for me to be a family man? What's the cutoff? Please be kind.

Your good buddy,

—Pauly Shore

As I was saying earlier in this chapter, "old" doesn't mean old anymore. In the past, we lived our lives in dog years. By the time you hit nineteen back then, you were a veteran of WWII and were married with two kids. Now we're living our lives in sea turtle years. You, Pauly, may be "The Weasel," but you're actually a sea turtle with plenty of time ahead of you to swim through the open sea. Plus, you have the bonus of being a male celebrity and a comedian, which means you can get married and start a family several years into old age. Look no further than the great Tony Randall, who had a kid at seventy-eight; Anthony Quinn, who banged out a boy at age eighty-one; or Larry King, who dropped his suspenders to create two boys with his seventh wife starting at age sixty-six. What I'm saying is that it's never too late. And if you have a daughter, God willing, you'd be there to "walker" her down the aisle. ∎

∙∙∙

What is with the cult-like obsession with Elf on the Shelf? My wife and I decided we don't want to start that tradition with the kids, and all my friends who are parents tried to convince me why we should. It's as if they are invested. I don't understand how something that wasn't around during our childhood is something we must do with our children.

Kevin, 36, Tucson, Arizona

I'm so glad my kids have outgrown this. It's a total pain in the ass and yet another reason to hate my parents. My folks never burned any calories on fun traditions at Christmas. For gifts, they'd stop at the Thrifty, grab something from the dollar bin, wrap it in the sports page, and kick it toward me. My dad never put an elf anywhere—not on a shelf, a counter, an ottoman, a fireplace. The construction of the dump I grew up in was so poor and my dad was so incredibly unhandy that if he *had* put the 1.5-ounce elf on a shelf, the shelf would probably collapse. There were gingerbread houses that were more structurally sound than my childhood home. Here's how the Elf on a Shelf conversation would have gone in 1972, when my parents were still married: "Hey, Jim, there's something called Elf on a Shelf." "What's that?" "It's for kids. You go to the store and buy a stuffed elf…" "Pass."

My wife and I had superserious discussions about the stupid Elf on the Shelf. We'd go down to the war room, look at the quarter-scale model of our house, and move pieces around like we were planning the Normandy invasion. We'd fight. She'd be like, "No, that's too obvious. Natalia will figure it out!" and I'd shout back, "Good. Then this living nightmare can end!" Inevitably, we'd get drunk one night and forget to move it, and then have to make up an excuse about how the elf liked that spot and didn't want to leave.

It just goes to show how shitty kids are. We have to invent this stupid doll stuffed with cat hair to monitor them so they won't be assholes for a couple of weeks a year. That tells you everything you need to know about human nature and motivation. I'm sure the dipshits that want to defund the police and worry about Big Brother monitoring your text messages are happily doing this with their kids. ■

I am a divorced, fifty-seven-year-old mother of four grown children ages twenty-six to thirty-seven. I raised all of my children with conservative values and took them to church multiple times per week all of their lives. Funny enough, after they grew up and went out into the world, they stopped going to church and so did I. My youngest daughter and I have always been very close, and she pursued and excelled at very girly things growing up, which I fully supported, such as cheerleading, dance, and fashion. Now that she is grown, (twenty-six years old), she has bought into the "woke religion"...hook, line, and sinker. A month ago, she sent me a lengthy text about how she is coming out as nonbinary and wants to be referred to with the pronouns "they" and "them." She said she has made up her mind and for me not to try and talk her out of it. She said when she identifies as a woman, it is like putting on a costume; one that she really tries hard to believe. She now realizes she has always viewed herself as "neutral." My response was, "Whoa! I did not see that coming! I do not know much about this subject, but I do know that I love you big. I love you the way you were, the way you are, and the way you will be... and nothing can change that." I meant every word of it.

I want to remain close to her, but I also believe in science and the fact that there are only male and female genders. I think this idea of a nonbinary gender is horse manure that does absolutely nothing to better her life or the lives in her community. I am proud to be a woman, but I put it low on the list of important facts about the real me. I wish she would work on her character and values and not worry about her gender. Should I play along and hope it's a phase, or should I tell her how insanely ignorant this makes her look?

I would love to know how you would react if Natalia came to you with the same news.

Dani, 57, Austin, Texas

I would voice my concern about it, but not because I would care about having two sons versus a son and a daughter. I would just want to go on record as saying this has more to do with the zeitgeist of our time than gender dysphoria, so later on, when "they" switches back to "she," I could be in the history books as correct. I'd then turn the page and get on with life.

In general, we've gone off the deep end with the gender stuff, and this seems like as good a place as any to go off on a rant.

When I was growing up, there were men and women. Some were gay, some were lesbians, and that was fine. There were even a handful of transvestites, or crossdressers, and even fewer who went through with the surgery and were transexuals. At a certain point we added the bisexual category, which was also cool (especially if it was the right kind of bisexual in the right kind of porn). Then "transvestite" fell out of fashion, and "transgender" came in to replace that and "transsexual." Then, all these groups decided to band together and become the LGBT community. (By the way, I would love to have been in the meeting where the "Ls" and the "Gs" fought it out for top billing.) It continued to progress from there. We added "Q" for queer, "I" for intersex, and eventually "A" for asexual. I can understand how being gay, lesbian, and trans can be an identity. That affects a lot of a person's life. But asexual? OK, they're not into sex. Fine. Do they need to build a community around it? In keeping with the alphabet theme, why do they need to ID as not being DTF? Even this patchwork "community" got annoyed and were running out of characters in their tweets, so they just added "+" at the end of LGBTQIA.

Former New York governor Andrew Cuomo's daughter announced in 2021 that she was "demisexual." Like the rest of America, I had to look it up. I thought it had to do with being sexually attracted to Demi Moore. I've seen *Striptease*; I was Demi-sexual watching that. Here's the definition from WebMD:

Demisexual people only feel sexually attracted to someone when they have an emotional bond with the person. They can be gay, straight, bisexual, or pansexual, and may have any gender identity.

We're now at the point where we're announcing "no shit" shit. Coming out as demisexual is like coming out as a person who likes pizza and adding your favorite toppings to your email signature. Not wanting to have sex with someone until you form an emotional bond with them? I'm pretty sure that's called being a chick. There are zero straight dudes claiming to be demisexual. Imagine being a dad today and your daughter came out as demisexual. Your head would be swimming as you sprint to the computer to google that shit. But think how relieved you would be when you discover the definition. *I thought she wanted to fuck people who dressed as demons*, you'd think. *Thank Christ, she's just an old-fashioned girl who wants to get to know the guy first.*

Gender issues are starting to creep into government regulations too. Much has been made about the bathroom bill in North Carolina, but California couldn't be left out of the mix. Last year,

Governor Gavin Newsom, in his never-ending quest to find shit to focus on other than homelessness, traffic, wildfires, and housing prices, found time to sign into law a bill requiring stores to offer sections of gender-neutral toys. Aren't there already tons of gender-neutral toys? I'm pretty sure Monopoly doesn't give a shit if you have a dick or a pussy. The game pieces are already gender-neutral—there's a race car, a hat, an iron. Not a vagina or testes figurine among them. Play-Doh is pretty fucking gender-neutral, though I guess you could shape it into a penis. Hey, Newsom, a little less woke-us and a little more focus. That's just what we need, a government bureaucrat going into businesses to make sure the toy aisles have gender-neutral offerings, though I did come up with a fantastic name for said section: The Androgenous Zone.

A sexual identity issue even made it to the Supreme Court. The owner of Masterpiece Cakeshop in Lakewood, Colorado, had a dilemma. A gay couple had come in asking him to make a cake for their wedding. He said he was deeply religious and couldn't do that, so they sued him and the Colorado Civil Rights Commission sanctioned him for refusing to make the cake. The case went all the way to the Supreme Court, where the judges ruled 7-2 in the bakeshop owner's favor, saying that the Colorado Civil Rights Commission had violated his right to freely exercise his religion. Don't get me wrong; I'm open-minded and cool with same-sex marriage, but God forbid you open a business and try to run it the way you want to in America. I'm big on small government.

The more I got to thinking about it, I realized it was a sting. Two gay guys and one of them can't bake? I don't think so. Find me two gay guys, neither of whom can whip up something worthy of *The Great British Baking Show*, and I'll give you ten thousand dollars. Now, two lesbians? That I'd believe. But with two gay guys, the chances are better that they're both master bakers than that neither of them is. I smell cake...and a rat. Now people keep going into the Masterpiece Cakeshop and ordering cakes the owner won't do so they can sue him. The latest incident happened when someone went in to order a cake celebrating their gender transition. So the owner said, again, he was religious and couldn't do it—and, again, he was sued. What does a transition cake even look like? Do you need to talk to a therapist before you cut into it? If I were the baker and someone tried to come at me with this shit, I'd just hand them a pumpkin pie, and when they ask, "What's this?" I'd say, "This pie identifies as a cake."

Last year Canadian prime minister Justin Trudeau (who I identify as a pussy) tweeted the following:

People across the country are lighting candles to honour Indigenous women, girls, and 2SLGBTQQIA+ people who are missing or have been murdered.

This looks like the automatic Wi-Fi password your computer tries to give you before you change it to your birthday or something you can remember. Why are there two "Qs" and what does "2S" stand for? I looked it up, and "2S" is for "two-spirit" people—they have both a masculine and feminine spirit. We're now including those seven groups? No one gives a fuck about anyone's spirit. We care about whether people litter and pay taxes. (Though if I were shopping for auto insurance, I would definitely use the female spirit.)

I was tweeted a list of 111 genders and sexualities recently. By the time you read this, the number will be four digits. Eventually we're all going to have our own personal sexuality. I'm a Carollasexual, meaning I'm only attracted to big-titted brunettes who are into comedy, cars, and Hungarian food. My community of one demands representation and respect! ■

. . . .

Been listening for ten years and now I have a young daughter.... I totally agree with not wanting to bum the kids out with all the negatives in the world, but I'm wondering where you draw the line between letting them enjoy their childhood and making sure they're informed of how the world works?

Greg, 38, Orlando, Florida

I don't think you have to draw a line between letting kids enjoy the world and informing them how it works. You can integrate it. Weave the life lessons into the things they enjoy, even if you don't enjoy it. Which brings me to a hopefully inspirational story. Like you, I have a daughter. She plays volleyball. This has led to both enjoyment and many teachable moments.

The first is about showing up as a parent. I'm now on my sixth book, and I think every one has contained a bit of smack talk about how my parents didn't go to my Pop Warner or high school football games. This will be no exception, because as a father I'm now forced to drive to and attend volleyball tournaments that last longer than Woodstock. Door to door, it takes from five thirty a.m. to four p.m. It's the whole Saturday. We have to leave before the sun's up because the tournaments are always a million miles away. For the most recent one I went to, I asked Natalia where it was, and she replied, "I don't know. Somewhere far." She was right. It was in Temecula. You don't even need to live in Southern California to know that's far. It just sounds far. Volleyball tournaments and outlet malls: They're always at least forty miles away from wherever you are.

We had to be there at seven a.m. even though nothing starts at seven fifteen, or even seven thirty. The tournament starts at eight, and the girls warm up for ten minutes. At 6:55 a.m., the place is locked. But Natalia insisted that we get there "on time."

They should tell all the people who have to schlep there that it starts at eight and let them do the math. To make it worse, Natalia slept all the way out there.

Because the journey to the tourney started before the rooster crowed, when we finally got home at five, we were gassed. It's not like, "Now that I got that out of the way, it's time to assemble that modular furniture and put the finishing touches on that screenplay." No. It's time to drink and nap. I'm a busy fucker. I don't have seven and a half minutes in my schedule, never mind seven and a half hours.

And the sheer volume of games is baffling. Natalia had a tournament in Tustin that was eleven games in a row. That's a whole season. Is seven hours of volleyball necessary? The Kentucky Derby is two minutes long. The Boston Marathon is two and half hours. The goddamn Super Bowl is three hours. Do we need to triple the Super Bowl? Couldn't my daughter's volleyball games merely double the length of the most beloved sporting event in our nation?

I grew up in a world where one seven-inning Little League game lasted ninety minutes. When I played Pop Warner, my home field was the nearest high school. Away games were a half hour away at most. There were four ten-minute quarters. All-in, with drive time and half time, it was about the length of a Pixar movie. Now, the new world order is that parents have to hang around for the length of a Ken Burns documentary.

I harbor a fantasy of gathering all the organizers together and saying, "Would you like to see me do stand-up comedy?" When they reply yes, I'll say, "OK, how about for nine hours?" There would be silence. "Oh, really? That' doesn't sound fun?" I'd say. "Maybe you're just not a fan of mine. How about Seinfeld? Would you want to watch him do observational comedy for half a day? No? Well, I'm a professional. These kids are amateurs."

Don't get me wrong; it's enjoyable. These girls are good. And, as you'll soon read, Natalia had a journey to get on that team, so some fatherly pride is involved. But doughnuts and cigarettes are good too. That doesn't mean you should eat a baker's dozen or smoke a carton in one sitting. All those *Twilight Zone*–style interpretations of hell are about torturing you with too much of something you love. This is that. Except that I don't love it. I like it. Force me to watch or participate in 24,000 Hours of Le Mans and you'll have a Rod Serling–worthy ironic plot twist.

Quick pro tip for any of my fellow parents forced to go to these interminable tournaments. Show up in surgical scrubs. Just go to any medical supply place and pick some up. It'll be the best thirty-eight dollars you ever spend. People will think you're a winner, you'll get cred for leaving something important to see your kid lose at volleyball, and if you want to duck out early, you can just check your phone really quickly and say there's an emergency. No one is going to ask for your hospital ID. You can just say you work at Huntington Memorial, and if on the odd chance the person questioning you happens to have a relative who works there, you can just say, "Oh, I'm at the satellite campus in Arleta." All these hospitals are now franchising and spreading like Starbucks, so no one would ever be the wiser. The only problem would be if someone has a heart attack in the bleachers and they all look to you. You'd be shouting to the heavens, *"Live, damn you! Not on my watch!"* while pounding on their thigh.

One redeeming factor is at least I'm a dude. Every time I go to these tournaments, I pass by the ladies' bathroom and see a long line of poor fidgety women waiting to empty their bladders. I always feel bad for them, but it dawned on me the other day that the average woman lives seven years longer than the average man. I bet if you added up all the time a woman waits in line to use the bathroom over the course of her lifetime, it would add up to exactly seven years. Women always complain about how long they wait in line and say it's not fair. But the reason the lines are so long outside the ladies' room is that they get to keep their dignity. They get their own stall with a door and a lock. Men hook arms in front of a giant trough and grab the dick closest to their right and all pee at the same time. If the women's bathroom just had a giant pit in the center of it and all the women went back-to-back, there'd be no line.

Anyway, on to the inspirational tale about how Natalia got on the team. I came home one night when she was in seventh grade, and she was in her bedroom crying because she had tried out for the volleyball team and hadn't made the cut. When I asked her what had happened, why she hadn't made it, she said, "The coach hates me." Normally, when my kids try to tell me something about their lives, I'll say, "There you go," and head to my office to watch *SportsCenter*, but I decided to have a parenting moment. I wasn't going to let this victim identity ruin her. I couldn't let her think that no matter how hard she tried, if the coach didn't like her then it was all for naught. This is the pabulum that the politicians are currently feeding many different "marginalized" communities, and it is hobbling them. (It's ironic that the communities being told most often that the deck is stacked against them and the game is rigged are the ones most prone to gambling and playing the lottery. It's actually true, in those cases.) Even if it were true, people should stop thinking it. The playing field is never level, but people can operate within the margins.

I sat on Natalia's bed with her and asked, "How many people tried out?" She said, "Twenty." I asked, "How many people made the team?" She said, "Ten." Then I hit her with the tough question. "Where were you in that group? If you were a stranger who had just wandered into the gym and saw you and nineteen other girls trying out, where would you rank you amongst those twenty?" She gave me an honest answer: "Ten." Then I dropped the truth bomb. "You admittedly had yourself at ten. There's only eleven on the team. Do you really think it was that he hated you, or could you have worked harder to get yourself into single digits and removed any possibility of not making it? What's in it for him to not field the strongest team possible on the hardwood?" She got it.

Two years later, I came home from a work trip, and my wife told me that Natalia had made the volleyball team. I was then told to pretend that I didn't know and to act surprised when Natalia told me herself. (I was on a cruise when the roster was announced.) I'm a better actor than people give me credit for. Independent films, not so much. But when it comes to domestic acting, like acting as if I'm engaged or interested in my kids' lives, I'd win an Oscar.

I was actually impressed, so I didn't have to act. But I did have to stifle my confusion and irritation when she explained the ridiculous number of team levels. It goes Rochambeau, Elite, Thunder, and Lightning. I put those in order from highest to lowest level to prove my point and hopefully annoy and confound you as much as I was. Why is Elite not first? What and/or who the fuck is Rochambeau? And in the real world, lightning comes before thunder. You see a flash of lightning and wait for the sound of thunder. But in volleyball team levels, it's the opposite. I'm not sure which one she made, but it was a traveling squad, which has been great for her self-esteem and bad for my weekends and the mileage limit on my car lease.

The inspiring point is that after my lecture, she worked harder and made it onto the Thunder. Or the Lighting. I don't fucking remember. All I know is that, as you read this, not only is she on the intramural club team but she is going into the eleventh grade and is on the high school varsity team. So, as a parent I was clearly Rochambeau. ∎

....

What do you think the long-term effect of the pandemic will be on kids?

Neil, 37, Haverhill, Massachusetts

A significantly worse infection than the coronavirus has been going around for the past two and a half years harming kids: the virus of indoctrination into a fear cult.

The COVID-causing virus has no effect on any kid without a preexisting condition. But the effect of being told constantly that they're going to die if they leave their house is much more harmful than anything the coronavirus could do. It's insidious. The harm of keeping kids in lockdown and out of school was not that they missed out on a social studies test. Hell, with the critical race theory bullshit getting infused into schools, it's probably better if they don't go to class. It was that we were teaching them to live in fear. That is the worst thing you can do to a person. And COVID has presented a perfect opportunity for the politicians and the media to immerse our kids in fear. Like, if you want to teach a kid a second language, you do it when they're young. Their brains are much more malleable then, and they learn to think in that second language. Well, we're teaching our kids to think in the language of fear.

At the height of the lockdown panic, I saw that this had infected Natalia. She was trapped in a fear cult. She had to turn to CNN, MSNBC, Gavin Newsom, Dr. Fauci, and the idiots at the L.A. Unified School District to tell her she was OK. I shit you not, at a certain point she demanded a video of me at the grocery store wearing gloves before she would let me back in the house.

The government, with the media's able assistance, has spent the past two and a half years indoctrinating kids into a fear cult so that it can control them. It's the same reason the government gives kids free lunches and health care: to create dependence so it can maintain control.

Doing things that make sense is science. Doing shit that doesn't make sense is control. If you had a roommate and you asked him to do something sensible, like cleaning up the dishes after he made lasagna, that would not be you trying to control him. That would just be asking him to be courteous. If you told your roommate that every time you passed him in the hallway, he needed to drop and give you twenty, that would be control.

In California, we went nuts trying to "protect" ourselves from the coronavirus. We bulldozed beach volleyball courts, dumped sand into skate parks, and welded rebar across basketball hoops to keep people from enjoying the outdoors. We shut down outdoor dining, although no one can produce a study that shows the virus is transmitted outdoors. But that's applying logic. Stop trying to make sense of the crazy edicts. The government's agenda is not to make sense. The agenda is to get kids brainwashed early and get them to stop questioning edicts so when the real crazy shit comes around, they'll comply.

My fifteen-year-old boy, Sonny, told me that every time he takes his mask down to sip water at his school, they make him leave the classroom. In what world does this make any sense? I told him to drink as much water as possible. I demanded that he get kicked out of the classroom as much as his bladder could handle. It's the first time I've ever been concerned about hydration. I wish this had existed when I was a shitty student and needed excuses to get out of Mrs. Tani's math class. As a father, I needed Sonny to know that if he didn't get kicked out of class at least six times daily, I'd be disappointed.

Check out this madness. I drove Sonny to school towards the end of last year, and it was raining cats and dogs—which, as you probably know, is a rare thing in L.A. He was lamenting the fact that they still had to eat lunch outside. They had a freshly remodeled cafeteria that they couldn't utilize because of arbitrary nonsensical rules about masks and social distancing. Statistically, nearly zero kids have died of COVID-19, and those who did had preexisting conditions. I was onto this early in the pandemic. My last book had just hit the shelves as the virus hit the news, and I started asking, "What are the ages of the people who are dying?" I couldn't get a straight answer. People would give me some bullshit about how they couldn't reveal the ages because of HIPAA and privacy laws. That's not true. Revealing a name and a birthdate is a breach. Revealing the age of an unnamed person in a hospital is not a violation. But we never heard that statistically it was affecting the elderly the most. Which stat have you heard fewer times: the average age of people who have died of COVID or the number of white guys killed by the so-called racist bastard cops? As with that latter stat, the media doesn't want you to know that the average age of a person who dies of COVID-19 is the same as the average age of a person who owns a bathtub with a door on it.

So why was the media hiding the ages? Because then we wouldn't be scared. We had to think that kids could die of this virus. We understand that old people die. We might not like it, but we get it. If an eighty-year-old dies, it's sad; but if an eight-year-old dies, it's a tragedy. Think about it like this. Let's say you and your spouse are pregnant, and when you go into the hospital, there's a big wheel like on *The Price Is Right* but with a bunch of different ages instead of dollar amounts. You get to spin that wheel to determine how old your kid was going to live to be. If it were to land on nineteen, you'd be devastated; but if it were to land on eighty-seven, you'd be jumping up and down and hugging. Inherently, we know that life ends and that the more life we get the better. So, if the media and the politicians are going to try to scare us into compliance, they have to use the kids.

The obsession with keeping kids out of school and getting five-year-olds vaccinated when the potential side effects of the vaccine are worse than the virus is about one thing: crate training.

You can't crate-train a middle-aged dog. It's too late. You have to train dogs when they're puppies. So, not only did the government and the media have to gin up a lot of fake fear to get the parents to watch the newscasts with "grim milestones," but they also had to get the kids to comply so they'd be obedient later.

But the crate is an illusion of safety. It's not actual safety. The dog could feel safe in the crate, but the crate could be in the middle of the living room in a house that's on fire. COVID is random. If you think you're controlling it, then you probably think you're controlling the car at Autopia at Disneyland. That car is on a carriage bolt. You're doing nothing; it's on a track. But you can turn the wheel and feel like you're in charge. Guess what? COVID decides who gets it or not. The thing you are in control of is how much the government and the media are in control of you. ■

Chapter 12

Get a Job and Fight to Keep It

Most of my fans know that I came from humble beginnings career-wise—construction, carpet cleaning, custom closet installation. Now I'm a millionaire, so I feel well-qualified to give career advice. To prove the point of how low I started and how far I've come, I offer this brief yet incredibly pathetic tale.

The first time I went to The Body Shop, the famous strip club on Sunset Boulevard in L.A., I was nineteen. People under twenty-one couldn't order a beer, but those over eighteen could get in and order a soda while watching the featured dancer.

At a certain point, the strip club DJ was making mediocre jokes, doing his patter. "Hey, kids, Kitten Natividad is coming up. Quit your grinnin' and drop your linen. We've got a cleanup on aisle you. Ha ha. We're gonna need a new janitor here."

This is how desperate I was. After the show, I walked up to the DJ and asked, "Do you really need a janitor? I could be that man." That would have been an awesome job for me at nineteen. Mopping up The Body Shop after the businessman's lunch was aspirational for me. The DJ just shook his head before telling me to fuck off.

That's where I was then. But this is where I am now, so successful that I can give you advice in my sixth book.

• •

What do you do when you are thirty-seven and still have no idea what you want to do as a career?
Scott, 37, Glendale, California

This is simultaneously the blessing and the curse of our current society. It used to be that you'd just get a job at a mill or factory to provide for your family, and that would be enough. That would give you status. Now we're inundated with Oprah, Tony Robbins, and commercials for energy drinks and herpes medications, all telling you you're not out there getting yours—that you have to do or be something more. That's the curse. But the blessing, and this makes me hate the America haters even more, is that in our current society you can go out there and get yours.

I'd say figure out what you'd do for free. What do you do the most of when you're not being paid? Whatever you'd naturally do in your free time is worthwhile to pursue as a career. Then you have to be creative as to how to get there.

I know what you're thinking. *How do I get paid to play video games and masturbate?* Very few people get paid for that, especially dudes. For chicks, it's got to be the salad days if they're looking to find a way to get paid to masturbate. OnlyFans has really opened things up. I believe a lot of the "Great Resignation" that's happening now is not due to the extended unemployment benefits, but from chicks figuring out that they can get paid to diddle themselves on camera and never have to leave the house. If only that option had existed for Jeffrey Toobin.

Quick side note on that story. If you don't recall, as time flies when you're having a government-enforced lockdown, in the fall of 2020, CNN legal analyst Jeffrey Toobin got caught masturbating during a break on a Zoom meeting with his *New Yorker* magazine colleagues. He was subsequently fired by the *New Yorker* and probably wished CNN had fired him, given how Alisyn Camerota humiliated him on air upon his return to the commentary chair. (Google this for the most uncomfortable two minutes of television you'll ever witness.)

Here's my take on this situation. First, say what you will about Jeffrey Toobin; he's a multitasker. That is a guy who gets shit done. But more important, since he got caught beating his meat on a Zoom call, we no longer have to call him Jeffrey. That's a Jeff move. He lost the right to the noble-sounding name. Jeffrey is one of the knights of the Round Table. Jeff works at Round Table Pizza.

Anyway, just like Jeff Toobin, you've got to do what you love. If you love cooking, playing an instrument, or taking care of pets, then you can figure out a way to get paid for that. Even if it's tangential. You might not get a job in a philharmonic, but you might get a job working *at* a philharmonic and be able to soak up the Stravinsky. You have to be realistic. If you want to play shortstop for the Yankees, you might have to settle for working the concession stand at Yankee Stadium. There are only so many shortstop jobs. But at least you'd be in the ballpark of your dream, literally.

The best method I can offer you to determine that dream is to ask yourself, "What would I write a book or make a documentary about?" I was talking with Maria Menounos about a time when a publisher approached her to write a book, and she was unsure what to write about. She asked me how I came up with ideas for my books. I simply said I write about what I'm interested in.

It reminds me of when I was a boxing instructor and I'd ask people what their "cross" was. Which was their power hand? That would determine their stance. They never knew. They'd know the hand they wrote with but not the hand they'd punch with. So I'd ask, especially the women, "If I stomped on your foot right now, which hand would you punch me with?" They'd immediately know the answer, and that would be their power hand.

So, Scott, if a book publisher came to you today and offered you a healthy advance to write about anything, what would it be? Whatever answer just came into your head, start heading in that direction. ■

How do you cope with a toxic coworker and/or boss who is playing every trick in the book to undermine you when quitting the job is not an option?

—Maria Menounos

As far as narcissism and toxicity, it would be nice to think people could knock it the fuck off and just be reasonable, but alas, that's too much to ask. You've got to read the room. There are people you argue with who are never going to admit defeat, who are never going to give up. Don't engage. Don't poke those bears.

I also know, Maria, that you have a motor and that it drives you nuts when people around you don't. Maybe ask yourself if your coworker or boss is undermining you and being toxic, or if the person is just a lazy fuck compared to you, with your get-up-and-go. ■

. . . .

What's the quickest fix most people could do to improve their likability?

Collin, 42, Nashville

Show up early with doughnuts. Everyone likes that guy.

Plan B is getting really good at your job, and then people don't have to like you. They will endlessly tolerate anyone who's good at their job. That applies to everyone from radio personalities to metal fabricators. You can be a dick, but if you're great at your gig, you become such a precious commodity that the boss and the company won't want to get rid of you. Your ultimate insurance against workplace hostility is not being the most likable; it's being the most effective.

People love other people's enthusiasm for the shit they're doing. If someone decides to build a pergola in their backyard, don't tell them about the time you tried to build one and it didn't work out, or ask, "Aren't you worried it's going to collapse in the next high wind?" Just say, "That sounds awesome," and keep walking. Enthusiasm is infectious. Just like with a virus, you have to be positive to spread it. ∎

• •

Like you, I'm pretty athletic. I play high school football and baseball but suck at school. Thinking about going into the military. Should I? Why didn't you?

Trevor, 17, New Hampshire

I was definitely physical enough to do it and certainly had nonexistent self-esteem—I didn't care whether I lived or died—but I just never signed up. I came from a very liberal family. Not that I gave a shit what my family would think, or that they'd even notice that I was gone on a tour of duty. I imagine two lieutenants showing up at my house after Operation Desert Storm, giving my folks a flag folded into a triangle, and telling them that I had been killed in battle. They probably would have shouted toward a room I hadn't occupied in four years, "Adam, there's some soldiers here to see you."

The problem was that I was born in 1964. I grew up in the Vietnam and post-Vietnam eras with soldiers being spat on and called baby killers. Even in the '80s, when I would have been eligible to enlist, being a soldier was not cool. It was like being a cop now. It wasn't until after the Gulf War and "Stormin' Norman" Schwarzkopf that it started to get some cred, and then, post 9/11, these guys became heroes again in the public eye. So, I think the prevailing attitude when I could have joined up hindered me. Consciously or not, I didn't think it was a good way to get laid. That said, the idea of the free haircut was appealing.

In all honesty, I was weirdly homesick as a late teen and in my twenties when some of my friends went off to college. Not actually homesick, but friendsick. My friends had raised me; they were my safety net. I'd eat and sleep at their houses. My parents weren't there for me, but my buddies' parents were. And there's a natural fear of leaving the nest. Just because my nest was feathered with my friends and not my own family members doesn't mean it wasn't a nest and it wasn't scary to leave behind. Four years when you're eighteen feels like a lifetime.

And the Army wasn't doing themselves any favors by running that stupid ad saying, "We do more before nine a.m. than most people do all day." I had been on the fence until I saw those ads; then I was like, *Fuck that, I want to sleep in.* You can't entice seventeen-and-a-half-year-olds to defend our country by showing footage of guys hustling and drinking coffee out of tin cups while the sun is barely up.

I wish I had done it. I don't know where I'd be now if I had, but I certainly would have been happier, or at least more fulfilled, digging a trench in Fallujah than digging ditches on construction sites in Sun Valley. It seems like it might be the right time for you, Trevor. We just got out of the never-ending war in Afghanistan, and there's not a strong appetite for war in our country right now. Some serious shit would have to go down for us to gas up the Humvees again. Our next war will be fought with predator drones and cyberattacks. So join the military, get a free education, get in shape, then come home and get laid. ∎

....

I often hear people asked about what drives them. The person will give some undoubtedly heartfelt but entirely overdramatic answer along the lines of, "All I have to do is look into the eyes of my two baby girls...[pretending to need a moment]...and I just want to give them the best of everything." Having a family is something that does not seem to be in the cards for me, and while I have aspirations, I find myself more and more wondering why I would even attempt to achieve them. So what advice can you offer a childless bachelor on what to use as a motivator?

Mike, 47, Las Vegas

I don't think that people should look for external motivating forces. If you need to be motivated by something that lives outside of your loins, you're probably looking in the wrong places. Kids, God, the girl you're trying to impress. Nobody you admire was ever motivated by family members, revenge, or a class reunion. You're all the motivation you need. You shouldn't do something right because you're enticed into doing it. Having the career you want should be your motivation, not what you'd get out of the career. Motivation should be internally generated. You could be motivated for thirty years to make your dad proud, but what happens when he's dead and you find out he was a pedophile?

And, by the way, attempting to make a family is the best part. Never deny yourself that experience. You'd be missing out on some pretty good sex, getting laid with a purpose. ■

....

How do I respond to all the intersectional identity politics at work? It's not even about being treated equally anymore—if you are in the "wrong" demographic, then you have to admit you're a racist and that you need to just shut up and let the others tell you what's up. Except that it's just too exhausting for them to have to explain it all to you. If

*you don't innately get it (which you cannot do, by defini-
tion), it's just more proof of your hopeless racism. This stuff
is crazy and absolutely scary. If I didn't have a wife and
daughter to support, I would be less risk-averse about this.*

Bobby, 53, Metairie, Louisiana

I'd say start your own business. As your own boss, you're not
going to force yourself to do antiracism training.

It's weird that identity politics has crept its way into the
workplace. This nonsense was formerly relegated to liberal arts
colleges. Now it's gotten into corporate America. Like a virus from
a Wuhan lab, it has escaped and mutated and now has variants.
We should have locked down the colleges to stop the spread.

Here's my take on all of this, and it's less about race and more
about employment practices. So much race discussion happening at work means not a lot of work is going on. Guys who work
on deep-sea oil rigs aren't talking about "white fragility." I worked
in carpet cleaning. I didn't know people's last names, never mind
who they voted for. I couldn't talk to my coworkers, because the
steam cleaner was so loud I couldn't hear myself talk. Guys working in factories and at logging camps don't give a fuck about race
discussions. They're trying to avoid getting killed by the machin-
ery they're operating. They don't have time to care about the race
of the person next to them; they care only about whether that guy
secured the safety line so they don't get crushed.

It's corporate America's fault for calling the chick making eight
dollars an hour stirring the beans at Taco Bell a "team member."
It implies she has a say. I was a goomper who worked my way up
to being a glorified goomper. "Hey, idiot" was how I was greeted
most days on the construction site. Now everyone is a "valued
associate," "partner," or "colleague." Language like that levels the
field and implies an opening for a conversation about your pronouns and gender identity, or about race and microaggressions.

If inmates in a maximum-security prison were referred to as team members, and the warden talked about striving to create an inclusive place where everyone's voice would be heard, a day wouldn't go by without a guard being taken hostage.

Worker euphemisms hit peak absurdity last year for me when I noticed a sign outside a Jimmy John's sub joint.

No wonder the Great Resignation is happening. Jimmy John's is hiring rock stars. Who'd work as a bank teller and be a "team member" when they can go across the street to Jimmy John's and be a rock star? As far as euphemisms go, this even beats Disneyland's calling the failed musical theater student in the Pluto costume a cast member. Obviously, Jimmy John's workers are not literally rock stars. Slash and Dave Grohl aren't slinging the composite-meat products behind the counter. They're shredding on their guitars, not shredding iceberg lettuce. But even figuratively, "rock star" doesn't apply. People in sales or advertising are called rock stars when they close a big account or do something else that's outstanding. How can someone stand out when they're assembling sandwiches and will soon be replaced by a robot? It's all part of the failure of the self-esteem movement. You can't give someone self-esteem. It has to be earned. We can change the language, but it doesn't change the job. Calling someone a rock star doesn't make them one. We can rename herpes "happies," but it doesn't change the fact that it's a sexually transmitted disease.

But I think it's too late. This shit with race discussions and ridiculous euphemisms for workers is just going to continue. Workplaces will continue to become wokeplaces, and intersectional identity politics will become part of corporate culture. But on the bright side, like those OSHA-mandated signs in the breakroom advising workers of their rights and the safety mandates of the building, they'll become like wallpaper that you don't even notice. Though I do look forward to seeing a sign next to the one that reads "115 Days without an Accident" declaring "28 Days Since Last Misgendering." ∎

I am a pretty driven person. I work a lot. And pretty damn hard. I had wonderful parents as role models and I like to work, but sometimes I wonder if my drive comes from something less than "pure." I know it sounds stupid, but I think I've pretty much pinpointed where much of my motivation comes from, and it might reveal a character flaw that I don't love.

Back when I was around sixteen or seventeen, my friends and I had gone to a party in Great Neck—a wealthy village on Long Island about forty minutes from my home. It was a friend-of-a-friend-of-a-friend situation. I didn't know whose house it was, but it was really nice.

There was an older kid at the party sitting outside with a guitar. He wasn't very good. I was uncomfortable in a stranger's house where I knew nobody, so I went outside to talk to this dude. He was, in short, a dick. He thought he was too cool to be at a high school party, and he kept talking about his band—they were going to call themselves Ugly Chicks—the joke was that they were so good, it would be the only time people would pay money and wait in line to see ugly chicks. The guy thought he was really clever and special, and I realized he was not the kind of person I'd want to hang out with. So I tried to make small talk and gracefully exit the conversation. I said something along the lines that I had never taken guitar lessons, or any music lessons for that matter. The guy looked at me condescendingly and said, "You've never had any music lessons? You're not from Great Neck, are you?"

As I mentioned, Great Neck is a wealthy area. He was basically saying, "You don't have any money. If you did, you'd have gotten music lessons—like everyone in Great Neck."

I have always had a blue-collar chip on my shoulder. I come from a family of bust-your-ass, work-with-your-hands-and-your-legs-and-your-back people. My parents broke their tails to give me everything I needed as a kid. But what that kid said to me, and the way he said it, I realize now, might have affected me as much as any loving advice I ever received or any examples I ever saw set for me.

I don't know this guy's name or who he is. All I know is I still think about him—decades later—and how I allowed myself to be affected by a throwaway comment he probably doesn't even remember.

So now, when I'm working 110-hour workweeks on average, and I ask why I'm doing it, I have several answers: for my parents, who did so much for me; for my grandparents, who came to America with nothing; because I love it; because I love the people I get to work with...but when I am being truly honest with myself, I also know that chip on my shoulder is the size of New York, and I just want to cram it up that guitar player's ass. And that is (once again, if I'm being totally honest with myself) pretty lame. I know

> *I should just be happy I get to work—and be thankful I love my work—and not turn it into an "up yours" situation.*
>
> *But I still think about that guy. And how what he said still motors me thirty years later. And I ask myself, "What the hell's wrong with me?"*
>
> *And now I ask you the same question: What's wrong with me? Why can't I let this kind of stuff go?*

—Nick Santora

I don't worry about you, Nick. This is a blemish on an otherwise spotless record of having all the keys to success. In fact, even your question is exhibiting the most important quality a person can have—the ability to internalize and self-correct. You're asking this question because, like Walter White in *Breaking Bad* trying to create meth that is 100 percent pure, you're trying to make your motivation and drive 100 percent pure. And, as with meth, 100 percent pure is unachievable. You can do the right thing for the wrong reasons. That's OK; the majority of your drive comes from the best place. You're like a beautifully made mahogany table. A well-made wooden table is going to have flaws, but we call them character. They're how we know the table is real and handcrafted and not some composite, too-perfect bullshit.

That's what I love about you, and that's why I'm using you as an example of having the key to success. So, I'll close this chapter on career and motivation, and this book, with another email exchange we had. Because it lays out everything people need to know about how to be a success.

Just to set things up for my readers. Nick has had quite a lot of success by reading newspapers and magazines, finding interesting individuals, tracking down the subjects, and acquiring the rights to their stories. That was how he got the show *Scorpion* on the air.

In 2015, I kept seeing billboards for the Will Ferrell and Kevin Hart movie *Get Hard*, in which Hart's character prepares Ferrell's white-collar-criminal character for life in prison. It occurred to me that about five years before, Nick had told me about an article he had read in the *L.A. Times* about a guy who prepped people for prison. Nick told me how he had tracked the guy down and purchased his life rights. I knew that *Get Hard* had to be Nick's project.

So I emailed him to see if he was producing it or if he had at least made some cash selling the premise. This is what he wrote back.

> *Yes, that Get Hard idea was the one I'd been running around with for years. But this movie isn't mine. I don't think anyone stole it. Wasn't exactly what I was going with. I had a different premise. Someone else wrote it...more power to them. I'm just pissed at myself for not getting it done sooner. My fuck-up. I deserve to lose this one. Ain't gonna happen again.*

First, he didn't externalize and say, "Oh, those bastards stole my idea," and then lawyer up. The premise was so similar that I thought it was his based on a conversation we'd had over lunch five years prior. He could have sued and created enough of a nuisance to maybe get paid to shut up. But he didn't let himself be victimized. He said, "This one's on me." He took personal responsibility for a mistake—or in this case, an uncaptured opportunity. No amount of money is worth acting like a victim when you're not. Dignity doesn't have a price tag.

But the most important part is the last line: "Ain't gonna happen again." This is the thing that separates winners from losers—learning from their mistakes and getting their ass in gear to make sure it never happens again. I can't tell you the number of retards I'm on my thirty-fifth conversation with about making the same mistake.

He literally said, "My fuck-up" and "Ain't gonna happen again." He did critical self-assessment and made plans to change. Imagine the utopia we'd be living in if every whiny bitch on Twitter and college campuses could be that honest with themselves. Hopefully you, dear reader, are that person. This is what successful people do. ∎

Acknowledgments

You know what? Fuck this. I've done six books, and they always end with *me* thanking people. You, the reader, should be thanking them. You should thank Anthony Ziccardi and Post Hill Press for giving you the chance to read my sixth book. You should thank Jacob Hoye for working so diligently on editing it. You should thank the copyeditors, proofreaders, and design team for making it look so good. You should thank my assistant Matt Fondiler for managing my schedule while I wrote it and dealing with all the communication. And you should thank Chris Laxamana, Gary Smith, and Superfan Giovanni for some archival audio and photo-finding assistance. But you should also thank yourself for supporting assholes like me.

About the Author

ADAM CAROLLA is best known as a comedian, actor, radio personality, television host, and *New York Times* bestselling author. He currently hosts *The Adam Carolla Show*, which holds the Guinness World Record for "Most Downloaded Podcast." Launched from his home office in February 2009, *The Adam Carolla Show* now receives more than thirty million downloads a month.

Adam began his career on the nationally syndicated radio program *Loveline* with Dr. Drew Pinsky. MTV ran a television version of the show for five seasons (1996–2000).

With his partners Daniel Kellison and Jimmy Kimmel, Adam created and starred in two hit Comedy Central shows, *The Man Show* (1999–2003) and *Crank Yankers* (2002–2005).

In 2010 Adam became a *New York Times* bestselling author for the first of three times with *In Fifty Years We'll All Be Chicks*. He has since released five more bestsellers, including *Not Taco Bell Material; President Me; Daddy, Stop Talking!;* and 2020's *I'm Your Emotional Support Animal*, which shot to number two overall on Amazon.com and held the number one Political Humor spot for several days.

Adam also cowrote, produced, and starred in two independent feature length films: *The Hammer* (2007) and *Road Hard* (2015), a crowd-funded comedy that raised over a million dollars in a single month. Through his venture Chassy Media he produced the inspirational documentaries *Winning: The Racing Life of Paul Newman, Uppity: The Willy T. Ribbs Story*, and *The 24-Hour War*, which documents the battle between Ford and Ferrari in the 1960s for racing dominance at Le Mans.

In 2019, Adam began touring a new show, *Adam Carolla Is Unprepared*, in which he improvises a stand-up act based on one-word audience suggestions pulled at random. And in 2022 he launched a new series of comedy specials for DailyWire.com titled *Adam Carolla: Truth Yeller*.